BECOMIN

After an MA in clinical psychology, Dr Nimmi Hutnik founded, along with four other people, a therapeutic community that operated in New Delhi for many years, serving people with mental health problems and substance abuse issues. She also taught at Lady Shri Ram College for twenty years. During this time she won the Commonwealth Academic Staff Fellowship to study social and developmental psychology at Oxford University in the UK. After completing a doctorate at Oxford, she returned to India and practiced as a clinical psychologist for a number of years. At the time she took a qualification in transactional analysis.

Now living in Britain, she is an accredited cognitive behaviour therapist and a chartered counselling psychologist. Till recently she was an associate professor at London South Bank University where she taught cognitive behavioural therapy to postgraduate students. She provides therapy, coaching and supervision in person and via Skype. Her website is www.cbtintheuk.com.

Advance Praise for *Becoming Resilient*

'This is a book with no pretensions. Its detailed, practical and authentic content is based on thirty years of Dr Hutnik's learning and her therapy practice. However, it is the lived wisdom that draws on her long and ongoing spiritual journey that adds a special flavour and additional depth to CBT principles and makes this a book with a difference.'

—**Gloria Burrett**, integrative and transpersonal
psychotherapist, New Delhi

'A fascinating blend of cognitive behaviour therapy with positive psychology, this is a compelling book for both the general and professional reader … full of illustrative examples of normal life distress, snippets of personal experiences and inspirational quotes from widely admired individuals. Written in an almost conversational style, it is easy to read and offers sustenance for the reader.'

—**Nigel Sage**, consultant clinical psychologist in
cancer and palliative care, UK

'This is a very engaging, accessible book. It is full of helpful examples and diagrams and there are a number of exercises for you to complete as you go, so that this is a true self-help book.'

—**Professor Jamie Hacker Hughes**, vice president,
British Psychological Society

'I would recommend this to anyone who wishes to enlarge their repertoire of possible ways of dealing with personal distress, as well as to those academics and others who wish to broaden their knowledge of how Western psychological techniques can be applied in non-Western, in this case Asian, cultural settings.'

—**Professor Suman Fernando**, visiting professor, Faculty of Social
Sciences and Humanities, London Metropolitan University and
professorial fellow, Institute of Mental Health,
University of Nottingham

BECOMING RESILIENT

Cognitive Behaviour Therapy to Transform Your Life

NIMMI HUTNIK

First published in India in 2017 by Harper Element
An imprint of HarperCollins *Publishers*

Copyright © Nimmi Hutnik 2017
Illustrations Copyright © Nimmi Hutnik and Tanya Hutnik 2017

P-ISBN: 978-93-5264-132-1
E-ISBN: 978-93-5264-133-8

2 4 6 8 10 9 7 5 3 1

HarperCollins *Publishers*
A-75, Sector 57, Noida, Uttar Pradesh 201301, India
1 London Bridge Street, London, SE1 9GF, United Kingdom
Hazelton Lanes, 55 Avenue Road, Suite 2900, Toronto, Ontario M5R 3L2
and 1995 Markham Road, Scarborough, Ontario M1B 5M8, Canada
25 Ryde Road, Pymble, Sydney, NSW 2073, Australia
195 Broadway, New York, NY 10007, USA

Typeset in 11/14.2 Adobe Garamond at
Manipal Digital Systems, Manipal

Printed and bound at
Thomson Press (India) Ltd

To my Father who has been the light upon this work
To my daughters, Anna and Tanya, who have enriched my being
beyond any telling of it
To all my clients from whom I have learnt many of life's precious
lessons

Acknowledgements

This book would not have been possible without the quiet, unpretentious, unassuming, intelligent hard work and research of Imogen Hagarty who wove an initial web of wonderful words around the PowerPoint bullet points that I have created over many lectures and over many years. Imogen showed amazing grit, travelling many miles to our weekly meetings and spending many hours interviewing people. She has made this book come alive. Thank you, Imogen!

Thanks too, to Tanya Hutnik, my graphic designer daughter who helped me create most of the diagrams in the book and in particular the resilient and the non-resilient face diagrams. Your ability to unequivocally tell me what communicates and what doesn't is invaluable to me.

Thanks to Anna Hutnik, my elder daughter who supports and encourages me in whatever I undertake.

Thanks also to Martyn whose 'can-do' attitude and positive stance on life has taught me a lot about becoming resilient.

Thanks to those who have supported my CBT knowledge and practice over the years, in particular Nigel Sage, Ruth Cocksedge, Lorraine Nanke and Christine Padesky who have gently shaped me over many hours of supervision and consultation. Thanks are due, too, to Professor Sally Hardy who was my boss and head of department, mental health and learning disabilities, London South Bank University, for seeing the value in this project. I would like to thank Rukmini Chawla Kumar for her original vision for this book and for the vision she has to bring psychotherapy writing increasingly to India. Thank you, Rukmini.

Last but not nearly the least, I would like to thank my clients who have shared their lives with me. I am truly enriched by the journeys that we have taken together.

Contents

Introduction

Do you often wake up dreading the day, feeling quite low, tearful and with a lump in your throat that you can't quite explain? Are tiredness and fatigue daily experiences for you? Does it take quite a lot of effort to drag yourself out of bed and into the shower to get ready for work?

Do you find yourself waking up with a start in the middle of the night, heart pounding with the stress of things that haven't been done or things that you need to do? Do you find your head buzzing with the million emails you have to attend to and the thousand issues you have to address?

This book is for ordinary people like you and me who suffer slightly elevated amounts of depression and anxiety, and other difficult emotions such as anger, jealousy, panic, shame and guilt. It will enable you to learn to deal with difficult moods, manage stress better and improve your relationships. But it doesn't stop there. Once you are on a more even keel emotionally, it will enable you to develop an ability to become resilient, to flourish and to develop in a positive direction. All of this will lead to a higher level of happiness and will enable you to transform your life.

Ideas in this book are based on Cognitive Behaviour Therapy (CBT). CBT is a very successful form of psychotherapy and is based on the observation that our thoughts are intimately connected with our emotions, behaviour and physiological responses. For example, we see a dog on the street and we think, 'Best get out of the way! Dogs are dangerous; they bite and carry rabies.' We will feel anxious and afraid. We might even find our heart racing and our mouth dry, and we will probably take another route to avoid the dog. On the other hand if we think, 'Dogs are friendly, furry, cuddly animals!' we may feel relaxed and/or excited, and cross the street to pet the dog. Two different thought processes for the same situation lead to very different emotions, physiological sensations and behaviours.

This book will enable you to discover how your typical ways of interpreting the situations you find yourself in create feelings of depression and anxiety. It will help you get up again and start over with renewed feelings of vigour and competence. Soon you will find yourself experiencing more positive emotions like joy, love and optimism. Gradually, this book will teach you how to flourish in life.

But to get there, you will need to be passionately committed to your own well-being and you may need to undertake and persist at tasks that may sometimes appear difficult. This is what a psychologist named Angela Duckworth calls grit: the passion and persistence to achieve long-term goals. You will get from this book as much as you put into it. Skimming the book will not produce the results you would like to see in your life. So make a commitment to yourself not just to read the book but to do the exercises in it that are geared towards enabling you to feel happier and more fulfilled.

HERE IS THE WAY THE BOOK IS STRUCTURED:

Part 1: Describes depression and the various types of anxiety. It also includes questionnaires to enable you to assess whether you are suffering from depression and/or anxiety. If you are suffering from anxiety, ask yourself what type of anxiety you suffer from. Phobias, panic disorder, health anxiety (now called illness anxiety), social anxiety, and generalized anxiety are all different types of anxiety. I have also included Obsessive Compulsive Disorder (OCD) and Post-Traumatic Stress Disorder (PTSD), though strictly speaking they are categories of mental suffering in their own right and are no longer classified under anxiety.

Part 2: Once you know what type of problem you are suffering from, it is then important to begin treating that problem. Part 2 looks at the tools and techniques that CBT has evolved to enable people to tackle depression and the various anxiety states. The exercises in this section, if done well and practiced regularly, will indeed help you feel less sad and less stressed.

Part 3: Is designed to take you beyond anxiety and depression into the realms of contentment, resilience, flourishing and transformation. In this section we look at an age-old meditation technique drawn from the Buddhist and Christian traditions called mindfulness. We will explore an outgrowth of CBT, a newly developed therapy called Acceptance and Commitment Therapy, more commonly known as ACT, said as 'act'. We will also look at how to teach ourselves to bounce back when life knocks us down, i.e., develop resilience, and to spring forward into a place where we can truly say we are thriving or flourishing in our lives.

How to Use this Book

The good news is that you do not have to read the whole book. After reading Chapters 1 and 2, it would be sensible for you to read Chapter 3, which describes the fundamental principles of CBT. Then you will need to identify your primary problem. If it is depression, then read the chapter on depression (Chapter 4). If it is anxiety, then read only the sections of Chapter 5 that are pertinent to your particular type of anxiety. I have included questionnaires for you to be able to assess what you suffer from. Even though these questionnaires have not been standardized for the Indian population, they will serve as a guide to signpost you to specific chapters in the book and to get specific help from a therapist if required. These questionnaires, if taken regularly, will also give you an objective measure of whether you are improving or not. If more than one problem is present, ask yourself which is the problem that is most debilitating to you at this time. Then read the chapter or section relevant to that particular problem. It is important that you start somewhere. You may even find that addressing one problem will have a knock-on positive effect on the other problems you are experiencing, thereby alleviating them.

Whatever your particular problem, you will benefit from reading the chapters on Mindfulness (Chapter 6), Acceptance and Commitment Therapy (Chapter 7), Resilience (Chapter 8) and Flourishing (Chapter 9). These chapters are focused on your strengths and not your deficits. I trust that they will bring you renewed energy and hope. Chapter 10 brings all the threads together to show you how you are on the pathway to parivarthan or transformation.

You will reap the greatest benefit from this book if you discuss some of the issues with a friend or trusted family member. Get them to read the book with you and support you as you try to do things differently. But don't worry if you do not have such a person in your life. You can learn to be your own cognitive behaviour therapist.

If your depression and/or anxiety are very severe and you are unable to function adequately in daily life, I recommend that you find a therapist to help you. This book is for people who suffer from mild to moderate conditions.

If at any point you find yourself considering taking your own life, you should get immediate help from a mental health professional.

By engaging with the ideas and exercises in this book, you will be able to bring yourself to a much happier place in your life. I wish you every success in your journey towards resilience, flourishing and transformation.

For Mental Health Professionals

This book is also for mental health professionals. Considering that depression and anxiety are the prime maladies of our contemporary world, it is likely that you will see a lot of these in your practice. Sometimes, if you are like me, you will have wondered what to do next, what road to go down and how to get your client past a particular impasse. Have you sometimes longed for a therapy manual that will help you get over the stuck places in your journey with your clients? Even though this book is written primarily as a self-help guide, it will be useful to therapists as well.

Cognitive behaviour therapy has swept the UK, USA and the western world as the therapy of choice for depression and anxiety. This is because it brings swift results within a limited number of sessions and research shows that CBT does better than many other therapies in helping people become significantly less depressed and anxious for longer. Having said this, as a CBT practitioner, I am very respectful of person-centered therapy and existential therapy. There is also space for aspects of psychodynamic therapy, transpersonal therapy, gestalt therapy and transactional analysis in my practice of CBT. The fundamental assumptions of these therapies are different and I recognize that CBT does not suit everybody. However, for those it suits, CBT is a powerful tool towards greater well-being and contentment.

Some people think CBT is not suited to Indians, but I disagree. There is no question that CBT is fairly medicalized and is informed by DSM-V and ICD-10. Thus, depression and anxiety are seen as symptoms to be treated. CBT, based as it is on the assumptions of science, is focused on categorization, formulation, maintenance cycles, behavioural experiments, etc. It uses the principles of science to facilitate healing. Do we not as Indians use the principles of science to heal physical illness, to develop computers and to strive towards economic and political growth?

Unlike a medical situation in which the doctor is often seen as the expert, CBT is based upon a collaborative, equal, enquiry-based relationship with clients that is warm, empathic, genuine and offers clients unconditional positive regard.

One of the fundamental assumptions of CBT is that the symptoms of depression and anxiety are developed because of our interpretation of the situations we find ourselves in and our relationship with our thoughts. As you know this is a deeply philosophical position to take and it is found in many spiritual traditions of the East and the West. Thus, for a person who is both depressed and anxious because they have a huge debt to pay (say), CBT is useful for enabling the depressed or anxious client to get out of bed and get to work, so that the money keeps coming in. By accepting the things that cannot be changed and changing the things that we can, by developing helpful thinking styles even in the midst of what may seem at first inexorable situations (such as poverty or unemployment), CBT enables people to overcome the inertia of depression and anxiety and bounce back rapidly to full functioning.

If you are a dedicated and experienced cognitive behaviour therapist, you will probably only need six to twenty sessions to complete a good piece of work with your client, though it depends upon the complexity of the problem at hand. Even PTSD and OCD can be treated in sixteen sessions or thereabouts. This is good news for many clients who might not have the wherewithal to pay for long-term therapy. It makes therapy affordable for a greater proportion of Indian people.

This book aims only to provide a quick snapshot of the main tools and models that CBT therapists, academics and researchers use. It does not propose to be an in-depth exposé of CBT. For more detailed material, I have made references to different resources. I have included as many questionnaires, diagrams and forms as I have obtained copyright permission for. I hope you will find these helpful in your practice with your clients.

Good luck with it all!
Nimmi Hutnik

PART 1

Assessment of Depression and Anxiety

1

Understanding Depression

'If we can really understand the problem, the answer will come out of it, because the answer is not separate from the problem.'
– Jiddu Krishnamurti

'Mind is very restless, forceful and strong, O Krishna, it is more difficult to control the mind than to control the wind.'
– Arjuna to Sri Krishna in *Bhagavadgita*

In this chapter:

— What is depression?
— Symptoms of depression
— Is depression a new thing?
— How long does depression last?
— Different kinds of depression
— How is suicide linked to depression?
— Functions of depression
— Common theories of depression

- Dealing with other people
- I think my friend or relative is depressed, what can I do?
- What can I do to start tackling my depression?
- PHQ-9 questionnaire: Are you depressed?

Tara is a thirty-nine-year-old woman who has always 'been there' for her husband, children and extended family. Her husband became ill and had to leave his job, which left the family with financial difficulties. When Tara's mother died, this triggered terrible feelings of misery and loss of energy in her. People told her, 'Don't worry, you will feel better soon,' but Tara felt worse and worse. She felt angry and resentful that her husband and children were constantly demanding things from her when she had not had sufficient time to mourn her mother. She stopped eating properly and was hardly sleeping. Even though she had always been the one to help other people, when she spoke to friends asking for help, they did not listen. Eventually, after about a year, Tara went to a psychologist who suggested that she was suffering from depression.

Life is a spiral. There are regular events of loss and failure followed by periods of renewal, regeneration and revitalization. Deeply embedded in the very fabric of life is the fact of suffering. At some point in our lives, all of us will face the death of loved ones, difficulties in our jobs, a low point in our relationships, health difficulties and the like. There are many sources of stress in modern life. Some of us will collapse under the strain, while others will be resilient, quick to bounce back and quick to spring forward to embrace life anew.

The ideas in this book will help you cope with the inevitable loss and failure you will experience in life, such that you will be able to find your way to a place of growth and transformation. When you face the next loss and failure, you will approach it from a new and different perspective, having acquired some CBT skills.

Those of us who have had happy childhoods have a head start in being resilient. For those of us who have experienced real pain and difficulty in our primary families, it will take greater effort to learn how to become resilient. I did not have a happy childhood and thus this book is in many ways a reflection of my own journey to resilience, flourishing and transformation.

What makes some people fragile and others robust? There are myriad answers to this question. The one that I think has the greatest amount of weight is this: those of us who are willing to put effort into grappling with the 'necessary suffering' (Rohr, 2011) in our lives until we can wrestle a blessing out of it, are most likely to come out with a greater degree of resilience and transformation than those who push things under the carpet and hope that it will all just go away.

And so at sixteen, rather than go into medicine, I decided to take up psychology. It has been one of the most useful and productive decisions I ever made. I wanted to learn how to deal with my depression and anxiety. I wanted to learn how to become happier, how to become wiser, how to become a fuller person. This journey has taken me into the pathways of spirituality and psychotherapy. Though they are inextricably interwoven, in this book I share with you my insights into psychotherapy. Maybe one day I will write a book on spirituality.

It is so important to be able to understand what triggers our moods and the impact they have on us and others around us. Cognitive behaviour therapy is particularly good at this. I did not start with CBT. I started with Psychoanalysis and with Erik Erikson's theory of the life cycle, which I refer to later in this book. I then moved into Transactional Analysis, which I still find useful in helping me understand what is going on in our relationships. At the culmination of this journey is cognitive behaviour therapy.

This is because CBT gave me a way to replace my negative mental filters with ones that were more true to who I am as a person. In the past year and a half, I have lived through the deaths of three very important people in my life; my dearly loved mother, my brother-in-law and a very good friend. I have also changed job and house. All these things would seemingly lead to a meltdown. I have surprised myself with the level of resilience and the sense of flourishing that I have experienced in the face of this. I have drawn on the wisdom of the masters and it is this that I share with you now.

Because life is made up of 'necessary suffering', there will be times when you will feel sad or tense. As you work on yourself, you will find that you are able to bounce back quicker. Indeed if you devote yourself to your own psychological and spiritual development, you will come to a plateau where the balance of flourishing in your life outweighs the suffering. This is indeed a happy place.

The first step is to understand ourselves and our moods. Let us look at another example.

Sneha was a twenty-six-year-old office worker in Mumbai who found herself crying every day on her bus home from work. She felt like she could do nothing right at work and was constantly plagued with thoughts of not being good enough. When she arrived home, she would feel too miserable to cook or tidy up and would go straight to bed as soon as she got in the door, even at 5pm! She became depressed after moving away from her family and starting to work in a difficult office environment.

WHAT IS DEPRESSION?

Depression is one of the most widespread mental health problems in our society today. It can negatively affect our careers, family lives, feelings of self-worth, joy and just about every aspect of our lives.

There are two different meanings to the word depression. We use the word depression to express feeling low, blue, miserable and when life is a struggle. When used in this context, it is obvious that everybody gets depressed sometimes. This is very normal and part of the human condition. However, the word depression is also used as a clinical diagnosis to describe when people have a certain number of specific depressive symptoms for a long period of time and it affects their daily life. This is known as clinical depression.

Around one out of ten people in India have a depressive episode at some point in their lives that meets these clinical criteria. Recent estimates have shown that lifetime prevalence rates of clinical depression in India are between 8 and 13 per cent, which is similar to the rest of the world, but not quite as high as some more affluent countries (Nieuwsma, 2011; Kessler and Bromet, 2013). If we use the studies mentioned above as a guide, we could extrapolate that over one hundred and twenty-two million people in India (a tenth of the population) are depressed. So you are not alone!

Clinical depression is more than just feeling sad. When a person is depressed, they can feel like everything is pointless, life is empty and the future is bleak. These unhealthy and unhelpful thoughts are a hallmark of clinical depression. More often than not, people suffer low mood simply because life is often difficult. This type of low mood usually sets itself right in a few days after the person has had the rest and the exercise they need and is able to think through situations clearly and realistically. But clinical depression needs to be treated with extra support, which is why I have written this book. This book is useful to those who suffer clinical depression but it is also useful to help alleviate and manage low mood and common anxieties in people like you and me who are not clinically depressed.

This chapter contains information on what depression is, how people may feel when they are depressed, different kinds of depression and some initial advice on what you can do to feel better. My friend, Imogen Hagarty, interviewed a woman who had suffered from depression for many years in order to give you an insider view on depression. In fact, Imogen has interviewed several people and their thoughts and opinions have been included in italics in separate boxes throughout the book. They chose to remain anonymous and I have given them pseudonyms. The boxes in this chapter give Usha's opinion on what her depression means to her. This may be helpful for you and could resonate with your own experiences.

Q: Usha, what do you think depression means?

A: I think it means not being the person that I can be. I sometimes feel there's two me's; there's the me with depression and there's the me without depression. I get angry and I get short tempered and I cry and I can't do my job properly. I think the me with depression is about feeling completely flat. It's not really being sad – it's very different to being sad. I think it's personality changing, not from the inside, what you are inside stays exactly the same but how the world sees you and how you express yourself and how you live your life completely changes.

Depression is nothing to be ashamed of. Many famous and very successful people have suffered from depression or continue to do so. International figures such as Abraham Lincoln and Winston Churchill are known to have had episodes of clinical depression and Indian celebrities such as Parveen Babi and Guru Dutt are also thought to have suffered from the condition. More recently, Deepika Padukone has come out in public about being depressed, which is a good thing as it goes a long way to de-stigmatize the experience of depression.

All of us feel low at times. This is because the very nature of life means that we will have suffering. It is not that we feel low but *how we deal with feeling low* that is important.

SYMPTOMS OF DEPRESSION

People who are depressed might experience a combination of any of the following:
- Feelings of sadness, emptiness and hopelessness most of the day, nearly every day
- Diminished interest in all or almost all activities

- Significant weight loss even when not dieting or the opposite, i.e., weight gain
- Insomnia or hypersomnia
- Restlessness or agitation or its opposite retardation or being slowed down
- Fatigue or loss of energy
- Feelings of worthlessness or excessive or inappropriate guilt
- Inability to concentrate or indecisiveness
- Recurrent thoughts of death or suicide (though in mild to moderate depression no particular plan has been made)

Sometimes people experience physical symptoms like aches and pains, feeling tired all the time, not being able to sleep, not being able to eat or not wanting to have sex. If you are experiencing this but your doctor can't find a physical cause for your illness, do the PHQ-9 questionnaire (Kroenke, Spitzer and Williams, 2001) at the end of this chapter to give you an idea of whether you are depressed. Also, a friend or relative who is depressed might be feeling some physical symptoms alongside their emotional distress but feel unable to talk to you about their depression. Reach out to them, perhaps with this book.

Below, Usha describes how she feels when she is experiencing a depressive episode.

Q: What does it feel like when you are depressed?

A: Ordinarily, when I'm feeling depressed it's not too bad – I just feel a bit flatter than normal and then you get to feel monochrome, like everything is in black and white. But at other times it can get really bad.

I feel irritable. I'm really trying to be nice and kind and patient but I just have this huge irritation building up. Probably because I feel so bad about myself at the time I can't focus on anything and so when you have someone going on at you it's like someone is poking at you. I just can't tolerate it.

IS DEPRESSION A NEW THING?

The number of people diagnosed with depression in India has risen dramatically in the last thirty years but this does not mean that we have all suddenly become depressed. All evidence points to depression being around as long as humans have been. It is described in the texts of ancient Mesopotamia. In Western medicine, the ancient Greek doctor Hippocrates called it *melancholia*. He thought that depression was caused by an excess of black bile in the body, which is where the word melancholy comes from. Conversely, Cicero said that it was caused by anger, fear and grief. The ancient Greeks and Romans used a combination of diet, exercise and herbal remedies to cure melancholia. The Persian doctor Rhazes in Baghdad at the end of the ninth century thought that the brain was responsible for melancholia (Nemade et al., 2013).

Religious texts also discuss depression, although without using medical terminology. The Guru Granth Sahib describes how depressed people might lose interest in activities that they would normally enjoy and how colours may seem faded and washed away (Kalra et al., 2013). In the Christian Bible, many of the psalms as well as the book of Job detail depressed thoughts and feelings. The first chapter of the *Bhagavadgita* describes Arjuna's depression and despondency at the thought of fighting on the battlefield. Ayurvedic texts Caraka Samhita and Susruta Samhita discuss six different mental disorders, three of which have similarities to major depression, particularly *shokaja unmad* caused by excessive grief and *kaphonmad*, where sufferers are described to be apathetic, losing their appetites and wanting to be alone (Murthy, 2010).

Early studies of depression in India found very low rates of the condition but more recent studies show that it is just as common as in other parts of the world (Nieuwsma et al., 2011). Reasons for this are thought to be that many people in India express their depression through physical symptoms such as aches, problems with sleep, palpitations, tiredness and weakness (Pereira et al., 2007). For example, Inga-Britt Krause did a study of Punjabi women who reported a '*dil girtha hai*' feeling (my heart is sinking) Krause, 1989). Earlier studies failing to interpret these symptoms as depression may have underestimated the extent of depression in India.

How Long Does Depression Last?

This is a question that is impossible to answer because it depends on how quickly people recognize the key importance of thinking and interpretation in fostering and maintaining depression. People with long-term clinical depression often say that they have experienced symptoms all their lives. This is usually because they have not yet met a cognitive behaviour therapist who can help them develop different perspectives on difficult situations, thereby enabling them to change their emotions and their physiology. The good news is that people with clinical depression can overcome it through cognitive behaviour therapy.

DIFFERENT KINDS OF DEPRESSION

Every person is different and every case of depression will vary. There are a few main types of depression that people report, which will be explained in the coming passages.

Mild to Moderate Depression

If you experience mild depression, you may either experience low mood and sadness over a period of time or lose interest in activities that you once enjoyed. It might be difficult to go about your day-to-day life but you will still be able to function on a daily basis. Depression is classified as 'moderate' when you have more than five of the symptoms of depression mentioned earlier. It is likely to affect your day-to-day functioning more negatively than in the case of mild depression.

Q: What are you like when you're depressed, Usha?

A: I'm mostly very listless so what I'd look like to other people is lazy. I can't do anything so I can't be bothered to cook or clean the house or go out or see friends. I can't focus at work or concentrate on anything. That gets into a bit of a spiral because I feel like I'm not achieving anything and I'm being lazy. So then I feel really bad.

Many people get through mild to moderate depression without professional help but others prefer to seek professional help. Reading and doing the exercises in this book will definitely help.

SEVERE DEPRESSION

People who experience this feel like they have no energy, feel miserable and often suffer from low self-esteem during a depressive episode. Their low moods and other thoughts and feelings affect their work and family life in a negative way. They often cannot feel pleasure.

People with depression often also experience physical symptoms like headaches, tiredness and problems with eating or digestion. Many people who have major depression also experience anxiety and often meet the clinical criteria for depression as well as one or more of the anxiety disorders.

SAD

SAD stands for seasonal affective disorder. This is another name for a pattern of depression where the episodes re-occur at a specific time of the year. For many people, especially in Europe and the US, this occurs in the winter and could be triggered by the lack of sunlight or bad weather. However, SAD has been documented in India with more people experiencing it in the summer, perhaps due to hot temperatures and the necessity to stay out of the heat. (Tonetti, Sahu and Natale, 2012).

PREMENSTRUAL DYSPHORIC DISORDER

Many women experience mood swings, feeling suddenly sad or tearful in the week before menstruation. Or they may feel markedly irritable or anxious or a sense of being overwhelmed and out of control. They may experience fatigue and have sleep disturbances and an inability to concentrate. There may be feelings of being keyed up or on edge and there may be more interpersonal conflicts during this time. This improves in a few days after the onset of menses, becomes minimal or absent in the week post menses only to begin again with the next menstrual cycle. In order to meet the criteria for this diagnosis, at least five of the symptoms must be present in the week prior to menstruation.

POST-NATAL DEPRESSION

This is another name for a major depression that can affect women or men after the birth of a baby. It can also affect women who have had a miscarriage. Many women feel sad and tearful for a few days after having a baby. This is perfectly normal and happens to many people. It is also normal to feel irritated and tired due to the demands of a baby. However, post-natal depression is characterized when you experience the feelings as listed below:

- tired and cannot sleep even when you get the chance to
- angry towards your baby
- indifferent towards your baby

- hopeless
- irritable
- worthless

BIPOLAR DISORDER

This is when people have episodes of depression followed by episodes of mania. Mania is when a person feels extremely energetic, high and active. They might behave in an impulsive way, taking financial risks or going on spending sprees. Bipolar disorder is also called manic depression.

Sandeep started to feel he was worthless and unsuccessful. He began feeling very depressed. He could not sleep at night or concentrate on things happening at work. A few months later, he started feeling the opposite; like he had a lot of control over the events in his life, even believing that he could affect the weather and make the sun come out. He became driven to exceed his goals, which meant that he was overworked, often getting only two to three hours of sleep at night. He would pace his bedroom constantly and talked ceaselessly with imaginary others, causing his parents to worry about him.

People experiencing a manic episode might also want to eat or sleep much more than usual. Each episode can last for weeks or months and there could be a long delay between the depression and the mania. Sometimes when people have episodes of mania they feel very creative and positive. On the other hand, they could be irritable and tend to talk very quickly. In extreme cases, they might see or hear things that don't really exist.

There are other types of depression too, for example, dysthymia, medication-induced depression and depression that is due to another medical condition, which I will not go into here. If you suspect you have symptoms of bipolar depression or severe depression of any sort which is recurrent, I encourage you to seek the help of a psychiatrist who might suggest some medication. Taking medication on a regular basis will help stabilize severely depressed moods.

HOW IS SUICIDE LINKED TO DEPRESSION?

Q: How do you feel when you are very depressed?

A: The times it's got really bad, I have suicide fantasies. Not because I want to die but because it seems almost comforting to think about it and I can get quite fixated on death. It's everything from feeling a bit flat to feeling listless, lazy and unable to concentrate ... the other end (is) having suicide fantasies. It depends how far along there I get...

A person who is severely depressed is twenty times more likely to kill themselves than somebody who does not have depression (Harris and Barraclough, 1997). However, studies have shown that only one in ten people who suffer from depression will attempt suicide even if many depressed people have suicidal thoughts or fantasies (Hasin, Goodwin, Stinson, & Grant, 2006). Just because somebody is depressed does not mean they are going to kill themselves. Indeed, suicidal thoughts are common in clinical depression but the vast majority of people never act upon them.

Nevertheless, if you are thinking about suicide and making plans about how you might kill yourself, please do seek urgent professional help. The Samaritans are a crisis line that helps people who are feeling suicidal. In New Delhi, Sanjivini (www.sanjivinisociety. org) provides help for people in crisis. If somebody you know starts talking about killing him or herself, you should always take it seriously and help them get professional help. Do not think that they are just looking for attention. Some of the biggest warning signs for suicide are talking about it, seeking access to pills or weapons or threatening suicide. India has one of the highest suicide rates in the world, especially amongst young people aged fifteen to twenty-nine (Patel et al., 2012). This book is designed for people with mild to moderate depression and I would urge you to get direct professional help as soon as possible if you have any fear that you or someone you know may be suicidal. If you have made a specific plan for yourself about how you would commit suicide or you discover a specific suicide plan that someone you know has created for themselves, you should take immediate action. There are several risk factors for suicide such as having a current suicide plan and access to weapons or pills, previous suicide attempts, a history of suffering abuse, recent loss, drug or alcohol abuse, hopelessness and not having friends or family to connect with. There are also factors known to protect against suicide, for example, social support from friends and relatives, spirituality, positive coping, problem-solving skills and a sense of responsibility to family.

FUNCTIONS OF DEPRESSION

It seems funny to think that depression might have a function when it is such a debilitating condition. No one wakes up one day and just decides to be depressed.

M. Scott Peck writes about the 'Healthiness of Depression' in his book *A Road Less Traveled* (1978). Scott Peck was a psychiatrist and writer who experienced depression himself as a teenager and was interested in both mental health and spiritual growth. According to Scott Peck, depression fulfils a necessary function of signifying to us that we need to make changes in our lives. He saw depression as a condition that can usher in a period of intense personal growth, starting with the depressed person realizing that they need to make a major change in their life and continuing through psychotherapy to make those difficult changes. Scott Peck was talking here about episodes of depression where the person takes control of their condition and actively seeks help or tries to do something about it. He contrasts this with 'chronic pathologic depression' where the person is unable or unwilling to do this.

On a less positive note, Gillian Butler and Tony Hope (Butler and Hope, 2008) suggest that depression allows people to avoid facing certain problems in their lives. There may be things that they want to do such as going to college, travelling abroad or having children but they do not think they can cope with it. Depression could be the path of least resistance. Simply continuing as they are, not being able to do things because of their depression means that they will stay stuck where they are in their life, avoiding the fear of failure. This is paradoxical because staying depressed means they will never try the things that they always wanted to do and if they don't try, they cannot succeed.

COMMON THEORIES OF DEPRESSION

Sometimes people know what has caused their depression. It could be that someone close to them has died or they have lost their job. But most often, people are unaware of why they are depressed. There are different theories on why people get depressed that you may find helpful.

> **Q: What do you think the cause of your depression is, Usha?**
>
> A: *Obviously, when you have depression you think a lot about why you have it. I'm really sure that it's linked to having a damaged childhood. It feels really linked to it and I think it's to do with my dad and what he was like.*

Depression often results from different causes and triggers in a person's life. It could be the combination of bereavement, physical illness of yourself or a loved one, stress at work or home, breaking up with a romantic partner or any number of other triggers. It develops when a person gets into a downward spiral of negative thoughts. Some people may be more susceptible to depression than others due to genetics but this does not mean that they cannot overcome it or learn to manage their condition. We can see that there can be many different causes of depression. Just as there are many causes, there are also a variety of treatments. Some will work for some people and others will work for others. Whereas a physical illness can be pinpointed as caused by a specific virus or bacterium, depression is not one virus that invades our body and mind but a label we give to the impact of a variety of negative thoughts and interpretations.

CHILDHOOD EVENTS

Some people become depressed because they have suffered abuse or lack of love and support as a child. Research suggests that children's brains develop differently when they are brought up in a stable, loving environment to when they are brought up in an uncaring, neglectful or abusive home. This can affect the parts of the brain that are in charge of our feelings and moods, making these children more likely to become depressed both as children and later as adults (Gilbert, 2000). Being at the receiving end of bullying can also lead to the development of low self-esteem and negative opinions about ourselves. People can develop core beliefs about themselves such as:

- I am unlikeable and unlovable
- I am a bad person
- I am worthless
- I am a failure

This does not mean that if bad things happened to you as a child, you will always be depressed. Some people had difficult upbringings and have good mental health, showing remarkable resilience. Other people might have struggled with depression after having problems in their families when they were children but will then learn to manage their moods after a number of sessions of therapy and effort on their part. Hopefully, this book can show you ways to manage depression, no matter what has happened to you in the past.

Rajesh grew up in a household with an abusive father who threw things around the house, was constantly screaming at his wife and children and who often came home drunk and angry. His father would tell him that he was stupid and would never be successful. Rajesh left home when he was eighteen to study abroad but whenever he had to give a presentation or talk to a professor or a tutor, he would always hear his father's voice in his head telling him that he was worthless. This led to episodes of depression and social anxiety when he was an adult due to these core beliefs that he had internalized as a young boy.

Our core beliefs are formed not only during childhood but also during adulthood. Events in our personal and professional lives, such as an over critical boss, may lead us to believe that we are inadequate or weak or unable to cope.

DIFFICULTIES IN RELATIONSHIPS

Your relationship with other people is one of the factors that most strongly predicts if you will get depressed, how severe the depression will be and how long it will last.

Being depressed may often lead you to feel that you want to avoid family and friends because you just don't have the energy and motivation to have conversations and be in contact. If you avoid contact you will create an anti-social cocoon for yourself in which you will feel isolated and lonely and therefore even more depressed. It is really important that you continue to be in contact with people even when you don't feel like it. We will talk more about this in Chapter 4.

Being depressed will often have a negative effect on your relationships. Feeling bad and maintaining negative thoughts makes you a very draining and wearing person to be around. So not only do you want to avoid people, others may want to avoid you as well. Also, many people do not understand what depression is and think that it is possible for you to 'just snap out of it' or 'pull yourself together'. It is helpful to think that this is not because the people do not care about you but that they do not understand what is wrong.

If you have social support from those around you, this will really help. If you know someone with depression, your support could be very beneficial to him or her.

One of the most common causes of depression is related to difficulties that we experience in our relationships. I am currently treating a thirty-nine-year-old man who is in the middle of a divorce. A twenty-nine-year-old woman came to me because she had broken up with her boyfriend and is now feeling horribly alone and isolated. A thirty-seven-year-old woman spent an hour and a half shedding tears because the man she had met online had come to visit, she had fallen in love with him but he did not fall in love with her and had left her without much ado. So many of our hopes and desires are related to finding a good romantic partner, but the path to this is a thorny one and we spend time, energy and effort healing our wounds. In Chapter 9 we will talk about romantic relationships and how to acquire some basic skills in keeping them going. And how to know when enough is enough.

Loss

The famous psychoanalyst Sigmund Freud compared depression to mourning. According to him, depression is caused by loss. We can think of loss in terms of physical things that we lose but there are also psychological losses. For example, loss of a job might lead to loss of income, friendships and daily activity but also to loss of self-esteem, confidence, purposefulness and security. Loss of a romantic relationship will mean that the person you were going out with is no longer present in your life but may also be accompanied by loss of confidence in your own attractiveness, loss of feelings of safety and loss of your status as a person in a relationship. Today, most psychologists believe that loss on its own does not cause depression. Again, people can survive terrible losses and show incredible resilience. Loss results in normal and understandable sadness and low mood but only develops into depression due to a person's reaction to that loss.

Ambrish was a fifty-five-year-old clerk in a government office who had just retired after a minor stroke. He started to feel like there was no meaning in his life. No longer being the family's breadwinner, he felt a loss of status and self-esteem. The loss of the structure of the working day and the friendly conversations that he'd had with his colleagues also impacted him, leading to feelings of worthlessness that spiralled into depression.

GENETIC AND BIOLOGICAL EXPLANATIONS

There is some evidence that people can inherit a genetic vulnerability to depression, although environmental factors have more impact on the development of depression. All of our feelings and moods influence what happens in our brains and our brains influence our feelings and moods. It is not yet known what exactly goes on in our brains to make us depressed. However, it is likely to be related to neurotransmitter functions. A neurotransmitter is a chemical in the brain that carries signals from one area of the brain to another. Examples of mood-regulating neurotransmitters are serotonin, dopamine and noradrenaline. In somebody who is depressed, neurotransmitters do not work normally to regulate the person's mood.

Q: Do you find the biological explanation of depression useful?

A: I think there's a chemical cause but whether that is pre-existing or whether what happens in your brain is caused by life experiences, I don't know.

This is helpful because we need to remember that our body and our mind are inextricably linked. When things go wrong in our body, our thoughts and feelings can be affected. Conversely, when our thinking and feeling is imbalanced, our body will be affected. The most important piece of information to take away from this is that some people might just have brains with a biochemical makeup that means they are more likely to get depression. This does not mean that you cannot take responsibility for making a positive change or that you cannot learn to manage your moods in such a way that you feel significantly less depressed and much happier.

THE BIOPSYCHOSOCIAL MODEL

Many psychologists today do not put depression down to one particular cause but tend to view biological, psychological and social factors as interrelated. Our patterns of thinking (a psychological factor) will be affected by our upbringing (a social factor). These patterns of thinking will have an effect on our moods and thus our hormones (a biological factor), which might then impact our relationships with others. Although many depressed people find it very important and interesting to know what has made them depressed, it is not necessary to find a definitive cause in order to overcome depression. It is unlikely that there will be one specific cause and far more likely that a number of interlinked factors have come together to make somebody depressed.

THE CBT EXPLANATION FOR DEPRESSION

According to cognitive behaviour therapy, people get depressed because of their internal reaction to the difficulties they face. This book takes a cognitive behavioural stance that depressed people often have unhelpful ways of thinking about the situations they find themselves in. They find it hard to bring to mind the positive events they have experienced and everything seems to be coloured by negativity. This can turn into a vicious cycle where an unhelpful thinking style causes the low mood which then causes more negative thoughts and feelings, which in turn exacerbate the low mood, which again causes more and worse negative thoughts and feelings to arise. This way of explaining depression is called a cognitive theory because it deals with the thoughts that happen in our minds, which lead to the experience of difficult emotions like anger, sadness, anxiety and guilt.

When people are feeling low, they are likely to think and behave differently. For example, if you are stressed at work you might feel too down to see your friends and family, which will give you a greater chance of developing depression. If your relationship breaks down, you may experience low self-esteem, which might have a negative effect on how you study or work, thus making your performance worse. This might in turn make you more upset or miserable, which could then affect other areas of your life.

Aaron Beck, who founded CBT, realized that negative thoughts can cause these depressive symptoms. Sometimes we have a negative belief about ourselves, such as 'I am stupid', 'I am bad at my job' or 'I am a failure'. If you then lose your job, you see yourself as a failure and your future seems bleak. These are negative thoughts and can lead to depression. If you did not hold these negative beliefs, you would find it easier to be more philosophical about your situation: 'the recession has affected lots of people', 'now I have the chance to pursue a career I really have a passion for', 'thanks to my redundancy pay, I can have some time off to spend quality time with my children'. By doing CBT, a person who is vulnerable to depression can increase his or her resilience by tackling the negative thoughts and by becoming aware of their hidden strengths which can then be transferred into the difficult situation. Then, when a loss or another difficult situation arises, a depressive episode can be avoided.

According to psychologist Susan Nolen-Hoeksema, depressive symptoms can be made worse if we ruminate on them. She defines depressive rumination as 'repetitively and passively focusing on symptoms of distress and on the possible causes and consequences of these symptoms' (Nolen-Hoeksema et al., 2008). Have you ever started thinking negative thoughts about yourself and then found you couldn't stop? The more you repeat negative beliefs to yourself and the more you focus on your negativity, the more it becomes a self-fulfilling prophecy. This is different to thinking constructively about your depression and taking action.

Q: How does your thinking change when you are depressed, Usha?

A. I worry obsessively about people I love dying and I get very taken up about what will happen and how I would cope and what I would do. I also worry about what would happen if I die and the effect it would have on the people I left behind and how hard it would be for them to manage.

Q: Have you told people that you're depressed?

A: Not many people. My friend Savita is aware of it. I will actually ask Savita to monitor it if I start feeling bad. Savita can tell on the phone if I'm getting depressed and she can tell really quickly too, and that's quite helpful because she will say, 'You need to go to the doctor's.' Because when I'm depressed, I'm not in a state to really know.

When you start ruminating, it becomes a trap that it is extremely difficult to get out of. Negative thoughts come into your head automatically and you might not even notice that they are there or even worse, think that they are all true.

Malini was a young high school teacher in a big city. The first school she had worked at was great – the other teachers were supportive, the students she taught were mostly interested in learning maths and she liked the environment. After a few years she moved to another school where things were a lot more difficult. She got it into her head that she was a 'bad teacher' and that she was 'hopeless at her job'. These thoughts would circle round and round her head when she was in class, when she was on the bus to and from the school, when she was at home in the evenings and even when she was on shopping trips with friends on the weekend. As she sat on the bus on her way to school, she would repeat in her head 'I am a bad teacher, I am hopeless at my job, I am a bad teacher, I am hopeless at my job ...' Guess what? When she arrived at school and went in to teach her class, her negativity and inability to concentrate made it impossible for her to teach well.

She then started recalling how she had been shy as a child and thought to herself, 'Well, maybe I'm not just a bad teacher, maybe I am bad with other people as well. This made her think about her weekends and she would withdraw from social contact and not want to socialize. Her new motto became 'I'm bad with people', which adversely affected her successful friendships, relationships and professional life. Since the only job that Malini had ever done was teach, she concluded, 'Whatever job I do, I will fail.' Malini forgot that she had been popular at high school and university and dismissed her current friends as acquaintances whom she did not really get along with. She also missed out the fact that she had been excellent at her last job at the old school. Malini's destructive rumination on these unhelpful thoughts ended up in 'I am bad at life and I cannot cope with the real world'. She got herself into a very bad place where she no longer enjoyed seeing her friends because her self-esteem was so low, she cried every evening as she walked from the school to the bus stop and she felt like her whole life was a failure. She then looked at herself crying and feeling depressed and thought, 'Look at me, crying, depressed and unable to cope. I am rubbish.'

This is what we call depressive rumination in CBT. Malini let her destructive thoughts spiral out of control.

In therapy, Malini was made aware of depressive rumination. She was taught to consider the negative consequences of entering this rumination cycle, which she discovered were very high and to balance these against the advantages of entering the rumination cycle, which she discovered were very few. Gradually she learnt how to replace destructive thoughts with facts about herself that built her up and made her feel good about herself.

Sometimes friends, family and colleagues may not react in a constructive way to help someone with depression and because of this the depressed person often withdraws from social contact. You might be feeling emotionally isolated and lonely even when you are with other people. This could lead you to stop seeking out help from those people and stop being in contact with them. Despite this, making use of the social support systems available to you will help. If you have a friend, colleague or family member that you can talk to, you should do so. Even if they don't understand exactly how you are feeling, just to talk to someone else will give you a different perspective on your problems – two heads are better than one! If you do not have someone to talk to or your problems are so great that your friends and family cannot help, you need to see a professional. Having one person close to you that you can confide in cuts the risk of you developing depression by half. However, a critical, unsupportive and emotionally abusive relationship will increase your chances of depression.

I THINK MY FRIEND OR RELATIVE IS DEPRESSED, WHAT CAN I DO?

Firstly, you should congratulate yourself for caring enough about your friend to pick up this book and look for an answer. Depressed people can be difficult to be around. You might be encouraging your friend to think positively and healthily or to take action in their lives but they might not respond or might bite your head off when you suggest this! In any case, this is not really the thing to do when you notice someone you love being depressed.

Amrita was a fifty-year-old woman who had broken up with her alcoholic husband a year ago. She felt like her life was getting back on track and with a new relationship, new hairstyle and new outlook on life, the future looked bright. Amrita's twenty-year-old daughter, Vaishali, was at university in Delhi. One day she started crying on the phone to her mother, telling her that she could not cope any longer and was considering dropping out of her course. Amrita was shocked at first and told her daughter she needed to pull herself together and stay on the course. When Vaishali came home for the summer holidays, Amrita decided that to make her feel better, Vaishali needed to do some volunteer work and help with the housework – moping around was only going to make things worse! She did not understand why her daughter was thinking in such a way. Of course, moping around did not help but eventually Amrita realized that Vaishali was too depressed to continue in her course or to get a job and together mother and daughter negotiated for Vaishali to take a year off and continue her studies the following academic year. Vaishali came home and Amrita cooked her favourite meals, spent time with her every day and arranged for Vaishali to see a therapist.

The most important thing is to listen and to keep caring and being there for your friend or relative even if you do not feel like it. Since you are not depressed yourself, you cannot really understand exactly how they feel – admit this but try to be as understanding as possible. Spend time with them, be kind and caring and don't expect that you can cure them. You don't need to give advice or become a psychologist or counsellor. In fact, if you try to do this without knowing what you are talking about, you might make things worse. Just be there for that person, listen to what they have to say and give positive encouragement. As Mother Teresa said in her Nobel Peace Prize acceptance speech (1979), 'Maybe in our own family we have somebody who is feeling lonely, who is feeling sick, who is feeling worried, and these are difficult days for everybody. Are we there to receive them, is the mother there to receive the child?' In this way, we do not need to provide a solution, just be there to 'receive' our friend or relative.

At the end of the day, it is not your responsibility to make your friend or relative better – it is their responsibility. You might find that even just being there to listen to your friend is too much for you. If this is the case, you might have to set down some limits about how much you can take and say 'no' at times but try to point them in the direction of someone who can help.

WHAT CAN I DO TO START TACKLING MY DEPRESSION?

There are many different courses of action that you can take if you are depressed or if you recognize that you have suffered depressive episodes in your life. Physical exercise, antidepressants and Cognitive Behavioural Therapy (including behavioural activation) are among the most common ways of treating depression.

Q: What makes you feel better, Usha?

A: The main things that help me are having a dog, going for walks and getting fresh air. I know if I did more exercise, I'd feel loads better. Having a job I love is an essential part of it too. Having people around me who I love and who love me is really important. Being in good environments, feeling I do things well, sleeping.

PHYSICAL EXERCISE

Physical exercise is a safe and healthy way to fight your depression and comes with very few risks. When you exercise, your body releases endorphins and neurotransmitters that carry signals to your brain, blocking pain and increasing pleasure. This is what happens when you experience a high after going out for a run or participating in a difficult fitness class. You can exercise on your own or join a class – both have benefits for your physical and mental health. Some people like to go for long runs on their own outside. The benefits of this are that you get fresh air as well as exercise. Running can feel particularly healing and invigorating if you can find a pleasant natural environment to exercise in. Many people like to listen to their favourite music as they run or they make a playlist of songs that make them feel joyful. Alternatively, you might want to join an exercise class or a sports team – this has the added benefit of meeting new people and forming new relationships, which can make you feel better.

If you are not ready to take up a sport, there are gentler forms of exercise that you can do. Going for walks outside, especially in a natural environment, can be very helpful. This is a particularly good way of getting physical exercise because it can be practiced in a way that is gentle or challenging. Also, focusing on your breath and staying mindful of your body is a good way of stopping unwanted negative thoughts entering your mind.

Try to be creative in finding a form of physical exercise that works for you. Think of what you enjoyed when you were at school. If you are not the sporty type, you could try gardening or get a dog that you have to take out for walks. Sometimes, if you don't have a natural talent or interest for sports, it's easier to take up an activity or exercise where there will be lots of beginners, like rock climbing, trampolining or deep sea diving.

In order to make exercise work for you, you need to plan it into your day. This is why it often helps to join a class or team scheduled for a particular time. If not, make a plan of when you are going to exercise and what you are going to do, otherwise you are unlikely to stick to it.

There is considerable evidence that physical exercise helps us feel more mentally healthy (Helmich et al., 2010). Being physically active enhances the way the neurons in our brains function, making us happier and decreasing the likelihood of dementia in old age. Some studies have even found that physical exercise had the same effect on making depressed people feel better as taking antidepressants did (Blumenthal et al., 1999). It is recommended that adults from age nineteen onwards do at least one hundred and fifty minutes of moderate activity per week. This can be any kind of sport or physical exercise including walking. Here is a list of different physical activities that you could consider:

- rapid walking that will increase you heart rate
- going to a gym to train
- taking up a sport such as football, tennis, badminton or swimming
- exercise classes
- dance
- yoga
- martial arts

The main thing in depression is to get the endorphins coursing around the body again and to keep the level as high as possible.

ANTIDEPRESSANTS

Antidepressants are medications that alleviate the symptoms of depression. Most antidepressants are relatively safe and some people respond well to them, whereas others do not. You should only take antidepressants if they have been prescribed by a doctor and do not stop taking them without talking to your doctor first. Antidepressants often work in relieving the symptoms of depression. This is because of the way events in our lives and our reactions to them and interpretations of them are likely to change our brain chemistry. Antidepressants can be necessary in cases of severe depression but on their own, i.e., without self-help or CBT, the research shows that they are not very effective. If depression is quite intense then it is recommended that you take antidepressant medication as long as you go in for therapy as well. This is because antidepressants do not tackle the underlying cause of depression and you need to continue taking them in order for them to have any effect. They will not cure your depression in the way that a course of antibiotics can cure an infection.

Considerable research has looked at comparing CBT and medication treatments for depression. A recent study found that the group of people taking an antidepressant but no CBT were less depressed after six months of treatment, but that after one year of treatment, the group who had CBT but no antidepressant were less depressed (Siddique et al., 2012). Additionally, CBT has a longer lasting effect and people who have CBT are less likely to relapse into depression, compared to people who take antidepressants and then stop (Dobson et al., 2008; Hollon et al., 2005).

Cognitive Behavioural Therapy, Mindfulness and Acceptance And Commitment Therapy

One of the most effective treatments for many people is CBT. This book is based on CBT, so the exercises given here constitute a Cognitive Behavioural self-help programme. Other 'talking therapies' exist such as psychoanalysis and various kinds of counselling and these can also help, though the evidence is not as strong for the effectiveness as it is for CBT. However, the quality of therapy provided is very variable, therefore, if this book does not help your problems, I would recommend that you see a therapist or psychologist who is qualified in cognitive behaviour therapy.

It is important that you trust and respect the person that you go to see. You may already have in mind the kind of therapist you would like to see. You might prefer to talk to a spiritual leader such as a guru or a priest. This is fine if you trust them and are willing to take their advice. Sometimes it helps just to have someone to talk to who will listen to you and challenge any negative beliefs you may have about yourself. However, remember that if they are not a qualified cognitive behaviour therapist, they may not be able to provide the same level of professional therapy.

The exercises in this book will help you to deal with unhelpful thought patterns and learn different ways of coping. You can work through cognitive behaviour therapy on your own with the help of this book. This book also provides exercises for you to increase mindfulness and includes a section on acceptance and commitment therapy (ACT). These methods are safe and healthy ways to help yourself if it is difficult for you to see a psychologist or if you feel like you do not need professional help. In Europe and the US, yoga, meditation and mindfulness techniques originating from India are being used more and more frequently to tackle mental health issues. Mindfulness can be particularly useful for dealing with depressive rumination – when we repeatedly think negative thoughts about ourselves and the fact of our depression over and over again, focusing on depressive symptoms (Ramel et al., 2004). There have been several randomized clinical trials of these techniques that have shown them to be successful in helping people overcome depression.

If any treatment, therapy or positive action that you are carrying out is not making a difference after six months or is making you feel worse, stop and try something else. Every individual is different and what works for one person may not work for another. Perhaps it is time to seek out professional help.

Are You Depressed?

This short questionnaire will help you work out if you are depressed or not. It is known as the PHQ-9 (Kroenke, Spitzer and Williams, 2001) and is commonly used to screen for depression. Circle the answer that seems to best describe how you feel. After you have answered question 9, count up your score and write it at the bottom.

OVER THE PAST TWO WEEKS, HOW OFTEN HAVE YOU BEEN
BOTHERED BY ANY OF THE FOLLOWING PROBLEMS?

	Not at all	Several days	More than half the days	Every day
1. Little pleasure or interest in doing things	0	1	2	(3)
2. Feeling down, depressed or hopeless	0	1	(2)	3
3. Trouble falling asleep, staying asleep or sleeping too much	0	1	(2)	3
4. Feeling tired or having little energy	0	1	2	(3)
5. Poor appetite or overeating	0	1	2	(3)
6. Feeling bad about yourself, that you're a failure or you've let yourself or your family down	0	1	2	(3)
7. Trouble concentrating on things like reading a newspaper or watching television	0	(1)	2	3
8. Moving or sleeping so slowly that other people might have noticed, or the opposite, being so fidgety or restless that you have been moving around a lot more than usual	(0)	1	2	3
9. Thoughts that you would be better off dead or hurting yourself in some way	0	(1)	2	3

Total points = _____18_____

10. If you have any of these problems, how difficult have they made it for you to do your work, take care of things at home or get along with other people? Tick one of the boxes below.

☐ Not difficult at all

☐ Somewhat difficult

☐ Very difficult

☑ Extremely difficult

Now follow the next few steps to work out if you are depressed:

STEP ONE:

If you have answered 2 (more than half the days) or 3 (every day) for Questions 1 and 2 as well as 'somewhat difficult', 'very difficult' or 'extremely difficult' for the last question, you may be clinically depressed.

STEP TWO:

Look at your total point score from questions 1–9 (not including question 10).

STEP THREE:

Use the table below to work out the severity of your depression.

Score	Severity of Depression	What You Should Do
5–9	Minimal symptoms	Use this book to learn how to develop techniques to help you feel better
10–14	Minor depression or mild major depression	If you score 10, use this book to develop techniques to help you feel better, but if your symptoms persist for more than a month or you cannot function properly, go to a psychologist or therapist specializing in CBT for help
15–19	Moderate major depression	You should get help from a psychologist or therapist specializing in CBT, and you might also find this book useful
More than 20	Severe major depression	You should get help from a psychologist or therapist specializing in CBT, and you might also need to see a psychiatrist for some anti-depressant medication. You may find this book useful but if you are in the midst of an episode of major depression, you may find it difficult to concentrate enough to follow the exercises in this book

If you are feeling low a lot of the time or if by filling in this questionnaire you find that you are depressed, then read Chapter 3 followed by Chapter 4. I encourage you to do the exercises and help yourself to learn more helpful thinking styles. Chapters 6–10 will also be immensely useful to you as they will help you to quieten your agitation and depressive rumination by using mindfulness meditation, to bounce back after having been knocked down and to spring forward to embrace life with renewed vigour and vitality.

> **Key Points from This Chapter:**
>
> — Depression is a common problem suffered by many people all over the world
> — Depression is nothing to be ashamed of
> — Depression should be taken seriously – it is not something that you can just snap out of
> — There are many different causes of depression and in one individual there may be more than one cause at work
> — There are many different treatments for depression and you can use whatever works for you, but this book recommends cognitive behaviour therapy
> — If you are feeling suicidal, it is important that you get help immediately

REFERENCES

1. J.A. Blumenthal, M.A. Babyak, K.A. Moore, W.E. Craighead, S. Herman, P. Khatri, R. Waugh, M.A. Napolitano, L.M. Forman, M. Appelbaum, P.M. Doraiswamy, and K.R. Krishnan, 'Effects of Exercise Training on Older Patients with Major Depression', *Archives of Internal Medicine*, 159(19):2349–56, 1999.

2. E. Bromet, L.H. Andrade, I. Hwang, N.A. Sampson, J. Alonso, G. de Girolamo, R. de Graaf, K. Demyttenaere, C. Hu, N. Iwata, A.N. Karam, J. Kaur, S. Kostyuchenko, Jean-Pierre Lépine, D. Levinson, H. Matschinger, M.E. Medina Mora, M.O. Browne, J. Posada-Villa, M.C. Viana, D.R. Williams, and R.C. Kessler, Cross-national Epidemiology of DSM-IV Major Depressive Episode, *BMC Medicine*, 9(90), 2011.

3. G. Butler and T. Hope, *Manage Your Mind: The Mental Fitness Guide*, 2nd ed., Oxford: Oxford University Press, 2007.

4. K.S. Dobson, S.D. Hollon, S. Dimidjian, K.B. Schmaling, R.J. Kohlenberg, R.J. Gallop, S.L. Rizvi, J.K. Gollan, D.L. Dunner, and N.S. Jacobson,

'Randomized Trial of Behavioural Activation, Cognitive Therapy, and Antidepressant Medication in the Prevention of Relapse and Recurrence in Major Depression', *Journal of Consulting Clinical Psychology*, 76(3):468, 2008.

5. P. Gilbert, *Overcoming Depression*, 2nd ed., London: Robinson, 2000.

6. T. Gyatso, Compassion and the Individual, http://www.dalailama.com/messages/compassion> (Last accessed on 29 January 2014).

7. E.C. Harris and B. Barraclough, 'Suicide As an Outcome for Mental Disorders', *British Journal of Psychiatry*, 170:205–228, 1997.

8. D.S. Hasin, R.D. Goodwin, F.S. Stinson, and B.F. Grant, 'Epidemiology of Major Depressive Disorder: Results from the National Epidemiologic Survey on Alcoholism and Related Conditions', *Archives of General Psychiatry*, 62:1097–1106, 2006.

9. I. Helmich, A. Latini, A. Sigwalt, M.G. Carta, S. Machado, B. Velasques, P. Ribeiro, and H. Budde, 'Neurobiological Alterations Induced by Exercise and Their Impact on Depressive Disorders', *Clinical Practice and Epidemiology in Mental Health*, 6:115–125, 2010.

10. S.D. Hollon, R.J. DeRubeis, A.C. Shelton, J.D. Amsterdam, R.M. Salomon, J.P. O'Reardon, M.L. Lovett, P.R. Young, K.L. Haman, B.B. Freeman, and R. Gallop, 'Prevention of Relapse Following Cognitive Therapy vs Medications in Moderate to Severe Depression', *Archives of General Psychiatry*, 62(4):417–422, 2005.

11. G. Kalra, K. Bhui, and D. Bhugra, 'Does Guru Granth Sahib Describe Depression?', *Indian Journal of Psychiatry*, 55 (Supplement 2), 195–200, 2013.

12. R. Kessler and E. Bromet, 'The Epidemiology of Depression Across Cultures', *Annual Review of Public Health*, 34:119–138, 2013.

13. I. Krause, 'Sinking Heart: A Punjabi Communication of Distress', *Social Science & Medicine*, 29(4):563–575, 1989, http://www.sciencedirect.com/science/article/pii/0277953689902025 (Last accessed on 17 October 2016).

14. K. Kroenke, R.L. Spitzer, and J.B.W. Williams, 'The PHQ-9: Validity of a Brief Depression Severity Measure, *Journal of General Internal Medicine*,16:606–613, 2001.

15. Mother Teresa – Nobel Lecture, 2013, http://www.nobelprize.org/nobel_prizes/peace/laureates/1979/teresa-lecture.html (Last accessed on 29 January 2014).

16. R.S. Murthy, 'Hinduism and Mental Health', in P.J. Verhagen, H.M. Van Praag, J.J. Lopez-Ibor Jr, J.L. Cox, and D. Moussaoui (eds), *Religion and Psychiatry: Beyond Boundaries*, Chichester: Wiley-Blackwell, pp.159–180, 2010.

17. R. Nemade, N. Staats Reiss, and M. Dombeck, 'Historical Understandings of Depression', 2013, http://www.gracepointwellness.org/5-depression/article/12995-historical-understandings-of-depression (Last accessed on 29 January 2014).

18. J.A. Nieuwsma, C.M. Pepper, D.J. Maack, and D.G. Birgenheir, 'Indigenous Perspectives on Depression in Rural Regions of India and the United States', *Transcultural Psychiatry*, 48(5):539–568, 2011, http://tps.sagepub.com/content/48/5/539.abstract.

19. S. Nolen-Hoeksema, B.E. Wisco, and S. Lyubomirsky, 'Rethinking Rumination', *Perspectives on Psychological Science*, 3(5):400–424, 2008, http://pps.sagepub.com/content/3/5/400.abstract.

20. V. Patel, C. Ramasundarahettige, L. Vijayakumar, J.S. Thakur, V. Gajalakshmi, G. Gururaj, W. Suraweera, and P. Jha, *Suicide Mortality in India: A Nationally Representative Survey*, 2012.

21. B. Pereira, G. Andrew, S. Pednekar, R. Pai, P. Pelto, and V. Patel, 'The Explanatory Models of Depression in Low Income Countries: Listening to Women in India', *Journal of Affective Disorders*, 102:209–218, 2007.

22. K. Pilkington, G. Kirkwood, H. Rampes, and J. Richardson, 'Yoga for Depression: The Research Evidence', *Journal of Affective Disorders*, 89, 2005.

23. W. Ramel, P.R. Goldin, P.E. Carmona, and J.R. McQuaid, 'The Effects of Mindfulness Meditation on Cognitive Processes and Affect in Patients with Past Depression', *Cognitive Therapy and Research*, 28(4):433–455, 2004.

24. J. Siddique, J.Y. Chung, C.H. Brown, and J. Miranda, 'Comparative Effectiveness of Medication vs Cognitive Behavioural Therapy in a Randomized Controlled Trial of Low-income Young Minority Women with Depression', *Journal of Consulting and Clinical Psychology*, 80(6):995–1006, 2012.

25. L. Tonetti, S. Sahu, and V. Natale, 'Cross-national Survey of Winter and Summer Patterns of Mood Seasonality: A Comparison Between Italy and India', *Comprehensive Psychiatry*, 53(6):837–842, 2012.

26. M.S. Peck, *The Road Less Traveled: A New Psychology of Love, Traditional Values and Spiritual Growth*, New York: Simon and Schuster, 1978.

2

Understanding Anxiety

'I do not worry about yesterday for it is past and tomorrow is yet to come.'

– Mother Teresa

'There is nothing that wastes the body like worry.'

– Mahatma Gandhi

In this chapter:

— What is anxiety?
— Symptoms of anxiety
— Functions of anxiety
— How common is anxiety?
— When does helpful anxiety become unhelpful anxiety?
— Panic attacks
— Different anxiety disorders
   ○ Panic disorder (with/without agoraphobia)
   ○ Health anxiety

- o Generalized Anxiety Disorder (GAD)
- o Specific phobias
- o Social anxiety
- o Post-Traumatic Stress Disorder (PTSD)
- Common theories of anxiety
- What keeps anxiety going?
- What can I do to start tackling my anxiety?
- GAD-7 questionnaire: Do I have Generalized Anxiety Disorder (GAD)
- Penn State Worry Questionnaire: Do I have GAD?
- OCI: Do I have Obsessive Compulsive Disorder (OCD)?
- HAI: Do I have health anxiety?
- Phobia Scales: Do I have a Specific Phobia?
- SPIN: Do I have social anxiety?
- IES Qestionnaire: Do i have Post-Traumatic Stress Disorder (PTSD)?

Nandita was a competent driver but every time she got into the car, she felt nervous. Even though she had been driving for over twenty years, she had just moved to a new city and did not know the roads there. Every morning on her way to work, Nandita would feel nauseous and dizzy when she started to drive. She arrived at work with pounding headaches that she could not cure even with painkillers. One day she was so physically sick on her way to work that she had to turn around and go home. She avoided the crowded narrow roads of the city, choosing only the larger flyovers, even though this meant that her journey took an hour instead of twenty minutes. Nandita told herself, 'When I feel confident in my driving, I'll drive in the city.' She felt that her anxiety was the appropriate response to a terrible danger. After a few weeks, she quit her job that she loved because she was so afraid of driving. When she talked to her family about this, her mother suggested that it was Nandita's anxiety stopping her from driving rather than her ability to drive or the conditions on the roads.

Modern life is a complex affair and stressors potentially abound. We are exposed to myriad examples of serious human suffering on the news: floods, earthquakes, accidents, physical and sexual assault, serious illness or injury, sudden unexpected death of a loved one or even worse, a violent death of someone close. These set the scene for the development of any number of anxiety disorders, including post-traumatic stress disorder.

There are also lesser stressors that can threaten to crush us under their weight: a boss that has no understanding of time and capacity, an organizational culture in which gossip is rife, in-laws who are over critical and unwelcoming, children who are angry and rebellious. It would seem that anxiety would be a natural response to the many opportunities that present themselves in daily modern life. It is not for nothing that we are known to live in the 'Age of Anxiety'.

Some people are robust and resilient. They seem able to cope with relative ease despite all the demands that are placed on them. Others are more fragile and liable to crack under the pressures that they face. In this book we are not interested in why this is the case. What we will focus on is how to turn our fragility into flourishing. Chapter 2 will zoom in on anxiety and its various manifestations.

WHAT IS ANXIETY?

Anxiety is a normal, natural human emotion that everyone experiences. It is different to fear, which is the emotion we feel in the face of actual danger. We see a cobra in our path and it is natural to feel frightened and to run away. Or when we see our partner coming towards us with a rolling pin and an angry expression on their face, we experience fear.

Anxiety, on the other hand, is commonly conceptualized as a response to perceived threat (Lazarus, 1991). This threat can be real or imagined. If we are trying to get a piece of work completed by the end of the week and a small but crucial piece of information is still missing on Thursday evening, then it is natural to feel anxious. However, if we are feeling anxious about this on Monday morning, it is likely that we are overestimating the danger in the situation and underestimating our ability to cope with it and also discounting the resources we have at hand to solve the problem.

Christine Padesky, a leading psychologist in CBT, expresses this as an equation:

$$\text{Anxiety} = \frac{\text{Overestimation of danger}}{\text{Underestimation of ability and resources to cope}}$$

We need moderate levels of anxiety in our contemporary world in order to function optimally. This means that we need to teach ourselves to realistically estimate the danger we face and school ourselves to be aware of the skills and the resources that we have at hand to cope with the situation.

SYMPTOMS OF ANXIETY

Anxiety affects us on a physical as well as cognitive level. When we are anxious, we might experience these bodily symptoms:

- dizziness
- tiredness
- headaches
- muscle tension
- sweating
- a racing heartbeat
- high blood pressure
- faintness
- dry mouth

We will never be able to eliminate all of our anxiety and just like a low mood, anxiety is part of being human. If our levels of anxiety are too low, we under-perform. If our levels of anxiety are too high, we become paralysed. In order to lead a productive, fulfilling and happy life, we need to learn how to manage anxiety appropriately in different situations. This is about differentiating between when a situation is really threatening and when it is not. It also involves correctly gauging the extent of the danger and assessing whether we have the correct resources and skills at hand to cope with it. People often don't realize what their strengths are and how equipped they are to deal with difficult situations.

Unhelpful anxiety can be managed in order to feel better and live healthily and happily. Some signs that you are experiencing unhelpful anxiety could be that you are getting confused between dangerous and safe situations, if the anxiety is getting in the way of your work life, social life or home life and if the anxiety lasts for a long period of time, even when the immediate threat has passed.

Similar to the previous chapter, this one contains information on what anxiety is, how you might feel when experiencing it and some primary advice on what to do about it. In Chapter 5, I will go into much greater detail as to how to deal with anxiety from a cognitive behavioural therapy perspective. Kiran, a woman who had suffered from anxiety for many years, was interviewed for this chapter in order to obtain an insider view on the condition.

Q: What is your anxiety like, Kiran?

A: I'll get a pattern of intrusive thoughts and images that are particularly anxiety provoking and a particular sick feeling. Anxiety is a very familiar companion because I've had it since childhood and it will come back and it just floods in. If the anxiety is allowed to develop, it will become overwhelming so I'm thinking about it all the time.

It's fear. Just being really, really frightened that something terrible is going to happen. There are two levels of anxiety, there's the normal and there's the obsessional, ridiculous, over-the-top anxiety. For me, it doesn't seem to be the response to a specific individual stimulus; it's more like a response to life.

FUNCTIONS OF ANXIETY

The physical symptoms of anxiety are remnants of the 'fight or flight or freeze' response. Historically, humans used to live in an environment where there were many physical dangers such as dangerous animals. In this context, when danger is spotted, the person needs to stand up to the physical attack (fight) or run away as quickly as possible (flight). Freezing is another reaction when you stand so still that you hope the animal will not see you. We now live in fairly safe cities but these responses are still strong within us. Dangerous animals come these days in the form of bosses or partners or children or from our own expectations of ourselves.

When a person feels anxious, the 'stress hormone' cortisol sends signals to the adrenal glands to produce more adrenaline and noradrenaline, which encourage the body to prepare for fight or flight. The person starts to breathe faster in order to take in more oxygen and the heart will beat faster to pump the oxygen all around the body, especially to the largest muscles that the person will need to use to get out of danger. The diagram on the following page illustrates the effects of the 'flight or fight' response on the human body.

This physical response is very helpful when a person has to escape from physical danger but if you have an exam or an important job interview, only moderate levels of fight, flight or freeze response will help. We need just enough to motivate us to perform well. Cortisol is a necessary and important hormone in charge of regulating our cycles of sleep and wakefulness. Having high cortisol levels for short bursts is very helpful in certain situations. But it is particularly unhelpful to maintain high cortisol levels over a long period of time. If you feel constantly anxious over a long period of time, it is detrimental to both your mental and physical health. It is called chronic anxiety and can lead to all sorts of health problems such as muscle pain, headaches, heart disease, stroke, weight gain, skin conditions as well as, of course, anxiety disorders.

> **Q: Is your anxiety accompanied by any physical feelings, Kiran?**
>
> **A:** I have that sick, sinking feeling that is there all the time. And if it's very acute, I will get shudders through my body. It's that feeling of not being able to rest or relax in any way because you're in a state of heightened anxiety all the time and feeling frightened.

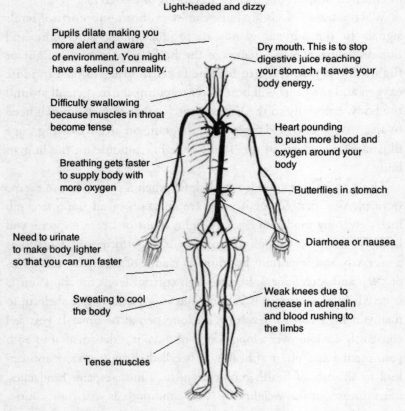

Light-headed and dizzy

Pupils dilate making you more alert and aware of environment. You might have a feeling of unreality.

Dry mouth. This is to stop digestive juice reaching your stomach. It saves your body energy.

Difficulty swallowing because muscles in throat become tense

Heart pounding to push more blood and oxygen around your body

Breathing gets faster to supply body with more oxygen

Butterflies in stomach

Need to urinate to make body lighter so that you can run faster

Diarrhoea or nausea

Sweating to cool the body

Weak knees due to increase in adrenalin and blood rushing to the limbs

Tense muscles

Figure 2.1: The Fight or Flight Response – Bodily Symptoms of Anxiety

In the example at the beginning of the chapter, Nandita's anxiety about driving was not in line with the situation. If she had looked at the facts (she had never had an accident in twenty years of driving), she would have realized that she was well equipped to cope with all the dangers on the Delhi roads and she would have felt less anxious about driving.

HOW COMMON IS ANXIETY?

Anxiety exists in all cultures and in both rural and urban settings. Different countries report varying rates of anxiety across the population. However, we do not know if this means that people in those countries suffer less anxiety or if they are just less likely to report it. Trivedi and Gupta (2010) found that in three reviews of studies on anxiety in India, between 16.5 per cent and 22.6 per cent of those surveyed suffered from anxiety. This is very similar to findings in the US, Australia and Great Britain (Clark and Beck, 2011). Even children and young people experience anxiety. Deb, Chatterjee and Walsh (2010) surveyed adolescents in schools in Kolkata and found that 20.1 per cent of boys and 17.9 per cent of girls there were suffering from anxiety. This means that if you are experiencing anxiety, you are not the only one. It is a very common condition that about a fifth of people across the country, i.e., over two hundred and forty four million Indians, share with you.

The main difference in accounts across cultures is not the frequency or severity of anxiety reported but the symptoms experienced. Researchers have found that people in Goa who suffered from anxiety used the terms 'tension', 'worry', *'maka zalem'* (tension) and *'khub chintalon'* (worry) to describe their condition (Andrew, Cohen, Salgaonkar and Patel, 2012).

But they also found a tendency among these patients to describe anxiety only in physical terms (palpitations, headaches and giddiness). However, when asked about the cause of these physical symptoms, their patients often reported emotionally distressing events, social difficulties and worrying too much. Thus, many people will only report the physiological reactions that they are experiencing rather than the emotion that accompanies that reaction. This can sometimes be misleading and may encourage worried parents or partners to get medical help rather than just realizing that their child or older parent is suffering from anxiety. As mentioned in Chapter 1, anthropologist and psychotherapist Inga Britt-Krause (1989) spoke to people from the Punjab who were living in Bedford, England. They told her about a condition they called 'sinking heart' or '*dil ghirtha hai*'. This term was used both to describe physical conditions of the heart and psychological issues such as depression, anxiety and stress.

Helpful Anxiety

Anxiety is not always the enemy. There are situations in which it is important to feel anxious and take appropriate precautions. Let's take another example:

Maulik had just learnt to drive. He didn't have enough money to buy a new car, so he normally borrowed his brother's old car, which sometimes stalled when he was driving and needed the brakes replaced. It was June, during the monsoon, so the roads were flooded and the heavy rain made it difficult to see. Maulik wanted to take his brother's car round to a friend's house twenty kilometre away. He felt very worried about getting in the car and extremely anxious when he imagined the danger. Maulik decided to stay at home that night.

In this situation, Maulik's emotional response helped him make a decision that, given the circumstances and the state of the car, was a wise one.

When Does Helpful Anxiety Become Unhelpful Anxiety?

Anxiety becomes unhelpful when we begin to avoid situations that might provoke it in us, just to escape feeling anxious. As a lecturer I am required to deliver PowerPoint presentations to classes of students and this sometimes makes me feel anxious. My anxiety is helpful because it keeps me on my toes, makes me alert to questions and open to new information. If I abandoned my students and stopped turning up at my lectures altogether, I would classify my anxiety as unhelpful because it is making my life dysfunctional. We might also engage in behaviours that give us a feeling of safety for a short while but in the long term, they do us no good. In Nandita's case, she avoided narrow, crowded roads and thus was never able to prove to herself that she had the skills to drive in these situations. Her safety behaviour was to drive only on flyovers even if it took her much longer to get to work than was necessary. She also ultimately gave up work in order to avoid driving. Both of these behaviours restricted her life and were life-limiting. Thus, avoidance and engaging in safety behaviours are two hallmarks of unhelpful anxiety. Unhelpful anxiety will show itself in the following ways:

- Avoiding anxiety-provoking situations
- Bodily arousal: physiological symptoms of fight or flight
- Worrying (particularly in GAD)
- Overestimating danger
- Engaging in compensatory safety behaviours
- Underestimating coping strategies
- Underestimating resources at hand to cope
- Inability to effectively solve problems
- An aversion to thinking through issues in a rational frame of mind

CYCLES OF ANXIETY

We feed and nurture our own anxiety, often without even being aware that we are doing so. We do this by:
- Predicting the worst possible outcomes, even if a positive outcome is more likely in reality
- Living in the future or in the past rather than in the current moment

- Seeing mistakes as complete failures
- Seeing life events as catastrophically bad and really important

There are many other ways in which we perpetuate cycles of anxiety, using unhelpful thinking styles. In Chapter 3, I will explain how CBT can help you manage your anxiety by using a more helpful thinking style to counteract it. Here are a few examples of unhelpful thinking styles that can make people feed their anxiety:

- Seeing yourself as a complete failure if you do not produce an absolutely perfect dinner party
- Thinking of the worst possible reason for an unpredicted event, for example, your wife is late home from work by over an hour and you think she must have had an accident

The above examples are of 'all or nothing' thinking and 'catastrophising' which we will look at further in Chapter 3. Recognizing these unhelpful thinking styles and labelling them as such is the first step towards breaking a cycle of anxiety. The next step is to replace them with a more helpful thinking style.

ANXIETY AS FUTURE-ORIENTATED THINKING

Clark and Beck (2011), leaders in cognitive therapy, write that anxiety and fear are both future-orientated emotions. This is because when we are worried, anxious or fearful, our thoughts and feelings are focused on something terrible happening in the future. We think in terms of 'what if' the worst comes to pass. Problems arise when we live in the future instead of in the present moment. This has long been recognized in Indian thought patterns. For example, Swami Chinmayananda discussed this in his translation of and commentary on the *Bhagavadgita* (1996). Chinmayananda writes about anxiety as coming about when we are too focused on the future instead of on the present:

'Burning anxiety for the fruits-of-action is an unprofitable channel of dissipation of the sacred and vital human energy. Fruits belong to future periods of time, and to waste the present in anxiety over the future, is indeed an unintelligent policy of existence.' (Chinmayananda, 1996, pg 1102)

This is karma yoga, the way of actionless action. Here, Chinmayananda describes one of the central messages of the *Bhagavadgita*, taking action without becoming attached to the outcome of your action, but trusting it to God. As Krishna explains to Arjuna:

'Let your concern be with the act alone and never with its consequences. Do not let the consequences of the act be your concern, and do not be attached to inaction.' (Bhagavadgita, II. 47)

This will be explored in more depth in Chapter 6, which explains the ideas behind and the technique of mindfulness.

PANIC ATTACKS

Any type of anxiety can be accompanied by panic attacks and anyone can have a panic attack. It is worth understanding what a panic attack looks and feels like so that you can recognize one if you or someone you know has one.

As with all anxiety-related issues, panic attacks have physical and psychological symptoms. When you are having a panic attack, you might feel like you are being overwhelmed by fear and have a sense of impending doom. Having a panic attack is common in most anxiety disorders. This is not the same as having panic disorder (See below).

Luckily, a panic attack will not harm you in any way. However, during the panic attack, you might experience these symptoms:

- dizziness, light-headedness or vertigo
- chest pains
- feeling faint

- nausea
- shaking or trembling
- pounding heartbeat
- hyperventilating
- chills or hot flushes
- shortness of breath
- feeling of choking

Although they will not cause you any lasting harm, the physical symptoms of a panic attack are real.

DIFFERENT ANXIETY DISORDERS

Anxiety is regarded as a disorder when it is excessive, becomes difficult to control, lasts more than six months and has a significant impairing effect on daily life (American Psychological Association, 2013).

We get into the realms of anxiety disorder when we:

- check our bodies repeatedly for signs of diseases or ill health (Health/ Illness anxiety)
- misinterpret physical symptoms of anxiety to mean that something catastrophic is happening to us like a heart attack or fainting or even death (Panic disorder)
- avoid going out of the home because we fear we will have a panic attack (Panic disorder with agoraphobia)
- let our worries spiral out of control that we are worrying about practically everything and are exhausted by the process (Generalized Anxiety Disorder)
- develop debilitating fear about specific things like spiders or being in a lift or flying in a plane (Specific phobias)
- become very self-conscious in social situations, such that we avoid social interactions as much as possible (Social anxiety)

One very debilitating type of mental health issue occurs in some people after they have been through a traumatic event like war, rape or the unexpected death of a dear one (post-traumatic stress disorder). This used to be classified in the diagnostic and statistical manual (DSM IV) as an anxiety disorder but in DSM V it occupies a category on its own. This is because people with PTSD suffer a whole range of emotions (terror, guilt, shame) and not just anxiety.

Another issue that is now in a category by itself is obsessive compulsive disorder where people repeatedly look for germs or return many times to the house to check if they have turned off the gas or locked the doors.

Even though they are no longer classed under anxiety, we will look at both these syndromes in some detail as they are so common. Christine Padesky divides these disorders into two main categories: the danger disorders and the coping disorders.

The danger disorders: in these disorders people tend to overestimate danger within the situation:

- Panic Disorder (without agoraphobia)
- Panic Disorder (with agoraphobia)
- Obsessive Compulsive Disorder (OCD)
- Health/illness Anxiety

The coping disorders: in these disorders people tend to underestimate their ability to cope and the resources available to cope:

- Generalized Anxiety Disorder (GAD)
- Specific Phobias
- Social Anxiety

Padesky sees PTSD as both a danger and a coping disorder.

Recognizing different kinds of anxiety problems could help you to take control of your anxiety before it takes control of you! Use the exercises and techniques described in this book to do this. Anxiety disorders are just anxious feelings, thoughts and behaviours taken to an extreme, which affect your daily life in a negative way. Having an anxiety disorder is very, very common. There is no human being who does not experience anxiety, even extreme anxiety, at some point or the other. However, if you feel that you have one or the other of these anxiety disorders, first read this book and go through the exercises. If your anxiety is still very strong then it would be wise to get in touch with a cognitive behaviour therapist in your locality who will help you get over some of the excessive anxiety that you are feeling.

People often suffer from multiple anxiety disorders and also suffer from depression or other mental health problems at the same time. So if you read the following descriptions of anxiety disorders and think that more than one may apply to you or somebody you know, this could very well be the case. They all have some features in common. However, as well as recognizing this, it is important to differentiate between them since varying kinds of anxiety disorders are treated in different ways. The cognitive behavioural therapy strategies used for generalized anxiety disorder will be different from those used for specific phobias. If you think you might be suffering from multiple anxiety disorders, you should try to identify what thoughts and feelings are causing you the most distress or if there is one particular type of anxiety that is more prominent than the others.

DANGER DISORDERS

These are anxiety disorders that arise from overestimating danger like:

> **Q: Have you experienced panic attacks, Kiran?**
>
> A: I used to have very severe panic attacks. They would be particularly bad outside the house. The first one that I recall having was in a theatre and I was sitting in the circle of the theatre in the middle of the row. I remember thinking I was going to die, I was going to faint and if I didn't die it would be a miracle. It was the worst feeling in the world. Looking back,

it's laughable. But at the time I was trapped in a row in this theatre and I couldn't get out. And that was when I realized I needed help.

I've had panic attacks since my post-natal depression, after the birth of my first two children. But after that first time in the theatre, I knew what they were. When you know, it's still awful but it's not quite as bad. You do start to believe that you will survive it. Although that's hard to hold on to in the moment because you don't think you will.

PANIC DISORDER (WITHOUT AGORAPHOBIA)

When people have recurring panic attacks that seem to come out of the blue and they then think they are having a heart attack, or that they are going to die or faint (or some other catastrophe), this constitutes a panic disorder. Having one panic attack does not mean that you have panic disorder. However, if you suffer from panic attacks on a regular basis and are quite convinced that something very bad is happening to you physically, you may have panic disorder. This may then lead you to circumscribe your behaviour in order to keep yourself safe. Understanding the symptoms of panic attacks can help somebody with panic disorder recognize that the situation they are in is not dangerous. Rationalizing the situation can lead to a reduction in anxiety. I once treated a man who used to have sixty panic attacks in a week. This came down to two after therapy and he realized that these attacks were just symptoms of anxiety.

PANIC DISORDER (WITH AGORAPHOBIA)

Agoraphobia is often linked to panic disorder and can develop from it. Much of the time, agoraphobia develops when people have panic attacks outside of their homes and then come to associate their panic attacks with those places. Panic disorder with agoraphobia develops when people fear having panic attacks in public spaces. This is often related to the physical symptoms at first. You might worry that you will look stupid in front of others if you have a panic attack; that others might stare at you or think you are insane. You might also think that a panic attack will be life threatening. Both of these were the case for Kiran when she had her first panic attack. Since then, she has been able to rationalize her experience of panic after it occurs and then recognize the symptoms as panic, rather than something more catastrophic like dying or fainting, thereby avoiding the development of panic disorder.

Many people think agoraphobia is a fear of open spaces. It is more complex than that. Agoraphobia is thought to be due to an underlying fear of situations where people may not be able to escape or get help. Thus people with agoraphobia might avoid going to shopping centres, using public transport, visiting the supermarket or even leaving the house at all.

Aashi was out walking her dog one day and she suddenly started shaking and feeling dizzy. She didn't know what was happening to her. She was fearful that she might faint and embarrass herself in public. Later that week Aashi was out shopping when she had a similar attack of dizziness. Over the next few months, Aashi continued to have these bouts of dizziness and her fear that she would faint in front of other people grew. She went to the doctor to check out the dizziness and the doctor did a number of tests and pronounced that she was well. Despite this the dizziness continued and so she started staying at home all day and left her job. Gradually she stopped going out at all and because of her anxiety that she might faint, she stopped seeing her friends altogether. She went back to her doctor who suggested that she might be suffering from panic disorder with agoraphobia and suggested that she see a cognitive behaviour therapist.

Alternatively, agoraphobia could be linked to general feelings of anxiety and not panic disorder. It may be caused by an individual's fear of terrorist attacks, crime or accidents. Much of the time, these feelings go hand in hand with panic attacks. When you start feeling overly anxious about one issue, it can easily spread to other areas of concern in your life.

OBSESSIVE COMPULSIVE DISORDER (OCD)

This is a type of disorder where a person experiences obsessive thoughts ('I am going to kill my son') and/or engages in compulsive behaviours like hand washing or repeatedly checking the gas or mental acts like counting (1, 2, 4, 5, 7 skipping the number 3 or multiples of it because the person thinks that 3 is particularly unlucky for them). OCD is a disorder that develops from an overestimation of external danger. The person who has these obsessions knows that it is only in their mind but still cannot control them. They might try to ignore them or to stop them with compulsive behaviours and mental acts. Common obsessive thoughts include:

- fear of contamination from dirt, germs or chemicals
- fear of harm from having forgotten to lock doors, turn cookers off, close windows, etc.
- inappropriate sexual thoughts that you feel ashamed of
- inappropriate religious or blasphemous thoughts
- thoughts that urge you to behave in a socially unacceptable way
- violent thoughts

People with OCD try to deal with these unwelcome thoughts through compulsions. These are actions that they feel they have to repeat again and again. They often know that they don't make sense but people with OCD might feel that it is the only way they know to control their anxiety or that something terrible will happen if they do not carry out these compulsions. Common compulsive behaviours or mental acts are:

- repetitive hand-washing
- checking and rechecking that doors are locked and electrical appliances are switched off
- repeating a particular word in your mind or out loud
- ordering items in a very specific way
- counting

Naresh was always concerned that he would get sick from touching something dirty. If he thought that he had come into contact with dirt or germs, he washed his hands. Whenever he went to collect the post, he would put gloves on his hands. When he was showering in the morning he would take two hours in the bathroom because he felt he first had to clean the whole shower area and basin. He covered his hands with a towel before raising the toilet seat every time he wanted to urinate and then put the towel for wash and washed his hands vigorously afterwards. He used about sixteen towels in a day. His hands became red, sore and cracked from washing them over seventy times a day. He knew deep down that he was washing his hands too often but could not stop. Naresh was always late for work and this made his boss very angry.

These compulsive behaviours are very time-consuming. OCD will affect a person's life, work and relationships in a significant way. Whilst the obsessions and compulsions of OCD were first documented in the US, Girishchandra and Khanna (2001) confirmed very similar symptoms in their Indian study.

HEALTH/ILLNESS ANXIETY

Health anxiety (which was once known as hypochondria and is now classified as Illness Anxiety in DSM V) is another 'danger disorder' that people can experience if they build up problematic beliefs about health and illness. A person with health anxiety may worry about having cancer, becoming HIV positive or any other physical or mental health condition. They may worry about contracting the disease or condition themselves or they might become concerned that a family member is becoming ill.

Of course, we all worry about getting sick from time to time, but illness anxiety becomes a disorder when the worry is out of proportion to the threat. People with illness anxiety typically check their bodies repeatedly for symptoms of illness, read books and search the Internet looking for information on illnesses, go for frequent medical appointments and ask for reassurance from family members. Anyone might very sensibly have a concern about a lump that could be cancerous but after visiting the doctor and having it checked out, most people would stop worrying. However, somebody with illness anxiety would persistently seek reassurance from medical professionals despite negative results.

Dinesh had worried a lot as a young person but it wasn't until his dad was diagnosed with cancer that the worry became uncontrollable. Dinesh started to find it difficult to concentrate at work and came home in the evenings tense and irritable. Dinesh's dad made a full recovery but this only partly relieved Dinesh's symptoms. He couldn't sleep and started to worry about other areas of his life too. He spent the evenings searching the Internet for information on how cancer develops in the body and reading articles about people who had been fatally misdiagnosed. He continually made medical appointments to check various lumps on his body but when the doctor told him that he was perfectly healthy, Dinesh decided that the doctor was making mistakes. Dinesh's anxiety was unhelpful and out of proportion to the threat of getting cancer. He overestimated the danger.

COPING DISORDERS

These are disorders that arise from underestimating your ability to cope and discounting the resources you have to help you cope.

GENERALIZED ANXIETY DISORDER (GAD)

Generalized anxiety disorder is a condition in which people experience high and upsetting levels of worry. People with GAD report feeling constantly worried and stressed about anything and everything. Sometimes they will know that there is no logical reason for their anxiety but will feel it anyway. They might not know what triggers their anxiety. They might also feel that worry is just part of their personality and feel as if they cannot change this. Whilst everyone feels anxious and worried from time to time, GAD is characterized by excessive and disproportionate worrying. People with GAD often worry about hypothetical situations in the future, imagining the worst. They tend to ask themselves 'what if' questions, such as 'What if I am in a car crash?', 'What if I fail my exam?', 'What if my son gets ill?' Often they will hold core beliefs that cause them to perceive many different situations as threatening. They will engage in chronic worry over a number of different situations and their worry spirals out of control leaving them feeling exhausted, tired and weary of living.

GAD is the most commonly diagnosed anxiety disorder and people who have this have been experiencing anxiety that affects their daily life in a negative way for nearly every day over a period of six months. 'What if' thinking is a hallmark of GAD. You may feel:

- restless
- irritable
- fidgety
- tired or fatigued
- distracted
- intense feelings of dread
- unable to relax
- unable to concentrate
- chronically nervous and tense
- unable to get a good night's sleep

Kim had always been a worrier. She remembered how when she was at school she used to constantly ask herself 'What if I forget my homework?', 'What if my mum forgets to pick me up?', 'What if I fail this test?' The worries had always gone round and round in her head. As an adult, she would worry about her husband such that she was phoning him at work several times a day to make sure he was okay. Her parents lived quite far away and she always worried about what would happen if her mum fell ill. She would text her brother and his wife at least once a day to remind them to check on their parents.

SPECIFIC PHOBIAS

Common phobias are a fear of spiders, snakes, flying, particular animals, heights, storms, driving, vomit and many more. When somebody has a phobia, they know that their fear is excessive or unreasonable but they will not be able to control it. Most people will feel nervous when they climb to the top of a high building. If fears are managed so that they do not have a large impact on your life, then it is not a phobia. However, someone who has a phobia of heights might avoid climbing stairs at all and feel intense fear, anxiety and distress and even have a panic attack if they are required to go up an escalator. Specific phobias lead to avoidance behaviours and tend to interfere in the person's daily life because they go to great extents to avoid that which they fear. Again, this is a 'coping disorder' because people with specific phobias believe that they will not be able to handle coming into contact with their fear. For example, Anand's fear of flying means that he has not visited his son who is studying abroad even though he has plenty of time and money to do so. He once booked a flight, travelled to the airport and then felt so anxious that he went back home. Thinking about going on an airplane makes Anand feel physically sick. This has become a phobia for him, since it is affecting his life in a negative way.

SOCIAL PHOBIA (SOCIAL ANXIETY DISORDER)

Most people feel nervous at times when they have to engage in social interaction in a public place. However, if the anxiety becomes so extreme and persistent that it stops a person from living their life the way they want to, it is classified as social anxiety disorder or social phobia. This is another very common anxiety disorder that affects many people all over the world. People who have social phobia often try to avoid social situations because they are worried about being humiliated in front of others. They will typically worry a lot about what other people think of them. Activities that they might avoid or dread include:

- giving presentations or speeches in front of others
- speaking on the telephone
- going to parties or social gatherings
- talking in a group of people

- getting to know new people
- speaking to strangers

Social phobia is classified as a coping disorder because people who have it underestimate their ability to deal with social situations effectively. If you have social phobia, you might convince yourself that other people think you are stupid or boring. This may lead to you having low self-esteem and worrying that your friends, colleagues and family do not really like you or want to spend time with you. You may also be scared of negative criticism from others and take it very personally.

Often these unhelpful cognitions will be accompanied by some of the physical symptoms of anxiety as detailed above.

Padma disliked going to birthday parties as a child but never knew why. As she grew older, she never enjoyed going out with friends or to family occasions because she felt very anxious. She felt very self-conscious and arrived at any gathering sweating and trembling. Sometimes she would spend all day worrying about a social event that evening and arrive at the event with her head pounding. She was very worried about what other people would think of her and felt that she was always making a fool of herself in front of friends and family. Padma reached her late teens but could not bear to go to college. She could not work in a job for more than a few months because she did not know how to tackle her social anxiety. This made her more ashamed and unhappy.

POST-TRAUMATIC STRESS DISORDER (PTSD)

After a traumatic event, it is common to feel frightened and for images of the event to play back in your mind. This normally subsides after a few weeks but for some people it can continue for months and years. In this case, it is known as PTSD. People can develop PTSD after a road accident, being a victim of a violent crime, physical or sexual abuse, natural disasters, being in military combat or witnessing violence or death. It could be any event that involves actual or threatened death or serious injury. People can also develop PTSD just by hearing about someone else's trauma, especially if they are a close family member. Traumatic events do not always cause people to develop an anxiety disorder and some people have already built up their resilience to a level that they come away from the traumatic experience with minimal symptoms. PTSD tends to be very painful and upsetting and it is recommended that people with PTSD work through their anxiety with a cognitive behavioural therapist.

PTSD has been well-documented in India, for example, in people who survived the Mumbai bombings in July 2011. There are many Indian mental health professionals who have worked with people suffering the symptoms of PTSD especially after the December 2004 tsunami in Kanyakumari district (Pyari et al., 2012) and with people involved in the conflict in Kashmir (Margoob et al., 2006).

PTSD can become a problem fairly soon after the trauma or it can be several months or years until it surfaces. People with PTSD often suffer from:

- Re-experiencing flashbacks, nightmares or vivid memories of the traumatic experience
- Emotional numbing – pushing the traumatic experience out of their mind, avoiding people linked to the trauma, feeling emotionally numb, feeling distant from others
- Hyperarousal – feeling constantly on guard, being irritable, losing their temper quickly, being easily startled, finding it hard to relax, having problems sleeping

Sandeep, fifty-three, was in the Zaveri bazaar in Mumbai during the 2011 bomb blast where twenty-six people were killed and 130 were injured. He quickly took shelter under a table to avoid the falling debris. He was knocked unconscious by the blast and woke up afterwards in a state of confusion. He became very sensitive to loud bangs and noises and he started to avoid crowded places such as supermarkets, bazaars and marketplaces. A psychologist introduced him to cognitive behavioural therapy and this helped him come to terms with what had happened to him.

If we do an analysis of the probabilities that Sandeep might be in another bomb blast in his lifetime, they would come out as quite low. Had he not spent fifty-two years of his life not being the victim of a bomb blast? Thus Sandeep might be overestimating the danger of going to crowded places like the market. He is also underestimating his ability to cope; did he not take shelter under a table? This prevented him from being killed and kept him out of the path of danger.

Many people who experience trauma do not get symptoms of PTSD. PTSD is thought of as both a danger disorder and a coping disorder since people with PTSD both overestimate the danger to themselves and underestimate their ability to cope with it and the resources they have to help them cope. Psychologists enable people suffering from PTSD to regain lost awareness of their inherent strengths and coping strategies, thereby facilitating them to become resilient.

COMMON THEORIES OF ANXIETY

> ### Q: Why do you think that you get so anxious, Kiran?
>
> A: I think it's a combination of a genetic predisposition to anxiety but also the parenting style that my parents adopted. I got into this pattern of feeling that I had to be able to please other people and be a certain way and then feeling anxious if I couldn't be that way. My parents didn't really fill me with much self-belief and my mother in particular was always keen to point out my deficiencies. I remember the criticisms and the feeling that I wasn't quite good enough.

As in the case of depression, most psychologists believe that a range of biological, psychological and social factors will contribute to a person experiencing unhelpful levels of anxiety. According to cognitive behavioural therapy, it is not the events that have happened to you that cause your anxiety. It is your underlying beliefs and negative thoughts about those events and your current life challenges. Therefore, adherents of CBT would agree that Kiran's anxiety may be at least partly due to her genetics and her upbringing. However, they would emphasize that Kiran's own thoughts and underlying assumptions play an important role in perpetuating her anxiety and with help it is possible to change this.

VULNERABILITY TO ANXIETY

Possessing an underlying central nervous system sensitivity to anxiety has been termed 'neuroticism' (Eysenck and Eysenck, 1975), 'trait anxiety' (Spielberger, Gorsuch and Lushene, 1970) and 'anxiety sensitivity' (Clark and Beck, 2011). More recently Aron (1999) has coined the term 'highly sensitive person'. This can be regarded as a personality trait. Many psychologists believe that some of a person's vulnerability to anxiety is hereditary and genetic in nature. Psychological studies of families, including twin studies, have shown that there are likely to be genes responsible for this (Hettema, Neale and Kendler, 2001). However, a genetic predisposition to anxiety does not mean that an individual will develop problems with anxiety. Environmental factors are much more influential in determining whether a person will develop an anxiety disorder (Clark and Beck, 2011).

FAMILY HISTORY

Vulnerability to anxiety is also likely to come from childhood experiences. Various theorists have written reams about the impact of inadequate parenting upon children who later grow up to be anxious and depressed adults. I will not stop for too long to dwell on this. Children who are neglected or abandoned at a young age can come to experience more symptoms of anxiety at a later age. Additionally, parents who are overprotective, preoccupied with threats to their children's safety or who restrict their children's independence can contribute to a child developing unhelpful ways of dealing with anxiety. Parents who are over-critical and unable to express unconditional love are likely to produce children who are over anxious to please others.

Because CBT is a here-and-now therapy, there is an assumption that we can effectively use what is happening in the current moment to grow, become more fulfilled and happier. Though we do look into critical events in the distant past briefly to get a flavour of the whole picture, an efficient cognitive behaviour therapist would not spend much time on this, preferring to stay with the data that presents itself in the recent past and more commonly in the present 'now' moment. This is where CBT is different to psychoanalysis and transactional analysis.

LIFE EVENTS OR TRIGGERS

People can be triggered into anxiety after a particularly stressful event or development in their lives. This is what Rohr (2011) calls 'necessary suffering'. A particular lecturer bullies you or harasses you, your boyfriend rejects you for another person or your boss does not think you are doing very well at your job. Such kinds of events can be triggers for an episode of anxiety. But they need not be. Whether you become anxious or not depends on how you deal with the triggers.

LACK OF SOCIAL NETWORKS

Social support helps keep people mentally and emotionally strong. A lack of good relationships and friends or family members to confide in increases the risk of developing anxiety problems. It is important to share your problems with a sympathetic person who can give you support and advice when you are feeling upset or distressed.

It is normal when we are feeling anxious to look for reassurance from others to help us. This can be very helpful, especially if you are not sure whether your fear is justified or not. However, becoming dependent on reassurance from other people can be a safety behaviour (see later). Only tackling the anxiety by yourself will enable you to get on top of it in the long term.

What Keeps Anxiety Going?

Once we are in a cycle of anxiety, it seems to develop a life of its own. We keep going round and round, becoming more and more anxious and unhappy. The reality is that we proactively maintain our cycles of anxiety by our catastrophic interpretation, our avoidance and our safety behaviours.

Catastrophic Interpretation of the Situation

We have already talked a lot about this. Our tendency to catastrophise or overestimate the dangers of the situations we find ourselves in rather than seeing them in a helpful frame is often the reason that we become anxious. This is not to say that there are no catastrophes in life; there are! In India, poverty, debt, illness and death are very common catastrophes. It is our response to these catastrophes that will determine whether we will grow or whether our lives will become narrow and restricted. We need to ask ourselves, 'Is this a catastrophe that has a solution?' If so, we need to put on our problem-solving hats. If not, we will need to develop mindfulness and ACT skills to help us simply be aware of and accept the situations that we cannot change.

Avoidance

When Neha went shopping, she felt anxious and afraid. The crowds of people around her were too noisy and the mall was too busy. The next time Neha needed to buy food, she asked her daughter to go instead of her.

Neha's solution to her anxiety was avoidance. Whilst this might seem like a sensible strategy, avoiding the situation that makes you anxious will not help you overcome your anxiety in the long run. In order to beat your fear, you will need to face it. You might need support from other people at first but fear will never go away until you tackle it yourself.

If Neha were to go shopping in the crowded mall on her own again, she might realize that she can cope in that situation. If she relies on others and stays at home because she is too scared, she might never develop the ability to cope with that stressful situation.

Avoidance could be, like in Neha's case, staying away from the situation that makes her anxious and relying on the support of other people. Avoidance could also mean drinking alcohol before meeting work colleagues for a dinner party. Whilst you are still going out to meet them, you are avoiding facing up to the situation and tackling your fear. You might be worried about talking on the phone or receiving emails with bad news and thus avoid answering the phone or checking your emails. Avoidance could be much more subtle than this and take the form of avoiding thinking about your phobia or fear.

SAFETY BEHAVIOURS

Safety behaviours are little actions that we carry out, props that we take with us or ways of presenting ourselves, which reduce our anxiety in the short term but end up increasing our anxiety in the long term. Often when we are anxious or depressed, we adopt safety behaviours to protect ourselves from pain. Safety behaviours prevent us from teaching ourselves that the beliefs we have or the predictions we make about our reality are not accurate.

For example, somebody who is worried about catching a disease might never go out in public without hand soap. A person who is nervous at social gatherings might wear dull clothes and avoid making eye contact or speaking to new people. Of course, these safety behaviours are really avoidance by another name. Every time you avoid a difficult situation or carry out a safety behaviour, you are confirming your underlying assumption that the situation is dangerous.

Nita thought that her friends would think badly of her because she no longer had a job. So she just dropped out of the social circle of friends who had been a strong support to her. She became increasingly house bound and agoraphobic. She would not go out with her husband anywhere and stayed at home, dully watching TV and playing on the computer. In order to protect herself from the possibility that her friends might think badly of her for having lost her job, she developed the 'safety behaviour' of social isolation. While this made her less anxious in the moment, in the long run, the safety behaviour in itself became a further problem (agoraphobia) that she had to deal with. In therapy, she understood the importance of dropping her safety behaviours and she slowly began making contact with her friends again to find that they were sympathetic and even helpful in finding her a new job.

In summary, what maintains anxiety is a negative, catastrophic way of interpreting the situation that we find ourselves in. This leads to experiencing the emotion of anxiety and all its unpleasant physiological symptoms. When we experience anxiety we want to avoid the situation that makes us anxious and then develop safety behaviours to keep us feeling comfortable. When we avoid the situations that cause us anxiety and develop safety behaviours to protect ourselves from that situation, we remove ourselves from opportunities to disconfirm our hypothesis that the situation is dangerous and full of threat. When we come across that situation again, we therefore continue to have a negative interpretation of it. This is how our anxiety is maintained in a vicious cycle.

Here is a simple diagrammatic CBT model of anxiety. Notice how the individual's negative interpretation of the situation, rather than the situation itself, produces anxiety and the fight or flight response.

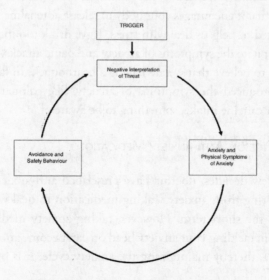

Figure 2.2: The CBT Model of Anxiety

Sometimes other people care so much about us that they want to help us with our anxiety. A mother might do her daughter's shopping for her if the daughter is scared of going out to the shops. A husband may do all the driving for the family if his wife is afraid of it. However, in these circumstances the more useful thing to do would be to gently enable and empower the person suffering from anxiety to conquer their fears themselves. Otherwise, the person 'helping' their friend or loved one is maintaining their cycle of anxiety and reinforcing the belief that they cannot cope.

ALCOHOL, CAFFEINE AND DRUGS

Drinking alcohol and taking drugs is another safety behaviour and avoidance mechanism. It may seem to help in the short term but will prevent you from tackling anxiety yourself in the long term. If you need to drink alcohol in order to face a family gathering, you are allowing yourself to become dependent on it. Also, as your body processes alcohol, it has the effect of making your body and mind experience more stress.

Caffeine, found in tea, coffee, chocolate and cola drinks, is a stimulant. This means that it encourages your body to release adrenaline, a hormone that is secreted to help us deal with stress. If we drink too much caffeine we can precipitate the symptoms of anxiety and panic attacks, which may then lead us to believe that we are having a heart attack. In fact, we have artificially produced the symptoms of anxiety, like palpitations of the heart via our caffeine intake, something to be aware of.

OVER-RELIANCE ON ANTI-ANXIETY MEDICATION

In the last few decades, doctors have prescribed anti-anxiety drugs to people suffering from anxiety. Taking medication to deal with anxiety can help in the short term. However, taking anxiety medication can stop you from tackling your anxiety head on can become another means of avoidance, thereby maintaining the anxiety cycle. It is better to use

CBT in order to deal with anxiety in the long term. However, if you need to take anti-anxiety medication, you should not feel embarrassed or as if you have failed. Many people are prescribed antidepressants since anxiety and depression often occur together. In these cases, some people report anti-depressants to be helpful in quelling their anxiety.

You should not stop taking a course of medication prescribed by your doctor without further consultation. Depending upon what it is, most doctors will help you taper off the medication rather than encourage you to stop it abruptly.

WHAT CAN I DO TO START TACKLING MY ANXIETY?

CBT has developed a number of techniques to help people manage their anxiety. These involve learning how to challenge your anxious thoughts effectively and learning to expose yourself to your most feared situations. Mindfulness and ACT offer complementary techniques for dealing with anxious thoughts and feelings. The remaining chapters in this book will detail these techniques so that you can use them effectively.

In the next section of this chapter, I have included a number of questionnaires that can help you determine if you have a particular anxiety disorder or not. If for example, you suspect that you have Obsessive Compulsive Disorder (OCD), fill in the OCI and score it. If your score is very high then do make an appointment to see a specialist. Likewise with the other questionnaires. If you suspect you have a particular anxiety disorder and your score is mild to moderate on the questionnaire related to it, then continue reading this book and do the exercises. If your scores have not improved despite diligent effort on your part, then it may be time to get specialist help.

DO I HAVE AN ANXIETY DISORDER?

Since there are many different anxiety disorders, there are many different questionnaires that can determine which type of anxiety you are experiencing. Just like with the previous chapter's questionnaire for depression, you cannot self-diagnose, but the questionnaires can provide a screening tool for you to do at home.

GAD-7 QUESTIONNAIRE: DO I HAVE GENERALIZED ANXIETY DISORDER?

This short questionnaire, the GAD-7 (Spitzer, Kroenke, Williams et al., 2006), assesses an individual for GAD. Circle the answer that seems to best describe how you feel. At the end, count up your score and write it in the box at the bottom.

Over the past two weeks, how often have you been bothered by any of the following problems?

	Not at all	Several days	More than half the days	Every day
1. Feeling nervous, anxious or on edge	0	1	2	③
2. Not being able to stop or control worrying	0	1	2	③
3. Worrying too much about different things	0	1	2	③
4. Trouble relaxing	0	①	2	3
5. Being so restless that it is hard to stay still	0	①	2	3
6. Becoming easily annoyed or irritable	0	1	②	3
7. Feeling afraid as if something awful might happen	0	1	2	③

Total score: _____16_____

8. If you have any of these problems, how difficult have those problems made it for you to do your work, take care of things at home or get along with other people?

[ ] Not difficult at all

[ ] Somewhat difficult

[ ] Very difficult

[✓] Extremely difficult

Now follow the next few steps:

STEP ONE:

If you have answered 2 (more than half the days) or 3 (every day) for questions one and two it is a good idea to tackle your anxiety.

STEP TWO:

Add up your total number of points from the whole table (not including question 8).

STEP THREE:

Use the table below to work out the severity of your anxiety.

Score	Severity of Anxiety	What You Should Do
0–5	Minimal anxiety	Use this book to learn how to develop techniques to help you feel better. You will benefit greatly from the chapters in Part 3 of this book

Score	Severity of Anxiety	What You Should Do
5–10	Mild anxiety	Use this book to learn how to develop techniques to help you feel better. If your symptoms persist for more than a month or you cannot function properly, go to a psychologist or psychotherapist for help, preferably one who practices CBT
10–15	Moderate GAD	If you score above 10 or above, you should think about seeking help from a psychologist or psychotherapist, preferably one who practices CBT, as well as use the techniques described in this book
More than 15	Severe GAD	If you score above 15, you should definitely get help from a psychologist or psychotherapist, preferably one who practices CBT, as well as use the techniques described in this book

PENN STATE WORRY QUESTIONNAIRE (PSWQ): DO I HAVE GAD?

PENN STATE WORRY QUESTIONNAIRE : DO I HAVE GAD?

This questionnaire is a more accurate measure of Generalized Anxiety Disorder than the GAD-7. I would encourage you to fill it in.

	Not at all Typical of Me				Very Typical of Me
1. If I do not have enough time to do everything, I do not worry about it*	1	2	3	4	5
2. My worries overwhelm me	1	2	3	4	5

	Not at all Typical of Me				Very Typical of Me
3. I do not tend to worry about things*	(1)	2	3	4	5
4. Many situations make me worry	1	2	3	4	(5)
5. I know I should not worry about things, but I just cannot help it	1	2	3	4	(5)
6. When I am under pressure I worry a lot	1	2	3	(4)	5
7. I am always worrying about something	1	2	3	(4)	5
8. I find it easy to dismiss worrisome thoughts*	(1)	2	3	4	5
9. As soon as I finish one task, I start to worry about everything else I have to do	1	2	3	4	(5)
10. I never worry about anything*	(1)	2	3	4	5
11. When there is nothing more I can do about a concern, I do not worry about it anymore*	(1)	2	3	4	5
12. I have been a worrier all my life	1	2	(3)	4	5

	Not at all Typical of Me	← →			Very Typical of Me
13. I notice that I have been worrying about things	1	2	3	4	(5)
14. Once I start worrying, I cannot stop	1	2	3	4	(5)
15. I worry all the time	1	2	3	(4)	5
16. I worry about projects until they are all done	1	2	(3)	4	5

This questionnaire by Meyer et al., (1990) is a bit trickier to score. All the questions marked with an asterisk (1, 3, 8, 10 and 11) are reverse scored since they are worded positively rather than negatively. Score as follows:

Questions 1, 3, 8, 10 and 11:

    Very typical of me = 1 (circled 5 on the sheet)
    Circled 4 = 2
    Circled 3 = 3
    Circled 2 = 4
    Not typical of me = 5

All other questions (2, 4, 5, 6, 7, 9, 12, 13, 14, 15, 16) are scored as in the table:

    Very typical of me = 5
    Circled 4 = 4

Circled 3 = 3
Circled 2 = 2
Not typical of me = 1

Now count up your score from all 16 questions.

Total score = _____73_____

If you have scored 45 or more, you may have Generalized Anxiety Disorder.

OBSESSIVE COMPULSIVE INVENTORY: DO I HAVE OBSESSIVE COMPULSIVE DISORDER?

Read each statement and select a number 0, 1, 2, 3 or 4 that best describes how much that experience has distressed or bothered you during the past month. There are no right or wrong answers. Do not spend too long on any one statement.

	Not at all	A Little	Moderately	A Lot	Extremely
1. Unpleasant thoughts come into my mind against my will and I cannot get rid of them	0	1	2	(3)	4
2. I think contact with bodily secretions (sweat, saliva, blood, urine, etc.) may contaminate my clothes or somehow harm me	(0)	1	2	3	4

	Not at all	A Little	Moderately	A Lot	Extremely
3. I ask people to repeat things several times, even though I understood them the first time	(0)	1	2	3	4
4. I wash and clean obsessively	0	(1)	2	3	4
5. I have to review mentally past events, conversations and actions to make sure that I didn't do something wrong	0	1	2	(3)	4
6. I have saved up so many things that they get in the way	(0)	1	2	3	4
7. I check things more often than necessary	0	1	2	(3)	4
8. I avoid using public toilets because I am afraid of disease or contamination	(0)	1	2	3	4
9. I repeatedly check doors, windows, drawers, etc.	0	1	2	(3)	4
10. I repeatedly check gas, water taps, light switches after turning them off	0	1	2	(3)	4
11. I collect things I don't need	(0)	1	2	3	4

	Not at all	A Little	Moderately	A Lot	Extremely
12. I have thoughts of having hurt someone without knowing it	0	1	2	3	4
13. I have thoughts that I might want to harm myself or others	0	1	2	3	4
14. I get upset if objects are not arranged properly	0	1	2	3	4
15. I feel obliged to follow a particular order in dressing, undressing and washing myself	0	1	2	3	4
16. I feel compelled to count while I'm doing things	0	1	2	3	4
17. I am afraid of impulsively doing embarrassing or harmful things	0	1	2	3	4
18. I need to pray to cancel bad thoughts or feelings	0	1	2	3	4
19. I keep on checking forms or other things I have written	0	1	2	3	4

	Not at all	A Little	Moderately	A Lot	Extremely
20. I get upset at the sight of knives, scissors or other sharp objects in case I lose control with them	0	1	2	3	4
21. I am obsessively concerned about cleanliness	0	1	2	3	4
22. I find it difficult to touch an object when I know it has been touched by strangers or certain people	0	1	2	3	4
23. I need things to be arranged in a particular order	0	1	2	3	4
24. I fall behind in my work because I repeat things over and over again	0	1	2	3	4
25. I feel I have to repeat certain numbers	0	1	2	3	4
26. After doing something carefully, I still have the impression I haven't finished it	0	1	2	3	4
27. I find it difficult to touch rubbish or dirty things	0	1	2	3	4

	Not at all	A Little	Moderately	A Lot	Extremely
28. I find it difficult to control my thoughts	0	1	2	3	(4)
29. I have to do things over and over again until it feels right	0	(1)	2	3	4
30. I am upset by unpleasant thoughts that come into my mind against my will	0	1	2	(3)	4
31. Before going to sleep I have to do things in a certain way	(0)	1	2	3	4
32. I go back to places to make sure that I haven't harmed anyone	(0)	1	2	3	4
33. I frequently get nasty thoughts and have difficulty getting rid of them	0	1	(2)	3	4
34. I avoid throwing things away because I am afraid I might need them later	(0)	1	2	3	4
35. I get upset if others have changed the way I have arranged my things	0	(1)	2	3	4

	Not at all	A Little	Moderately	A Lot	Extremely
36. I feel that I must repeat certain words or phrases in my mind in order to wipe out bad thoughts, feelings or actions	0	1	2	3	4
37. After I have done things, I have persistent doubts about whether I really did them	0	1	2	3	4
38. I sometimes have to wash or clean myself simply because I feel contaminated	0	1	2	3	4
39. I feel that there are good and bad numbers	0	1	2	3	4
40. I repeatedly check anything that might cause a fire	0	1	2	3	4
41. Even when I do something very carefully I feel that it is not quite right	0	1	2	3	4
42. I wash my hands more often or for longer than necessary	0	1	2	3	4

Since OCD can present itself in different ways, there are different subscales that correspond to these different presentations. You should add your scores up for each subscale as well as calculating a total score for OCD.

Add up your scores for each subscale:

Washing subscale score:
(Questions 2, 4, 8, 21, 22, 27, 38, 42)

$\boxed{3}$

Checking subscale score:
(Questions 3, 7, 9, 10, 19, 24, 32, 40)

$\boxed{12}$

Doubting subscale score:
(Questions 26, 37, 41)

$\boxed{3}$

Ordering subscale score:
(Questions 14, 15, 23, 29, 31, 35)

$\boxed{2}$

Obsessions subscale score:
(Questions 1, 12, 13, 17, 20, 28, 30, 33)

$\boxed{7}$

Hoarding subscale score:
(Questions 6, 11, 34)

$\boxed{0}$

Neutralizing subscale score:
(Questions 5, 16, 18, 25, 36, 39)

$\boxed{3}$

Total OCD score:

$\boxed{30}$

A total OCD score of 42 on this questionnaire by Foa et al., (1998) or more or a mean score of 2.5 or more on any subscale indicates that you could have OCD. To calculate your mean score for a subscale, divide your score by the number of questions in the subscale, for example, the Ordering subscale has 6 questions, so take your Ordering score and divide that by 6.

Health Anxiety Inventory: Do I Have Health/Illness Anxiety?

Each question consists of a group of four statements. Please read each group of statements carefully and then select the one which best describes your feelings over the past six months. There are no right or wrong answers. Do not spend too much time on any one statement. This assessment is not intended to be a diagnosis. If you are concerned about your results in any way, please speak with a qualified health professional.

1. a)   I do not worry about my health
   b)   I occasionally worry about my health
   c)   I spend much of my time worrying about my health
   d)   I spend most of my time worrying about my health

2. a)   I notice aches/pains less than most other people (of my age)
   b)   I notice aches/pains as much as most other people (of my age)
   c)   I notice aches/pains more than most other people (of my age)
   d)   I am aware of aches/pains in my body all the time

3. a)   As a rule I am not aware of bodily sensations or changes
   b)   Sometimes I am aware of bodily sensations or changes
   c)   I am often aware of bodily sensations or changes
   d)   I am constantly aware of bodily sensations or changes

4. a)   Resisting thoughts of illness is never a problem
   b)   Most of the time I can resist thoughts of illness
   c)   I try to resist thoughts of illness but am often unable to do so
   d)   Thoughts of illness are so strong that I no longer even try to resist them

5. a) As a rule I am not afraid that I have a serious illness
   b) I am sometimes afraid that I have a serious illness
   c) I am often afraid that I have a serious illness
   d) I am always afraid that I have a serious illness

6. a) I do not have images (mental pictures) of myself being ill
   b) I occasionally have images of myself being ill
   c) I frequently have images of myself being ill
   d) I constantly have images of myself being ill

7. a) I do not have any difficulty taking my mind off thoughts about my health
   b) I sometimes have difficulty taking my mind off thoughts about my health
   c) I often have difficulty in taking my mind off thoughts about my health
   d) Nothing can take my mind off thoughts about my health

8. a) I am lastingly relieved if my doctor tells me there is nothing wrong
   b) I am initially relieved but the worries sometimes return later
   c) I am initially relieved but the worries always return later
   d) I am not relieved if my doctor tells me there is nothing wrong

9. a) If I hear about an illness I never think I have it myself
   b) If I hear about an illness I sometimes think I have it myself
   c) If I hear about an illness I often think I have it myself
   d) If I hear about an illness I always think I have it myself

10. a) If I have a bodily sensation or change I rarely wonder what it means
    b) If I have a bodily sensation or change I often wonder what it means
    c) If I have a bodily sensation or change I always wonder what it means

d)   If I have a bodily sensation or change I must know what it means

11. a)   I usually feel at very low risk for developing a serious illness
     b)   I usually feel at fairly low risk for developing a serious illness
     c)   I usually feel at moderate risk for developing a serious illness
     d)   I usually feel at high risk for developing a serious illness

12. a)   I never think I have a serious illness
     b)   I sometimes think I have a serious illness
     c)   I often think I have a serious illness
     d)   I usually think that I am seriously ill

13. a)   If I notice an unexplained bodily sensation I don't find it difficult to think about other things
     b)   If I notice an unexplained bodily sensation I sometimes find it difficult to think about other things
     c)   If I notice an unexplained bodily sensation I often find it difficult to think about other things
     d)   If I notice an unexplained bodily sensation I always find it difficult to think about other things

14. a)   My family/friends would say I do not worry enough about my health
     b)   My family/friends would say I have a normal attitude to my health
     c)   My family/friends would say I worry too much about my health
     d)   My family/friends would say I am a hypochondriac

For the following questions, please think about what it might be like if you had a serious illness which particularly concerns you like heart disease, cancer, multiple sclerosis and so on. Obviously you cannot know for definite what it would be like; please give your best estimate of what you *think* might happen, basing your estimate on what you know about yourself and serious illness in general.

15. a) If I had a serious illness I would still be able to enjoy things in my life quite a lot

    b) If I had a serious illness I would still be able to enjoy things in my life a little

    c) If I had a serious illness I would be almost completely unable to enjoy things in my life

    d) If I had a serious illness I would be completely unable to enjoy life at all

16. a) If I developed a serious illness there is a good chance that modern medicine would be able to cure me

    b) If I developed a serious illness there is a moderate chance that modern medicine would be able to cure me

    c) If I developed a serious illness there is a very small chance that modern medicine would be able to cure me

    d) If I developed a serious illness there is no chance that modern medicine would be able to cure me

17. a) A serious illness would ruin some aspects of my life

    b) A serious illness would ruin many aspects of my life

    c) A serious illness would ruin almost every aspect of my life

    d) A serious illness would ruin every aspect of my life

18. a) If I had a serious illness I would not feel that I had lost my dignity

    b) If I had a serious illness I would feel that I had lost a little of my dignity

    c) If I had a serious illness I would feel that I had lost quite a lot of my dignity

    d) If I had a serious illness I would feel that I had totally lost my dignity

All groups are scored a = 0, b =1, c = 2 or d = 3 depending on the statement selected.

If more than one statement is selected, use the highest-scoring statement of those chosen.

Main section score (questions 1 to 14) = ☐

Negative consequences score (questions 15 to 18) = ☐

Total score = ☐

This questionnaire is by Salkovskis et al., (2002). In the 2002, a paper describing the development of both the full Health Anxiety Inventory and this current shortened eighteen item version, the following scores were reported for the shortened form in a series of different populations. The table below gives the average scores on the Health Anxiety Inventory for people with and without health anxiety. Compare your scores with the average scores here.

	People with health anxiety	People without health anxiety
Main section score	30.1	9.4
Negative consequences	7.8	2.2
Total score	37.9	12.2

PHOBIA SCALES: DO I HAVE A SPECIFIC PHOBIA?

Choose a number from the scale below to show how much you would avoid each of the situations or objects listed below. Then write the number in the box opposite the situation.

0	1	2	3	4	5	6	7	8
Would not avoid it		Slightly avoid it		Definitely avoid it		Markedly avoid it		Always avoid it

Social situations due to a fear of being embarrassed
or making a fool of myself

Certain situations because of fear of having a panic
attack or other distressing symptoms (such as loss
of bladder control, vomiting or dizziness)

Certain situations because of a fear of a particular object
or activities, (such as animals, heights, seeing blood,
being in confined spaces, driving or flying)

Scoring
4 or above on any item means that you have a specific phobia.

SOCIAL PHOBIA INVENTORY (SPIN): DO I HAVE SOCIAL ANXIETY?

Please check how much the following problems have bothered you
during the past week. Mark only one box for each problem and be sure
to answer all items.

	Not at All	A Little Bit	Somewhat	Very Much	Extremely
1. I am afraid of people in authority	0	1	2	3	4
2. I am bothered by blushing in front of people	0	1	2	3	4
3. Parties and social events scare me	0	1	2	3	4

	Not at All	A Little Bit	Somewhat	Very Much	Extremely
4. I avoid talking to people I don't know	0	1	2	3	4
5. Being criticized scares me a lot	0	1	2	3	4
6. Fear of embarrassment causes me to avoid doing things or speaking to people	0	1	2	3	4
7. Sweating in front of people causes me distress	0	1	2	3	4
8. I avoid going to parties	0	1	2	3	4
9. I avoid activities in which I am the centre of attention	0	1	2	3	4
10. Talking to strangers scares me	0	1	2	3	4
11. I avoid having to give speeches	0	1	2	3	4
12. I would do anything to avoid being criticized	0	1	2	3	4

	Not at All	A Little Bit	Somewhat	Very Much	Extremely
13. Heart palpitations bother me when I am around people	0	1	2	3	4
14. I am afraid of doing things when people might be watching	0	1	2	3	4
15. Being embarrassed or looking stupid are my worst fears	0	1	2	3	4
16. I avoid speaking to anyone in authority	0	1	2	3	4
17. Trembling or shaking in front of others is distressing to me	0	1	2	3	4

Scoring: add up your scores to get your total score. This questionnaire was constructed by Connor et al., in 2000.

Severity	None	Mild	Moderate	Severe	Very Severe
Score	Less than 20	21–30	31–40	41–50	51 or more

Impact Of Events Scale: Do I Have Post-Traumatic Stress Disorder?

Instructions –

Below is a list of difficulties people sometimes have after stressful life events. Please read each item and then indicate how distressing each difficulty has been for you DURING THE PAST SEVEN DAYS with respect to _____, which occurred on _____. How much were you distressed or bothered by these difficulties?

0 = Not at all; 1 = A little bit; 2 = Moderately; 3 = Quite a bit; 4 = Extremely.

The **Intrusion subscale** is the MEAN item response of items 1, 2, 3, 6, 9, 14, 16, 20. Thus, scores can range from 0 through 4.

The **Avoidance subscale** is the MEAN item response of items 5, 7, 8, 11, 12, 13, 17, 22. Thus, scores can range from 0 through 4.

The **Hyperarousal subscale** is the MEAN item response of items 4, 10, 15, 18, 19, 21. Thus, scores can range from 0 through 4.

	0	1	2	3	4
1. Any reminder brought back feelings about it					
2. I had trouble staying asleep					
3. Other things kept making me think about it					
4. I felt irritable and angry					
5. I avoided letting myself get upset when I thought it or was reminded of it					

	0	1	2	3	4
6. I thought about it when I didn't mean to					
7. I felt as if it hadn't happened or wasn't real					
8. I stayed away from reminders of it					
9. Pictures about it popped into my mind					
10. I was jumpy and easily startled					
11. I tried not to think about it					
12. I was aware that I still had a lot of feelings about it, but I didn't deal with them					
13. My feelings about it were kind of numb					
14. I found myself acting or feeling like I was back at that time					
15. I had trouble falling asleep					
16. I had waves of strong feelings about it					
17. I tried to remove it from my memory					
18. I had trouble concentrating					
19. Reminders of it caused me to have physical reactions, such as sweating, trouble breathing, nausea, or a pounding heart					
20. I had dreams about it					
21. I felt watchful and on-guard					
22. I tried not to talk about it					

Total IES-R score: _____

On this test which was created by Weiss in 2007, scores that exceed 24 can mean that you suffer from PTSD. High scores have the following associations.

Score (IES-R)	Consequence
24 or more	PTSD is a clinical concern. Those with scores this high who do not have full PTSD will have partial PTSD or at least some of the symptoms
33 and above	This represents the best cutoff for a probable diagnosis of PTSD
37 or more	This is high enough to suppress your immune system's functioning (even ten years after an impact event)

Key Points from this Chapter:

— Anxiety is very common and experienced by people all over the world
— Some anxiety is good, healthy and appropriate
— Feelings of anxiety that last over a long period of time and interfere significantly in a negative way with your life need to be tackled
— Anxiety cannot be eliminated from your life. Everyone needs to learn to manage their own anxiety in order to live a happy, healthy and fulfilling life
— Many people have anxiety disorders. This is nothing to be ashamed of
— People often use avoidance and safety behaviours to escape their anxiety. This is unhelpful
— The symptoms of anxiety are felt in our bodies as well as our minds. We often notice the physical symptoms before we realize that they are due to anxiety
— Anxiety disorders come about when we overestimate the danger and underestimate our ability to cope and the resources we have at hand to cope

- There are many different anxiety disorders such as GAD, social phobia, specific phobias, panic disorder, and illness anxiety. OCD and PTSD occupy a category of their own because the emotions related to them often involve more than just anxiety: guilt, shame, terror. All of these disorders can be classified as either danger disorders or coping disorders

REFERENCES

1. E.N. Aron, *The Highly Sensitive Person: How To Thrive When the World Overwhelms You*, London: HarperCollins *Publishers*, 1999.

2. G. Andrew, A. Cohen, S. Salgaonkar, and V. Patel, 'The Explanatory Models of Depression and Anxiety in Primary Care: A Qualitative Study from India', *BMC Research Notes*, 5(1): 499, 2012.

3. E. Behar, O. Alcaine, A.R. Zuellig, and T.D. Borkovec, 'Screening for Generalized Anxiety Disorder Using the Penn State Worry Questionnaire: A Receiver Operating Characteristic Analysis', *Journal of Behaviour Therapy and Experimental Psychiatry*, 34:25–43, 2003.

4. G. Butler, and T. Hope, *Manage Your Mind: The Mental Fitness Guide*, 2nd ed., Oxford: Oxford University Press, 2007.

5. S. Chinmayananda, *The Holy Geeta*, 10th ed., Mumbai: Central Chinmaya Mission Trust, 1996.

6. D. Clark, and A. Beck, '*Cognitive Therapy of Anxiety Disorders*', New York: Guilford Press, 2011.

7. K.M. Connor, J.R.T. Davidson, L.E. Churchill, A. Sherwood, R.H. Weisler, and E. Foa, 'Psychometric Properties of the Social Phobia Inventory (SPIN): New self-rating scale', *The British Journal of Psychiatry*, 176(4): 379–386, 2000.

8. M. Creamer, R. Bell, and S. Failla, 'Psychometric Properties of the Impact of Events Scale-Revise', *Behaviour Research and Therapy*, 41:1489–1496, 2003.

9. S. Debs, P. Chatterjee, and K. Walsh, 'Anxiety among High School Students in India: Comparisons Across Gender, School Type, Social Strata, and

Perceptions of Quality Time with Parents', *Australian Journal of Educational and Developmental Psychology*, 10(1): 18–31, 2010.

10. M.J Dugas, and M. Robichaud, *Cognitive Behavioural Treatment for Generalized Anxiety Disorder: From Science to Practice*, New York: Abingdon, Routledge, 2007.

11. E.B. Foa, M.J. Kozak, P.M. Salkovskis, M.E. Coles, and N. Amir, 'The Validation of a New Obsessive-Compulsive Disorder Scale: The Obsessive-Compulsive Inventory', *Psychological Assessment*, 10:206–214, 1998.

12. B.G. Girishchandra, and S. Kanna, 'Phenomenology of Obsessive Compulsive Disorder: A Factor Analytic Approach', *Indian Journal of Psychiatry*, 43(4): 306–316, 2001.

13. J. Hettema, M. Neale, and K. Kendler, 'A Review and Meta-analysis of the Genetic Epidemiology of Anxiety Disorders', *The American Journal of Psychiatry*, 158(10): 1568–1578, 2001.

14. R. Lazarus, *Emotion and Adaptation*, Oxford: Oxford University Press, 1991.

15. T.J. Meyer, M.L. Miller, R.L Metzger, and T.D. Borkovec, 'Development and Validation of the Penn State Worry Questionnaire', *Behaviour Research and Therapy*, 28:487–495, 1990.

16. C. Padesky, 'Anxiety Traps, CBT Antidotes', Workshop presented at the Institute of Education, London, 21–22 May 2012.

17. P.M. Salkovskis, K.A. Rimes, H.M.C. Warwick, and D.M. Clark, 'The Health Anxiety Inventory: Development and Validation of Scales for the Measurement of Health Anxiety and Hypochondriasis', *Psychological Medicine*, 32:843–853, 2002.

18. H. Sheth, Z. Gandhi, G.K. Vankar, 'Anxiety Disorders in Ancient Indian Literature', *Indian Journal of Psychiatry*, 52(3), 289–291, 2010.

19. R.L. Spitzer, K. Kroenke, J.B. Williams and B. Lowe, 'A Brief Measure for Assessing Generalized Anxiety Disorder: The GAD-7', *Archives of Internal Medicine*, 166(10):1092–1097, 2006.

20. J.K. Trivedi, and P.K. Gupta, 'An Overview of Indian Research in Anxiety Disorders', *Indian Journal of Psychiatry*, 52(1), S210–218, 2010.

21. D.S. Weiss (2007), 'The Impact of Events Scale – Revised. In J.P. Wilson & T.M. Keane (Eds.)' *Assessing Psychological Trauma and PTSD: A Practitioner's Handbook* (2 ed. pp. 168–189), New York : Guildford Press.

Part 2:

Treatment of Depression and Anxiety

3

The Nuts and Bolts of CBT

'Everything can be taken from a man but one thing – the last of the human freedoms – to choose one's attitude in any given circumstance, to choose one's own way.'

— Viktor Frankl (1959)

In this chapter:

— What is CBT?
— The relationship between thoughts and feelings
— The ABCDE of CBT
— Helpful and unhelpful thinking styles
— Negative Automatic Thoughts
— The Hot Thought
— Safety Behaviours
— Dealing with unhelpful thoughts

WHAT IS CBT?

Cognitive behaviour therapy or CBT as it is popularly known is everywhere. This is because CBT has been scientifically proven to be effective in helping people overcome states of depression, anxiety, obsessive compulsive disorder (OCD) and post-traumatic stress disorder (PTSD). Compared with other therapies, CBT has the most convincing evidence base. This is why institutions such as the National Institute for Health and Care Excellence in England (NICE) recommends CBT as the therapy of choice if people are suffering from depression (NICE, 2009), anxiety (NICE, 2014), obsessive compulsive disorder (NICE, 2005) and PTSD (NICE, 2005). It also produces better results with patients who have not responded to antidepressants and these effects are maintained over twelve months (Wills, London, Abel et al., 2014).

CBT Is a Brief Therapy

While CBT is useful in targeting and alleviating the above mentioned emotional states, it does not purport to tackle existential issues. If, for example, you have had early issues relating to your attachment towards your mother or father, CBT might not be the best place for you to find healing. Or if you have issues relating to a spiritual search or are looking for the meaning of life, one of the other therapies might be a more helpful starting place. You might want to enter into psychodynamic psychotherapy or into transactional analysis, gestalt therapy, person-centred therapy, transpersonal therapy or existential therapy. All of these therapies have tried methods to heal early memories and early decisions and to help people along their psycho-spiritual journey. These therapies, unlike CBT, are usually long-term therapies (some as long as ten years or more) and are focused on the development of insight. CBT on the other hand is usually short term, time limited, focused on addressing specific problems and achieving specific goals. There are some situations in which CBT is long term.

For example, when a person has been diagnosed with a personality disorder or psychosis, CBT takes longer than the usual six to twenty sessions of therapy that is recommended for depression, anxiety, OCD and PTSD. Also schema therapy developed by Jeffrey Young is a type of CBT that integrates the best of cognitive behavioural, psychoanalytic, existential and interpersonal therapies and looks at early developmental issues as they play out in current life. However, CBT is a brief therapy in general. The time limited nature of CBT suits many people who are comforted by the fact that the therapy they are receiving will fairly quickly come to an end and is therefore affordable. Because CBT is short term and fast acting, it is more practical than other therapies.

CBT IS A HERE-AND-NOW THERAPY

CBT is essentially a here-and-now therapy. It looks at current behaviour, thoughts and feelings without delving too much into the past. It recognizes that the past has an important role to play in the forming of our core beliefs and underlying assumptions about life but it generally looks at the out-workings of these in current situations. The assumption that CBT makes is that we have all the data we need for repair and transform in the way our beliefs and thoughts lead us to act or react in current situations. If our current styles of thinking and our current ways of behaving lead us into difficult situations and create destructive emotions within us, then we need to learn to change our thinking and do something differently.

THE FUNDAMENTALS OF CBT

Because thinking is so central to cognitive behaviour therapy, it is important to understand the nature of thought. According to Charles Fernyhough, professor at Durham University, if we introspect when we are thinking, we will discover that there is a 'flow of inner speech', which is conscious, active and capable of making connections and creating meaning. It is a kind of internal conversation between different perspectives (Fernyhough, 2010). We engage in a constant internal dialogue. Albert Ellis, the father of Rational Emotive Behaviour Therapy, called this 'self talk' (Ellis, 1977), while Aaron T. Beck, the founder of CBT, called this internal dialogue 'Automatic thoughts' (Beck, 1979). I was recently at a workshop in which the facilitator told us that we can have up to 6000 thoughts on any given day. Like gnats, thoughts buzz around your head all the time. In Beck's understanding, our automatic thoughts are often negative and he calls them negative automatic thoughts (NATs). Our NATs are as quick as lightening and like lightning, it can leave a great amount of emotional damage. Just underneath our NATs are our underlying assumptions about ourselves, the world and the future. These underlying assumptions and NATs drive much of our emotion, physiological sensations and behaviour.

At an even deeper level of our personality lie our core beliefs about ourselves, the world and the future. I liken these three levels to a tree. NATs are the most surface level, the branches and the leaves. Underlying assumptions are the trunk of the tree and core beliefs correspond to the roots. Core beliefs and underlying assumptions are often shaped during our childhood and have a significant impact on the way we act and feel in our current life. We will talk about underlying assumptions and core beliefs later in the chapter.

THE RELATIONSHIP BETWEEN THOUGHTS AND FEELINGS

The fundamental tenet of CBT is that the way we think about things determines the way we feel, and not the other way around. If we think helpful thoughts then we will feel good (or at least less bad) than if we think unhelpful thoughts.

The common sense model says that when something difficult happens we react to it with a negative emotion. CBT says that when something difficult happens, the thought we have about the event will determine how we feel about it (see Fig. 3.1).

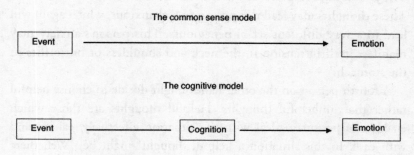

Figure 3.1: The Relationship between Thoughts and Feelings

Let me give you an example. Imagine a situation in which you are trying to get to work on time at 10 a.m. You have an important meeting scheduled for 10.15 a.m. Normally the flyovers are clear and the route is simple. You can easily get there within twenty minutes. But today things are different. There is a traffic jam and cars have backed up a long way. You cannot see what has caused the jam. All you know is that you are stuck, that you cannot move your car either forward or backward and that you will be late for your meeting.

One person might think thoughts like, 'Who is the idiot who has caused this?' This thought might lead to a feeling of frustration and anger, which in turn might lead to this person honking his horn loudly and aggressively. They will almost certainly enter the meeting hot and flushed with anger.

Another person might think thoughts like, 'Oh no! I should have anticipated that the traffic might be bad. I should have planned ahead and left earlier. I am such a stupid person.' These thoughts might make the person feel low and sad and this mood will affect their behaviour when they enter the meeting. They may come across as dejected and apologetic. They will probably experience a sinking feeling in their stomach and may even feel tearful as they enter the meeting.

A third person may wonder, 'What will they think of me? I am sure this will reflect badly in my performance review next month. The boss is sure to point out that I was late and tell me off for this.' These thoughts may lead this person to feel anxious, which again will lead to a very different set of behaviours. This person's anxiety may manifest itself in tension in the neck and shoulders or butterflies in the stomach.

A fourth person on the other hand, might decide to choose helpful rather than unhelpful thoughts. Helpful thoughts are those which enable the person to deal with the situation effectively, calmly and with ease. In this situation a helpful thought might be, 'Well there is absolutely nothing I can do to move forward or backward. I just have to wait till the traffic clears. I will call and let them know that I will be late. I have been meaning to listen to the CD I bought the other day. So here I go!' These thoughts lead to a productive phone call and a relaxed time of listening to the CD. When the person thinking these thoughts enters the office, they will do so with a sense of calm acceptance that these things happen in life and this sense of calm will positively influence their presence in the meeting.

Thus we see four different responses to the same situation. One is an angry response, the second is a depressed response, the third is an anxious response, each leading to different behaviours and even different physical sensations within the body. Each of these emotions came about because of the thoughts that preceded them. The fourth response of calm acceptance came through thinking helpful thoughts.

The relationship between our thoughts, emotions, physical sensations and our behaviour is usually expressed in what is known as the Hot Cross Bun (Padesky, 1995) (see Fig. 3.2). For example, when we think, 'I am such a useless person,' it might produce feelings of depression and when we feel depressed we might experience a heaviness in our chest or tearfulness and because of this we might shut down and withdraw from conversations or contact with our friends. Thoughts have produced emotions, physical sensations and behaviours. And each feeds back to the other.

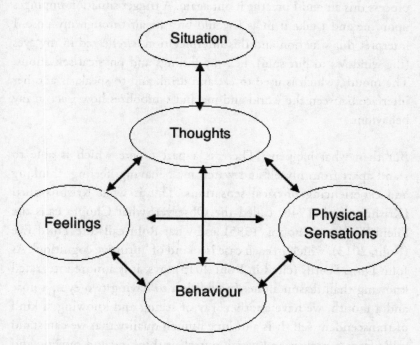

Figure 3.2: The Hot Cross Bun © 1986 Christine A. Padesky & Kathleen A. Mooney, www.MindOverMood.com

This model has served us well for many years. However, in my understanding we need a further addition to the above.

THE THIRD EYE: OUR CAPACITY FOR SELF-OBSERVATION

The Face diagram (see Fig. 3.3) incorporates our ability as human beings to be self-observing or self-reflective and this is absent in the

Hot Cross Bun. Let me explain the Face diagram. A difficult situation arises and immediately we think about what is happening to us. I have used the nose as a symbolic repository of our thoughts. In everyday life, the nose is the interface between the world and me. I take in air, I process this air and I breathe it out again. A trigger situation impinges upon me and I take it in as I would breathe air through my nose. I interpret this situation and this interpretation is reflected in my eyes (the windows to our soul), i.e., my feelings and physical sensations. The mouth, which is used to eat and drink and to speak, is another interface between the world and me and symbolizes how I act in my behaviour.

But then what happens? There is a part of me which is able to stand apart from myself and watch me behaving, feeling, thinking and experiencing physical sensations. This is what Krishnamurti (Krishnamurti, 1946) called the Observer, what Chopra calls the Silent Witness (Chopra, 1995) and what Rohr calls the Third Eye (Rohr, 2013), which in each case is a kind of 'intuitive cognition'. As John Duns Scotus (cited in Rohr 2013) says, it is a more integrated knowing than reason alone. In addition to having two eyes, a nose and a mouth, we have another way of seeing and knowing, a kind of transcendent self. It is a unique human quality that we can stand aside from ourselves and watch ourselves thinking and moving and having our being in the world. I am able to have both thoughts, feelings, physical sensations and behaviours as well as watch myself having those thoughts, feelings, physical sensations and behaviours. This ability to watch myself having these is what some psychologists call metacognition. If you look at the middle of the third eye you will see that it starts spiralling in one direction, then the spiral changes direction again and again. This is the ability of the third eye to look at things from different perspectives, integrating them all. When I can stand aside and watch myself thinking and feeling, sensing and behaving, I can then choose what to think, feel, sense and how to behave. The third eye enables 'choicefulness' within us. This is the good news. It is the hope of freedom; we no longer need to live at the mercy of our emotions, our thoughts or even our physical sensations!

Let me give you an example. Let us suppose you are a single woman of twenty-six. You have just joined a new company for work and have struck up a conversation with a colleague. It was an interesting conversation and he takes your phone number and promises to call you. You wait all evening for his call, but it never comes. What are your thoughts?

> Thoughts: obviously, he wasn't as interested in me as I was in him
> Emotions: low, feelings of rejection
> Physical sensations: tired and without much energy
> Behaviour: go to bed early

Third eye (standing apart and reflecting upon me having my thoughts, emotions, physical sensations and behaviours): look at me acting as if the world has come to an end! I have no idea why he did not call. Perhaps he is preoccupied with some work. My thoughts are just thoughts. They are not reality. Let me suspend my thoughts, judgments and all my anxiety and use this evening so that I am happy at the end of it. I will call Sushila and see if she is up for watching a DVD together tonight.

Using the third eye to act as an observer of ourselves having our thoughts and feelings, physical sensations and behaviour is useful because it enables us to gain just that little bit of objectivity that is needed to cope constructively with the situation. It enables us to take constructive action to move in the direction of our most deeply held values despite everything, and in this case not waste the evening moping.

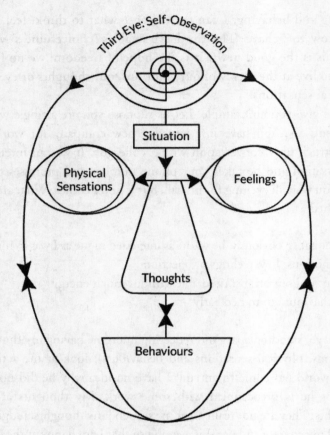

Figure 3.3: The Face

Exercise 3.1: Learning to use the Third Eye

Think of a situation in which you felt mildly criticized.

- What were your feelings? Hurt? Angry? Frustrated? Anxious? Write in the space below.

_____

_____

- What were your physical sensations?

_____

_____

- What were your thoughts?

_____

_____

- What did you do?

_____

_____

Now use your third eye to observe yourself thinking those thoughts and feelings, experiencing those physical sensations and behaviours.

What did your third eye lead you to conclude? Remember the third eye is the ability to think about your thinking, to think about your feelings and to think about your behaviour.

_____

_____

Congratulations if you were able to gain a little bit of 'distance' from your thoughts and feelings. If, however, you did not know how to use your third eye, don't worry. We shall be returning to this later in the book. Using your third eye is a skill that comes with CBT practice. It is not an easy thing to do but once the skill is mastered it becomes a very valuable tool in becoming resilient in the face of stress.

Occasionally, we use our ability to observe ourselves in a way that is not helpful for our well-being. When people become severely depressed or anxious, they tend to look upon themselves being depressed and anxious and attack themselves for being so. Their Third Eye has become unfriendly and unhealthy. Through CBT we can learn new habits and techniques that will turn an unfriendly, unhelpful Third Eye into a friendly helpful one.

THE ABCDE OF CBT

Let us concentrate on acquiring the rubrics of CBT. It is traditional to talk about the ABCDE of CBT. Let us take a common situation: the end of a relationship. Raja had been going out with Sheila for a number of years but recently Sheila told him that she no longer wants to continue with the relationship.

- A= Activating event: in this case it is the end of Raja's relationship with Sheila.
- B= Beliefs or thoughts: Raja finds himself thinking thoughts such as, 'Without her I am worthless. My life has no meaning anymore.'
- C= Consequences (emotional or behavioural): Raja experiences depression and withdraws from his circle of friends, he cries a lot in private and ultimately he is so depressed that he cannot bring himself to go to work anymore.

What are the D and the E of CBT? Because CBT is hinged upon the tenet that the way we think determines the way we feel, the D consists in disputing or battling with our thoughts in order to change the way we see a particular situation. When we are emotionally upset, our thinking system becomes closed and narrow and we develop a kind of tunnel vision, which excludes a lot of information. Disputing our thoughts enables us to open our minds up to new possibilities and to see the opportunities that are available to us.

CBT has evolved a number of ways in which we can dispute our thoughts. Raja has successfully disputed the thought that he is worthless and that his life has not got any more meaning without Sheila by looking at the evidence for and against this thought and coming up with a more balanced perspective on this situation. He asked himself a number of questions:

- Where is the evidence that I am worthless?
- How will believing I'm worthless help me find a new relationship?
- Would I call my best friend worthless if his relationship had ended?

Writing things down really helps a lot in the process of disputation so Raja writes down his answers to all the above questions. Later in the chapter we will look more closely at a well-respected CBT tool called the thought record, which you can use to battle with your thoughts and come up with a more balanced way of thinking about a situation. Having done the thought record Raja thinks, 'My life still has meaning despite Sheila not wanting to be in a relationship with me anymore. I can now concentrate on improving my batting in cricket and maybe even getting into the team. This is what I wanted to do before Sheila came along but I put it aside to be with her. Now I can take it up again. Yes, there will be times when I miss her but this does not mean that I am worthless. After being on my own for some time and finding myself again, I will begin to think about looking for a new relationship.'

When we have successfully battled with our thoughts, we become empowered even within difficult situations. We have renewed energy. This is the E of CBT. It is a natural consequence of managing our minds so as to learn to look at situations using helpful rather than unhelpful thoughts. Through disputing thoughts we can develop an effective outlook using reason and logic and this promotes an emotionally stable and balanced way of being and behaving.

In Raja's case, thoughts about taking up cricket again led him to join the local cricket club and spend his evenings improving his game. He made a new set of friends and this has led to a full and vibrant life. In a recent therapy session, he told me that he was interested in/attracted to a beautiful girl at the club he recently became a member of.

HELPFUL AND UNHELPFUL THINKING STYLES

Many of us develop habits of unhelpful thinking, not realizing how powerful these unhelpful thinking styles are in producing unhappiness. If we did understand the significance they have in creating our emotions, I think we would be diligent in dealing with them. In Raja's case, he schooled himself to think helpful thoughts, rejecting thoughts such as, 'I am worthless' and this opened life up for him.

Earlier we dealt with an example in which I asked you to imagine you were caught in a traffic jam. Learning to school ourselves to think helpfully about situations is so important that I think it is worth doing this exercise again with another example.

Imagine a situation in which you are walking to the market and your friend passes you and does not greet you. What are your thoughts, feelings, physical sensations and behaviours? Are they helpful or unhelpful?

	Unhelpful Thinking
Thoughts	She doesn't like me
Feelings	Dejected
Physical Sensations	Sinking feeling in the pit of the stomach
Behaviour	Withdraw/ sulk

Or you may have thought another kind of thought...

	Unhelpful Thinking
Thought	How dare she ignore me?!
Emotion	Anger
Physical Sensation	Hot and flushed
Behaviour	Confront her then and there

Here is yet another type of thought that you might have:

	Unhelpful Thinking
Thought	Have I done something wrong?
Emotion	Anxiety
Physical Sensation	Butterflies in the tummy
Behaviour	Ask her for reassurance that she is not annoyed with me

Thus, the same situation can produce very different responses depending on how you think about it. The first type of thought produced depression, the second produced anger and the third produced anxiety. The way we think about a situation will determine the way we feel and act. These thoughts described above are not helpful to us. They lead us down a route of withdrawal, worry or conflict. It is therefore very important that we learn to acquire a helpful thinking style.

If my friend passes by me on the street without saying hello, I might school myself to think a helpful thought such as, 'She looks a bit worried and pre-occupied. I wonder if everything is alright with her.' This thought might lead me to feel compassion and love and my feelings and physical sensations might lead me to reach for the phone and enquire if everything is alright with her.

	Helpful Thinking
Thought	She looks a bit worried and pre-occupied. I wonder if everything is alright with her
Emotion	Compassion
Physical Sensation	Closeness and caring
Behaviour	Reach out for the phone later and find out whether she is alright

Paramita is a top model, well-known in all the major cities of India. She is due to get onto the catwalk this evening at a show where she will be one among many top models. She knows that this is a make-or-break show that will determine her future as an international top model since the guest list includes a large number of famous fashion designers from different countries.

Paramita could choose to have a helpful thinking style or an unhelpful thinking style about the evening. An unhelpful thinking style might run something like this: 'I hate shows like this. I always mess them up and I am sure to mess this one up too. The shoes that I have to wear are ridiculously high heeled and I am sure to trip and fall especially when I am wearing that Rajasthani sari with the heavy border. Oh God! I wish the evening was over.'

These thoughts will lead Paramita to feel anxious, scared and worried. The energy she brings to her performance may reflect this anxiety about her social performance and she might easily sabotage her success by tripping on the heavy border of her sari in her high heels.

On the other hand Paramita might adopt a helpful thinking style about the evening: 'It is true shows like this make me anxious but I am not a top Indian model for nothing. I have practiced walking in those high heels in that sari at least a hundred times. So it is more than likely that I will do well this evening. I certainly will do my best and I will leave the results to God.'

This helpful style of thinking will lead Paramita to have a confident, buoyant presentation style while on the catwalk which will most likely produce the same feeling in her audience.

Thus, we see that helpful thinking styles produce a different and better quality of energy as we face the stresses that life brings.

HELPFUL THINKING IS NOT POSITIVE THINKING

Helpful thinking needs to be distinguished from positive thinking. It enables you to develop a soft and flexible approach that leads to an ability to feel good and make rational decisions about how to behave well in a difficult situation. Positive thinking on the other hand is relentlessly positive even in the face of evidence that shows it is unwise to be positive. Positive thinking can be unhelpful in some cases.

WHEN HELPFUL THINKING MEANS THINKING A NEGATIVE THOUGHT

A helpful thinking style is not about positive thinking, as Sage et al., (2008) point out. Imagine this scenario: in the previous example, Paramita is suddenly taken ill just before the show and you are asked to stand in for her. You have had some, but very little modelling experience. In this case the first thought that the shoes are ridiculously high, the border of the sari is very heavy and that you will probably mess up the performance is the *helpful* thought, not the unhelpful one. It leads you to assess the risks for yourself and calculate whether those risks are worth taking. In this case you might decide to decline the invitation and let someone else avail of it rather than risk the social embarrassment of falling on stage. The second thought, i.e., the positive thought (so it is more than likely I will do well this evening) will lead to a social failure that will be hard to recover from. Sometimes thinking a thought that seems negative is the helpful thought because you have calculated the risks realistically and looked at the situation rationally. Neenan (2009) points out that it is helpful to think the thought, 'I have had too much to drink,' even though it seems to be a 'negative' thought because thinking it will lead to constructive action like taking a taxi home rather than risking driving on the roads when inebriated. Thinking a 'positive' thought such as, 'I have a remarkable capacity when it comes to drinking,' is actually an unhelpful one because it puts one at risk of having an accident.

What is a helpful thought? There are many ways of looking at whether thinking is helpful or unhelpful. One way is to look at other people in a kind and generous way. Thus, you may, in the absence of sufficient data, give people the benefit of the doubt in situations where you suspect they may have mistreated you. This will lead to a trusting attitude and a relationship that continues on a relatively even keel, at least until the next time when there is even more evidence that this person has mistreated you. Here, in choosing to trust rather than mistrust the person, you lead yourself into good feelings of friendliness.

Another way of assessing whether a thought is helpful or unhelpful is to ask oneself, 'Does it work for me?' This is a pragmatic attitude to life that is useful most of the time. Thus, in the above example, you might decline the invitation, tempting though it may be, because it does not work for you. Unlike Paramita, you have not had the opportunity to practice walking the catwalk in high heels in a heavy sari over a hundred times. And so, albeit reluctantly, you tell yourself this is too risky and it does not work for me, thus choosing the helpful, though not positive, option.

While being pragmatic works in many instances, in some instances it leads to decisions that harm other people because of its emphasis on 'what works for *me*'. Let us look at an example. Sunita is a professor at a university in which research is highly valued and research money is hard to come by. Ajit is a senior lecturer in the same department doing work in the same field as Sunita. This threatens Sunita who sidelines Ajit and his work at every opportunity. This works for her because it has eliminated the threat in her career but it lacks ethics and moral quality because she actively harms Ajit with her behaviour.

In my opinion and experience we can assess a thought as helpful or unhelpful if its consequences lead us to move in the direction of our deepest and most cherished life values. Most spiritual traditions outline a set of values that people over the centuries have found to be useful guidelines for behaviour. In Chapter 7, we will talk much more about the importance of knowing our values and of marshalling our life so that it is moving in the direction of our values. It is suffice to say that we can judge whether a thought is helpful or unhelpful if it falls in line with the morality that we call our own. For now, in order to distinguish between a helpful and an unhelpful thought you might ask yourself, 'Does having the thought enable me to move in the direction of my most deeply held and cherished values?'

We will return to this when we talk later about ACT.

UNHELPFUL THINKING STYLES

Psychologists have been at pains to classify some common unhelpful thinking styles. Traditionally they have called these 'Cognitive Distortions' because of the somewhat distorting effect that our thinking styles have on our perceptions of reality. If you look at a number of CBT textbooks you will see that theorists have come up with quite a number of these cognitive distortions. In my opinion, many of them have over-lapping characteristics. I have chosen just a few of the most common one's for you to study. I first outline the unhelpful thinking style and then I suggest a more helpful way of thinking about the situation.

ALL OR NOTHING THINKING

Sometimes called Black and White thinking or Polarized thinking, this type of thinking leads us into trouble when we cannot see the nuances (or shades of grey) of a particular situation. Jivan demonstrates this type of thinking when he says to himself, 'If I am not chosen to play on the cricket team today, I am an utter failure.' Here he sees everything in all or nothing terms or black and white terms.

HELPFUL THINKING

Jivan could decide to think a more helpful thought such as, 'Even if I am not chosen to play today, I know the captain really values my abilities because he has said so on many occasions. In fact, just last week he complimented my batting. There will be a chance for me to play soon.'

CATASTROPHISING:

This refers to the tendency to see potential catastrophes in everything that happens. Sushila has had a headache for a number of hours. She thinks to herself, 'This must be a brain tumour. After all, did chacha not die of a brain tumour?' Some people live life lurching from one catastrophe to another. Can you identify anybody in your life that has a tendency to do this? Or perhaps, do you do this yourself?

HELPFUL THINKING

Sushila recognizes that she has been working very hard lately and that she has not had enough sleep. She attributes her headache to this.

MIND READING

You think you know what other people are thinking even without checking this out. You read between the lines to the level of what people are 'really thinking' or 'really feeling'. You don't take them as they are, instead you try to interpret their remarks and their behaviour instead of looking at things at face value. You question their motives and their intentions and you speculate about what they might do next.

Sandeepa had promised Raju that she would call him in the evening. When she did not call, Raju felt really low and sad, thinking, 'She must think I'm boring.'

HELPFUL THINKING

'Any number of things might have prevented her from calling me. Let me wait till tomorrow to see how she reacts.'

MENTAL FILTERING

This occurs when we filter out or selectively attend to only parts of the message that has been communicated to us. For example, Aditi is a university student who submitted a project for a degree in architecture. She has just had a tutorial that was a critique of the work she had done, which was designed to help her develop the work into a dissertation. Aditi came back feeling completely dejected. When her mother asked her how the critique went, she said, 'They thought my project was rubbish.'

HELPFUL THINKING

When Aditi's mother asked for more details, she discovered that the tutors had said seven positive things about her project. She counted them and showed her daughter how she had filtered them out and concentrated on the one negative thing they had said. Her tendency to filter things mentally left her feeling really depressed.

OVER-GENERALIZATION

This occurs when we use one or two examples and generalize from these to the whole of life. For example, Ramesh who came from Punjab was very keen on marrying Deepika who came from Kerala. Deepika jilted Ramesh after three years of being his girlfriend. Ramesh decided that he will be wary of all Malayali girls from now on.

HELPFUL THINKING

'I have had one bad experience with one Malayali girl. This does not mean that all Malayali girls will treat me the same. I will keep myself open to all women.'

BLAMING

This occurs when we feel over-responsible for situations and take the blame for anything that goes wrong. For example, if we throw a dinner party we feel responsible to ensure that everybody has a good time and we blame ourselves if even the smallest thing goes wrong. Or alternatively, we blame others for things that go wrong. When we blame ourselves for things we lead ourselves into a state of regret. Chavi got admission into a very good college and then she decided to go to a college which was not so high on the league tables but where her school friends were going. At this new college, she dislikes her course and her lecturers immensely and blames herself for having chosen this college instead of the other.

HELPFUL THINKING

'I could not have foreseen the fact that I would not like this course and these lecturers. There is no need to blame myself for making this decision. I might have hated the other college just as much.'

We see a lot of couples playing the blame game. For example, Susheela has gone over the monthly household budget which has exceeded their allotted figure of expenses. Suneel blames her, gets angry with her, criticizes her and does not look at the fact that this is the festive month of Diwali.

Were he not playing the blame game, Suneel would have recognized the fact that in a normal month Susheela is very good at managing the house on a tight budget.

Labelling

This occurs when we say to ourselves, 'I'm such an idiot', 'I'm stupid', 'I'm so silly' 'I'm such a rubbish person' or other such put-downs. Ramanathan started kicking himself when he filled diesel into the car instead of petrol. He labelled himself a fool and this thought led him to feel very frustrated, dejected and annoyed with himself.

Helpful Thinking

'I was temporarily absent-minded. Anyone could have made this mistake. It was an accident. There is no point in calling myself a fool.'

Or equally, we cognitively distort reality when we call others by derogatory names. Malay experiences a lot of road rage, calling other drivers 'idiots', 'fools', 'stupid drivers', making himself very angry in the process. He could spare himself this emotion by thinking, 'Everybody has different styles of driving. Their style is not my style, but that does not mean they are an idiot.' This thought leads him to a sense of calm and peace instead of anger and frustration.

Emotional Reasoning

Emotional reasoning occurs when we assume that feeling and being are one and the same thing. Tanuja feels fat even though she is not. She thinks she has too much weight on her calves and thighs. This means she goes to the gym every day after a long day at school, often neglecting other chores because of how long she works out.

HELPFUL THINKING

Tanuja could make her life easier by thinking the helpful thought: 'The tests show that I am healthy. Let me trust them. There are huge individual variations in the circumference of calves and thighs. Let me not be so critical of myself. Instead, let me use that energy to do something positive like get my homework done for tomorrow.'

BIAS AGAINST THE SELF

We use this unhelpful thinking style when we regularly put ourselves down. We have a self-critical bent of mind and are unable to silence the critic within us. We routinely overlook our strengths and focus on our weaknesses. Thus, we act as our own worst enemy.

Ashish had risen high in his company but he was not yet the CEO. He keeps berating himself for not achieving that status. Instead of focusing on what he has achieved, he focuses on what he has not yet achieved. He looks at this as failure. He often catches himself thinking, 'I am not really CEO material. CEOs are made of firmer stuff.'

HELPFUL THINKING

'I am a work in progress. There is still time for me to acquire the skills necessary to be a good CEO.'

Or

'Should I really be coveting the CEO's job? It really is an unenviable one. Leadership is lonely and the decisions a CEO has to take are hard on some people in the company. I am well-liked in the firm and I love my colleagues and they love me. So perhaps I am in a really privileged position now. I have a good amount of influence and do not suffer the dislike, hate and contempt that a CEO often has to suffer.'

THE TYRANNY OF THE 'SHOULD'S

Many people live their whole lives with 'should's and 'should not's, and 'must's and 'must not's, 'ought's and 'ought not's, 'do's and 'don't's. They have a very straight and narrow idea of what is right and wrong and this leaves them with very little freedom because they must always do what others expect them to. These people have very little sense of self. To be able to say, 'I want', 'I need' or 'I think' is a very selfish thing to them. Rajni's system of 'should's led her to a state of despair. According to her she should always be the perfect mother and the perfect daughter-in-law. This meant that when she was not running the children to and fro from various after-school classes, she was attending to her bedridden mother-in-law. She did not feel she could ask for any respite from her sister-in-law or from her husband as this would mean she was not a good wife and bahu (daughter-in-law) and she must always be a good wife and bahu irrespective of the situation and circumstances.

HELPFUL THINKING

'I need some help with my responsibilities or else I will really go crazy. This does not mean I am a bad wife or a bad daughter-in-law or sister-in-law. This merely means I'm taking care of myself enough so that I have the energy and good will to care for others.'

Leela regularly uses a tyrannical 'should' when she criticizes her husband's choice of which clothes to wear. She tells her therapist that the colours he chooses do not go well together and that he should learn to choose the right onces. But what are the 'right' colours? Some would argue that blue and green don't go together, others would say that pink and orange don't match well and yet we see these combinations of colours in so many of our Rajasthani prints. In fact, we see them in nature as well! Leela needs to learn that her husband might see colours differently from the way she does and that she may need to give him the space to be the person he is. She will have to forsake the tyranny of her 'should's.

It is always a challenge, learning to balance the needs of others against our own. However, to live a healthy, happy life, it is essential that we learn to do this. If we do not have our own needs met, we tend to become sulky, angry or resentful. Paradoxically, others are happy when we are happy. The old Christian adage, 'Love your neighbour as you love yourself' is really interesting here. It seems to suggest a certain proportionality to loving the self and loving others. It recognizes that self-care is important or it would not talk about loving oneself. Increasingly, however, some people in Indian society have become too self-focused. This is when the 'I want...' or 'I need...' verges on being selfish. The culture we live in is becoming more and more individualistic and less family centric, taking the unhealthy aspects of western civilization unquestioningly with the healthy aspects. Getting the balance right between loving ourselves and loving others is a real challenge, one that we may spend a life time learning.

THE HEALTHY SIDE OF COGNITIVE DISTORTIONS: APPREHENDING REALITY ACCURATELY

It is very important to realize that unhelpful thinking styles become unhelpful only when they get out of proportion to the facts. Thus, the tyranny of the 'should's refers to a situation in which a person's life becomes increasingly constricted, unhappy and inflexible due to having too many 'should's. In the normal course of life, we need the 'should's to guide our behaviour towards others and towards ourselves.

Likewise, we need black and white thinking for the justice system to operate effectively. For example, though there may be many shades of gray in a situation of crime or wrongdoing, the jury and judge must come to a decision of guilty or not guilty.

We need to be able to mind read so as to know how to react appropriately in social situations. Autistic people are unable to mind read because they are unable to apprehend visual cues such as eye contact and body language in the same way as people who do not suffer from autism can. Malcolm Gladwell in his book *Blink* (Gladwell, 2005) talks about how important it is to be able to mind read in everyday situations. For example, if after a heated argument your partner says, 'I forgive you,' but they are hidden behind a newspaper when saying it and do not meet your eye, you might accurately read the fact that your partner is not yet ready to forgive and forget. In many cases we accurately apprehend the non-verbal behaviour of other people. To be more accurate, we read other people's bodies. This is important for smooth social functioning. Thus, mind reading is an important human skill, but when it gets out of proportion it causes a terrible amount of anxiety and mental anguish. Gladwell cautions that it is very important to recognize that we can be wrong. When we develop a habit of mind reading without checking out reality as well we tend to bring ourselves to the brink of anxiety more often than not. The easier or perhaps more helpful option is to take people at face value or at least to check with our partners and our friends the accuracy of our mind reading endeavours.

We need to label things regularly or we will be flooded with too much stimulation. It is when we use the skill of labelling to categorize ourselves and others in a derogatory manner that labelling becomes a burden. Likewise, mental filtering is sometimes important if we are living with over-critical parents or a spouse who is routinely unappreciative of our endeavours. Here, if we did not learn to filter out a lot of the negatives, we would allow ourselves to be unnecessarily damaged. Catastrophes are not all in the mind, they do happen. The Bhopal tragedy, the Sri Lankan tsunami, the collapse of the Bangladesh garment factory that killed over nine hundred people, earthquakes, floods, fires. All these things produce real and immediate suffering. Poverty is real, debt is always difficult, unemployment or under-employment is demeaning. It is how we respond to real catastrophes that will determine whether we are resilient or not. Catastrophising, on the other hand, refers to the tendency to see situations as catastrophic when they are not.

If we make a habit of regularly using helpful thinking styles to interpret the things that happen to us, we will find that we build resilience within ourselves.

Exercise 3.2: Cognitive Distortions

Circle the cognitive distortion or distortions you think are present in each example.

The washing machine breaks down. A mother of small twins says to herself, 'I can't cope. This always happens. The whole day is ruined.'

a. Over-generalization
b. All or nothing thinking
c. The tyranny of 'should's
d. Mind reading
e. Mental filtering

He looked up from across the table and in a monotonous voice said, 'That's interesting.' I knew he was dying for breakfast to be over so he could get away from me.

a. Magnifying
b. All or nothing thinking
c. The tyranny of the 'should's
d. Mind reading
e. Bias against the self

A man was trying to get his girlfriend to be warmer and more supportive. He got irritated every night when she didn't ask him how his day was or failed to give him the attention he expected.

a. The tyranny of the 'should's
b. Mind reading
c. Over-generalization
d. Blaming
e. Catastrophising

A driver of a fairly new Mercedes feels nervous on long trips, afraid of having car trouble and being stranded far from home. Faced with having to drive 500 miles and back, he tells himself, 'It's too far, it will never make it. The car has 60,000 miles on it already.'

a. Over-generalization
b. Mental filtering
c. Mind reading
d. Catastrophising
e. Tyranny of the 'should's

Exercise 3.3. Cognitive Distortions

What are the unhelpful thinking styles that you most commonly use? Rate yourself on statements below from 0-10, where 0 is 'never' and 10 is 'absolutely all the time'.

Bias against the Self

1. I overlook my strengths
2. I focus on my weaknesses
3. I downplay my achievements
4. I am my own worst critic

Mental Filtering

5. I see things through dark-tinted glasses
6. I tend to focus on the bad in situations

Catastrophising

7. I predict that the very worst will happen
8. I seem to suffer more bad things than most of my friends

Mind reading

9. I think that others don't like me
10. I try to second-guess what others are thinking about me

Blaming

11. I always take the blame if things go wrong
12. I take things personally and to heart
13. I take unfair responsibility for things that are not my fault
14. I feel overly responsible for making everybody have a good time
15. Usually it is other people who are at fault
16. If things go wrong, then it is usually someone else's responsibility

Tyranny of the 'Should's

17. I make 'must', 'should' or 'got to' statements to myself
18. I use the words 'always', 'never' and 'typical' a lot to summarize things
19. I find myself using the words 'should not' and 'ought not' a lot when thinking about the actions of other people
20. Other people make me angry and frustrated because they violate the norms a lot

Add up your scores and divide this total by the number of items in each category. This will give you an average score for each category.

What do you conclude about your most commonly used unhelpful thinking styles?

_____

_____

_____

Dealing with Unhelpful Thoughts

If unhelpful thinking has been long standing and habitual, teaching oneself to think in more helpful ways is at first strange and may feel false. However, to be fully human we have taught ourselves many things that initially feel false. Brushing teeth doesn't feel natural to a two-year-old nor does mum's insistence that they sit on the pot to defecate when all along the nappy has been perfectly adequate. So in order to become resilient we need to unlearn habits of unhelpful thinking and learn habits of helpful thinking. This does not come naturally, but with practice it can be done. Here is a nifty little tool that you can carry about in your handbag or wallet to fill in as the days go by.

Exercise 3.4: Dealing with unhelpful thoughts

Think of a situation, preferably a recent one, in which you felt mildly upset. Write this down in column 1 of the table below. What were some of the feelings you had in this situation? Write this in column 2. What were the thoughts you had? Make a list of these thoughts and put them in column 3. Were these helpful or unhelpful thoughts?

Make a note of the type of unhelpful thinking you engaged in, in column 4. What thought would be more helpful in this situation? Note this down in column 5 which I have designated as my resilient response.

Here is an example:

Reshma felt upset when her father criticized her cooking which he felt was too salty.

1. Situation	2. Feelings	3. Thoughts	4. Helpful/unhelpful. If unhelpful, what type?	5. My resilient response
Dad criticized my cooking	Anger, resentment	I hate him. He is such a difficult person. Such a bastard	Unhelpful: labelling, over generalization	Dad sometimes criticizes me but usually with good reason. This does not mean that he does not love me. I did put in too much salt today. It might have been better if I had accepted that and apologized for my mistake

It is hard to jump from unhelpful thinking to helpful thinking. Sometimes we do not believe the helpful thoughts that we have created and so just creating them does not change anything for us. This is because we have not really looked at some important ingredients of CBT. Let us look at them now.

NEGATIVE AUTOMATIC THOUGHTS (NATS)

Negative automatic thoughts are unhelpful thoughts that are conditioned by family, friends and the media. They occur involuntarily, without reflection and seem very plausible at the time. They are negative in that they leave you feeling bad; they are automatic because they seem to be beyond your control. They often appear in shorthand. 'Oh damn!' which when unpacked might mean something like, 'I am useless, late again as always.' They don't have to be expressed in words, images are common. They are almost always believed, no matter how illogical. They have a truth-value similar to that attached to sounds or sights in the real world. They are experienced as spontaneous. They pop into the mind automatically, they are hardly noticed or analysed. They are often couched in should language; 'ought's or 'must's are common NATs. They tend to 'awfulize', to predict catastrophes, to expect the worst, to see danger where there is none.

For example, you see your partner talking animatedly to a beautiful woman and they briefly embrace. You immediately feel jealous. Your NATs: 'Who the hell is that? Why are they laughing so much? They are having an affair.' When your husband gets home you ask him and find out that the woman is a cousin whom he had not seen for several years. Your thoughts now are, 'I'm so stupid for jumping to conclusions.'

Another example: your partner is late coming home. You feel anxious. Your mind is flooded with disturbing thoughts and even powerful images of a car crash. Your NAT: 'What if he has had an accident?' Your partner arrives home safe and you realize that there was nothing to worry about at all.

NATs are pernicious and powerful and yet they are slippery and hard to catch. I liken them to eels because of this. But they are like a waterfall, cascading at the back of your mind. On the other hand, as I have said before you might visualize them as lightening. They strike unpredictably and leave a lot of damage behind. They are hard to turn off. They seem so plausible. They differ from our public statements. A man whose girlfriend has broken up with him might say to his friends, 'It was mutual. We both knew the relationship was not going anywhere.' But internally he may feel like a failure and think thoughts of suicide. NATs repeat habitual themes; anxious people's NATs are related to danger; depressed people's thoughts are related to loss; angry peoples' thoughts are related to being transgressed.

It is important that we school ourselves to become aware of our NATs. In any situation where we feel upset, angry, sad, anxious, guilty, jealous or any of the gamut of difficult emotions, we just need to ask ourselves what was going through our mind just before we began feeling the emotion. We then make a list of all the thoughts that have occurred just prior to the emotion.

THE HOT THOUGHT

In and amongst all the NATs that have occurred to you just prior to feeling the emotion is the 'hot' thought. It is the thought that drives the emotion (Greenberger and Padesky, 2015). It is the thought with the greatest amount of emotional charge. The one that made the most contribution to you feeling anxious or depressed. It comes with a quick flash of negative emotion and is responsible for the feelings we experience and the behaviours we exhibit.

In many instances, our hot thoughts are inaccurate misperceptions of the facts of a situation. Thus, it is really important that we challenge our hot thoughts by looking for the evidence for and against the thought.

In looking for the evidence for and against the hot thought, we put on the mantle of a scientist. We treat the hot thought as a prediction or a hypothesis in an experiment and look for factual evidence that supports the hypothesis or disconfirms it.

THE THOUGHT RECORD

Christine Padesky, a world leading CBT expert, developed the 7-column version of the thought record to enable us to challenge or dispute our hot thought.

Below is a sample thought record filled in by Sunita.

Nilesh and Sunita are a couple who have been married for a couple of years. Nilesh is an outgoing extravert; Sunita is more introverted and tends towards anxiety. Nilesh has been married once before but the marriage did not last. The reasons were complex but primarily Nilesh's ex-wife, Amrita used to have a drug problem, which left Nilesh feeling desperate and alone. Feeling this way, Nilesh had meet Niraja and had a passionate affair with her. But Niraja was seventeen years younger than Nilesh and ultimately Nilesh called off this relationship because he did not think he could keep up with a woman so much younger than himself.

Nilesh then met Sunita and fell in love with her. After going out with her for several months, he told Sunita both about his marriage to Amrita and his affair with Niraja. Sunita really appreciated his honesty and his willingness to be vulnerable. However, sometimes thoughts of Nilesh's past relationships return to haunt Sunita and her thoughts then spiral out of control.

It is Friday evening, the start of the weekend. Nilesh has not yet come home and Sunita has a flash of NATs that rush through her head. This is how she used the thought record effectively towards her own well-being.

Situation	Feeling	Thoughts	Evidence for Hot Thought	Evidence against Hot Thought	Alternative/Balanced Thought	Re-rate Mood
Friday night: Nilesh has not yet come home and it is late	Worry 80 per cent Low 75 per cent	Why is he so late? – Why hasn't he called to tell me he is going to be late? – He must be talking to Krishna (very attractive person at the office) – I am not as attractive as Krishna – Nilesh is flirting with Krishna and is going to have an affair This is the hot thought	He has had an affair once before he knew me – He told me last week that he finds Krishna attractive	He is meeting a deadline for Monday – We have been away on holiday two days this week so there might be a lot of work to catch up on – When we made love on Monday, he turned my face to look at him and with tenderness in his eyes, he told me how much he loves me	Even though he sometimes flirts with women, he constantly demonstrates his attraction to me in the way he meets my eyes when we make love, in the way he is unafraid to tell me the truth about his inner realities, in the way that he is on the whole reliable and responsible to us as a couple. There must be a legitimate reason why he is late and hasn't called and it is unlikely to be Krishna	Worry 10 per cent Low 5 per cent

In column 1 Sunita has identified the situation which has caused her to feel emotional. In column 2, Sunita has specified what these emotions were and has rated the intensity of these emotions on a scale of 0–100 where 100 is the most intense that she has ever felt of each of the emotions and 0 is the least intense.

Sunita has asked herself a number of questions about the nature of the thought that drives her mood of anxiety. This is quite a skill. She has written all the thoughts that occurred to her just before she started feeling the way she did. She then looked at her list of NATs and identified the hot thought.

Notice the accuracy with which Sunita has identified the hot thought and how devastating that is to her. As we said before, the hot thought is the thought with the highest emotional charge and it is responsible for creating the mood. In this case, the thought that Nilesh is going to have an affair with Krishna has made Sunita feel very low (75 per cent) and worried (80 per cent).

Using the techniques of CBT, Sunita has taught herself to take this thought to court and to look for the evidence for and against the hot thought.

In column 4 she looked for all the evidence that supports the hot thought and listed them.

In column 5, she looked for all the evidence that does not support the hot thought and wrote them down.

In doing these two columns, she has successfully identified facts (actual occurrences) and has avoided putting down beliefs and opinions in the evidence columns. So in the 'Evidence for' column, Sunita did not say things like, 'All men have affairs after they have been married for some time.' This is a belief and not a fact. Putting down a belief or an opinion rather than a fact is a common error. But doing this does not help us dispute the hot thought.

Finding evidence for the hot thought is not very difficult. However, finding evidence against the hot thought can be problematic because the hot thought feels like it is the truth at the time that we are thinking it. So when trying to find evidence against the hot thought Sunita asked herself what Maryam (her best friend) would tell her if she were here? Asking herself this question enabled her to step out of her skin and view her life as if it were the life of another person. This enabled her to look more objectively at the facts in her life and to come up with a more flexible, balanced view of the situation. Sunita captured this more balanced/alternative thought in column 6.

The final step in using the thought record is the critical one. Using the new balanced thought that she had come to, Sunita asked herself what she would have felt if she had thought this alternative thought in the situation that she found herself in on Friday night, in place of the hot thought. She realized that had she done this, her worry and low mood would have diminished to almost nothing.

Now try it for yourself.

I have made a simple modification of the thought record here so that it is clearer. I have also put the steps down in sequence. The idea behind the thought record is that we regularly use it by writing down information in each of the sections.

Exercise 3.5: The Thought Record

Step 1: Describing the situation

Describe the situation (in short) which caused you to feel upset.

_____

_____

_____

_____

Step 2: Specifying our emotions

What emotions did you experience? Be specific. Remember, all emotions come under four generic emotions: mad, sad, glad and scared. You might want to be a little more nuanced than this. Rate the emotions on a scale of 0–100, with 0 being no emotion at all and 100 per cent being the most intense that you have ever felt this emotion.

Emotion	Rating 0–100 per cent
–	–
–	–
–	–
–	–

Step 3: Identifying NATs

List the negative automatic thoughts that were going through your head just before you felt the emotion. Once you have done this, identify the hot thought, the one that seems to carry the most emotional charge that would have produced the emotions you listed in Step 2.
Put a circle around the hot thought.

_____

_____

_____

_____

Step 4: Evidence for the hot thought

Now look for all the evidence that supports the hot thought and write it down. Look for factual occurrences and put these down rather than beliefs and opinions.

_____

_____

_____

_____

_____

Step 5: Evidence against the hot thought

Now look for evidence that does not support the hot thought. Using the ability to look upon yourself as if you were another person is a critical skill to develop when learning to dispute our hot thoughts.

Again we are looking for facts and not for beliefs or opinions. This may be more difficult. You can ask yourself some questions like, 'If my best friend were to offer an opinion on my hot thought what would they say?' or 'If I were my best friend what would I be saying to myself?' or 'What evidence do I have from my past which indicates that the hot thought is not true?'

_____

_____

_____

_____

_____

Step 6: Becoming even-thoughted: crafting an alternative and more balanced thought

We again look at the evidence in columns 4 and 5. What do the facts say? Is the hot thought true? Does it stand up to the facts or does it have to be modified and balanced out a bit? Most likely, having considered the evidence for and against it, we will have to modify the hot thought to take into consideration the evidence that we found in column 5. So we craft an alternative or more balanced thought in Step 6. After this, we rate our level of belief in this alternative thought on a scale of 0–100 per cent with 100 per cent being total belief and 0 per cent being no belief at all.

Rate your level of belief _____ per cent.

_____

_____

_____

_____

_____

Step 7: Re-rating our emotions

The next step is a crucial one. If we were to re-enter the situation that we described in Step 1, thinking the thought we have crafted in Step 6, what would happen to the emotion we described in Step 2? Would we feel more or less sad/angry/anxious? How intense would this feeling be if we thought the alternative or more balanced thought in the situation that we described? What percentage rating would we give it now?

Put the same emotions down as you had before, in the column under 'Emotion' and re-rate these emotions on the same scale. Be careful to specify a percentage.

Emotion	Re-rating 0–100 per cent
–	–
–	–
–	–
–	–

The thought record is a powerful tool for changing our unhelpful thinking styles and battling with our NATs. If we do the thought record fifteen to twenty times in different situations with different emotions and thoughts, it will become an internalized habit to look for the evidence for and against our unhelpful thinking and ultimately we will no longer need to use the actual form. However, unless we actually use it for a substantial period of time, we will not be able to fundamentally change our thinking style. So I encourage you to practice with it as much as you can.

SOME COMMON MISTAKES IN DOING THE THOUGHT RECORD

There are a number of mistakes that people commonly make when doing the thought record. Correcting these mistakes will open you to the power of the technique to change your moods.

OUR HOT THOUGHTS OFTEN APPEAR IN UNTESTABLE FORM. MAKE THEM TESTABLE.

Pratap is a student of architecture. He is in the fourth year of a five-year course. He has submitted work for a paper titled 'Environmental Design' but has received a letter from his lecturer saying that the work he has submitted is not enough to pass this paper. He has found out that he is not alone and that 20 per cent of the class has received the same note from the same lecturer. He has been given an extension of another week till the following Monday to submit more work for this paper in order to be given the chance to pass. The issue is that next Monday is also the final submission date for his Main Project. He has undergone several 'crits' (critiques) for the Main Project and his lecturers have pointed him in the direction of substantial pieces of work. If he does not pass his Main Project, he cannot pass the fourth year. All of this has produced a very high level of anxiety and panic within Pratap. So he put his newly acquired CBT skills into practice and filled in a thought record. But he was not terribly successful. Here is what he did:

Situation	Feeling	Thoughts	Evidence for Hot Thought	Evidence against Hot Thought	Alternative/ Balanced Thought	Re-rate Mood
I have to hand in two pieces of work next Monday	Anxiety 90 per cent Panic 80 per cent Worry 90 per cent Low 80 per cent	I am doomed – I don't have the time	No time to complete the work – I don't know what is missing in order for me to pass – So many other things are more important	–	–	–

When he brought the thought record into therapy, he could not really understand why his mood had not changed.

The first thing we looked at was the hot thought. 'I am doomed' is really an emotionally laden thought which is difficult to test. After some questioning Pratap learnt to 'craft' the hot thought slightly differently. Instead of 'I am doomed', which is really very difficult to put to the test, he realized that 'I am doomed' could be unpacked to say 'I am going to fail the year'. Crafting the hot thought into a form which is testable is an important skill to learn.

PUTTING DOWN BELIEFS AND OPINIONS AS EVIDENCE FOR AND AGAINST. WE WANT FACTS.

In his failed attempt at doing the thought record, he looked for evidence for the hot thought.
- No time to complete the work
- Don't know what is missing in order for me to pass
- So many other things are more important

The mistake that Pratap was making in trying to fill in the thought record was to put down beliefs and perceptions as facts in the evidence for and against columns. Thus in this case, 'I have no time' is a belief or a perception rather than a fact. In fact, Pratap had seven days in which to retrieve the situation. But because he put 'no time' down as a fact, he did not do himself any favours and his mood did not change much. It is really important then to learn to distinguish between facts and beliefs.

A fact is something that has already happened. It is 'hard evidence'. So during therapy with me, he realized that he knew he had passed two papers. Of the two remaining papers, the results had not been declared for one of them and for the other one, his lecturer had contacted him asking him to submit more work within the week, so he had a chance of passing if he did this. When probed for more evidence, he could not find any other evidence that he had failed the year.

So he began looking at the 'Evidence against' column. Here he found considerable evidence against the hot thought that 'I am going to fail the year'. First of all, he realized that he has definitely passed two papers. For the other two, failing the papers does not mean failing the year. Each student is allowed to re-take those papers. So he can re-take the Environmental Design paper and the other one for which the results have not been declared, if at all he fails them this time. Also, he realized that the marks he has obtained in the Main Project during the 'crits' thus far have been high.

So now he was able to become more 'even-thoughted', i.e., to come up with an alternative, balanced thought. 'If I concentrate this week on doing sufficient work for the Main Project and some work for the Environmental Design paper, I will not fail the year because the evidence shows that I am unlikely to fail my Main Project judging from the marks that I have been receiving, and I can always re-take the Environmental Design paper and the other one, if I fail them.'

This decreased his level of anxiety to 40 per cent, feeling of panic to 30 per cent, worry to 50 per cent and low mood to 10 per cent.

He also recognized that it is critical he concentrates on finishing his Main Project because without passing that he definitely will not pass the year.

Here is a blank thought record for you to use on your own situations that cause you to be upset.

Thought Record Template
Step 1: Describe the situation
_____
_____
_____
_____

Step 2: Identify your moods and rate them from 0–100 per cent
_____
_____
_____
_____

Step 3: Listing your NATs. Don't forget to circle your hot thought
_____
_____
_____
_____

Step 4: Evidence for your NATs
_____
_____
_____
_____

Step 5: Evidence against your NATs
_____
_____
_____
_____

Step 6: Becoming 'even-thoughted'
_____
_____
_____
_____

Step 7: Re-rating your moods from 0–100 per cent
_____
_____
_____
_____

If at the end of a thought record the mood has not changed or has become worse, then the next step would be to look at how much you believe the alternative or balanced thought. If your belief in this alternative or balanced thought is not very high, then it is time to make an action plan to test out this thought. We do this by designing and undertaking a behavioural experiment.

BEHAVIOURAL EXPERIMENTS

You might ask, 'What is a behavioural experiment?' Well, human beings have two primary ways of knowing: through our thoughts and through our feelings. Sometimes it is easy to get our 'head' in the right place through cognitive restructuring or using the thought record, but our 'heart' is lagging behind and is slow to follow. We can help ourselves get our hearts in line with our heads by doing behavioural experiments. CBT is fundamentally scientific and we use scientific principles and strategies to help us feel better about ourselves. Just like in the thought record you have been encouraged to look for the facts (and not your opinions or beliefs about a situation), in behavioural experiments we will take a prediction, which in scientific terms is normally called a hypothesis, and test it out. A behavioural experiment is a process of self-discovery. You will teach yourself to design an action or series of actions to put your prediction to the test. Like any experiment, this is a procedure designed in uncertainty with no guarantees of success.

According to Bennett-Levy et al., (2004) behavioural experiments are planned experiential activities, the primary purpose of which is to test the validity of extreme or unhelpful thoughts. Behavioural experiments can also be used to construct and test out new, more adaptive thoughts in everyday situations in order to further you towards your goals. If at the end of your thought record your belief in the alternative or balanced thought is less than 60 per cent, it is time to use a behavioural experiment.

In order to design a behavioural experiment we need to craft our prediction or hypothesis in the form of 'if… then…' statements.

UNDERLYING ASSUMPTIONS

In CBT, underlying assumptions are the assumptions or rules that we have developed about how the world will treat us if we act in a particular way. They take the form of 'If... then...' statements. Some examples of 'If... then...' statements:

- If I sweat while giving my presentation, then I will not get good marks
- If I don't cook every night, Bunty will think that I am a bad wife and will reject me or humiliate me
- If I dress unfashionably, people will reject me
- If I fail my driving test, then my dad will be contemptuous of me
- If I don't please my tutors with the work I hand in, then they will think that I am rubbish

Ram is an anxious person, who is very frightened of public speaking. In his job as a finance analyst, he has been asked to make a presentation for some important senior members of his company. His underlying assumption is:

'If I don't take a beta blocker (an anti-anxiety drug) then I will have a panic attack in front of everybody.'

Ram's safety behaviour (see Chapter 2) was to take a beta-blocker every time he had to make a presentation in public. In behavioural experiments we encourage people to drop their safety behaviours and watch what happens. Usually when people find the courage to drop their safety behaviours, they discover that their predictions do not come true.

We could help Ram test out this underlying assumption by designing a behavioural experiment. He could first make his presentation to his wife and adult children without his beta blocker, which will not be threatening to him. Next, he could present it to his department colleagues while not taking his beta-blocker (moderately anxiety provoking). It is important when designing an experiment to make predictions about how anxious the person would feel in each of the situations and then to watch their levels of anxiety when carrying out the experiment. It is also import to anticipate obstacles that Ram might come up against during the experiment. He might find that all of his colleagues are too busy this week to give him the time to listen to his presentation. He can decide to overcome this by asking them when they might be free. Or he could choose some colleagues from a different department.

We would ask Ram to notice how anxious he felt before making the presentation, during the presentation and then after the presentation. We would then ask Ram to modify his underlying assumption in the light of this new evidence.

In this case, Ram discovered that even though he felt anxious he did not have a panic attack. Thus, his old belief was modified to a new belief: 'Even though I feel anxious when I do not take a beta-blocker, I am still able to make a presentation in public to colleagues at my level of seniority in my department.'

The next step would be to design an experiment to take Ram further so that he can risk making a presentation to senior colleagues without his beta-blocker.

Exercise 3:6. Designing a Behavioural Experiment

Shalini is single and twenty-eight years old. She has taken up a job in Mumbai and has left her family in Delhi. She recently bought her first home PC. She feels hopeless about learning to manage her home computer: the anti-virus software, the connections needed to install and re-install printers, buying the right ink cartridges and all the other technicalities. When she was living with her parents her dad or brothers always handled computer-related work. Her beliefs are that IT is men's domain. Her thoughts are, 'I am a techno-idiot and I am a woman. I will never be able to manage my home computer on my own.'

Design a behavioural experiment to test these beliefs. First craft an 'If… then…' statement. Then design an experiment to test this prediction or hypothesis.

_____

_____

_____

Can you think of any obstacles that Shalini might face in putting her 'if… then…' predictions to the test? What are these and how can she overcome them?

_____

_____

_____

_____

Exercise 3.7: Designing Your Own Behavioural Experiment

Can you think of any of your own 'If… then…' beliefs that you can put to the test in a behavioural experiment? For example; 'If my boss criticizes me, then I…' or 'If my boyfriend/girlfriend breaks up with me, then I…'

_____

_____

_____

_____

In designing your own behavioural experiment it is useful to look at all possible difficulties you might have in conducting the experiment.

Once you have done this, you need to think of ways of overcoming these difficulties.

Always write down the explicit hypothesis, rate how strongly you believe it and ask yourself, 'What is the worst possible outcome?'

It is really important that you design behavioural experiments that are safe, ethical and reasonable. Your experiments should never put you or anyone else at risk of being harmed.

Both thought records and behavioural experiments can be difficult to construct in certain situations. *Mind Over Mood* by Greenberger and Padesky (2015) is great for thought records and Bennett-levy et al., (2004) is a wonderful resource for behavioural experiments. If you find you are at a loss, then perhaps it is time to seek actual face to face help from an accredited cognitive behaviour therapist.

CORE BELIEFS

Core beliefs are deeply held beliefs about ourselves, others and the world. 'I am unlikeable, I am a failure. Others can't be trusted. The world is a hard place.' Negative core beliefs are sometimes developed from the experience of trauma. Most often they come from watching and modelling ourselves on our parents as school teachers or others who are important to us. Greenberger and Padesky, (2015) suggest that one way of identifying some of your core beliefs is to fill in the blanks below:

I am _____

Others are _____

The world is _____

Because core beliefs lie deep within our personality, they can be harder to change than negative automatic thoughts or underlying assumptions. They are normally experienced as 100 per cent true without question.

To change a core belief that is unhelpful for our well-being, we can challenge it in much the same way as we do a negative automatic thought. We can collect evidence to show ourselves that the core belief is not 100 per cent true.

Take one of your core beliefs as identified earlier and document the evidence that this core belief is not always true. For example, Malini thought of herself as a failure at her relationships. She had had three boyfriends and not yet been able to find a suitable life partner. She decided to collect some evidence to see if her core belief was not 100 per cent true.

This is what she wrote:

Core Belief: I am a failure at all my relationships
Level of belief in this statement – 100 per cent
Evidence or experiences that suggest the core belief is not 100 per cent true:

1. I was the one who broke up with Rajat and since I walked out I cannot call myself a failure here
2. I am more introverted than Nitin and so we were not working well together as a couple. This was just physiology
3. I am not a sporty person and Ramesh wanted a sports companion in a girlfriend. I could have tried to change myself but I chose not to as I prefer to do embroidery instead. This does not mean I am a failure at my relationships

At the end of the exercise, Malini re-rated her core belief that she is a failure at her relationships at 75 per cent. This may not seem a large change to you, but to Malini it was the first time she thought of herself in less negative terms. So to her this was a big change.

Another way of dealing with negative core beliefs is to collect evidence for an alternative belief. Nirmala entertained the core belief, 'Others always reject me'. She therefore believed herself to be unlikeable. She had become socially withdrawn and isolated. She never phoned any of her friends, always leaving it to them to phone her. As she tested this belief, she gradually came to the conclusion that while not everybody liked her, more people liked her than those who did not like her. She was beginning to substitute her negative core belief with the positive one that she was likeable.

She decided to test this belief out in a behavioural experiment:

Experiment	Prediction	Observation
She would approach Nimish and ask him out for a coffee	Her prediction was that he would say no	He accepted and seemed pleased that she had asked
She would phone Samira	Her prediction was that Samira would say she did not have time to speak with her	Samira did not say No. She was in the middle of her assignment when Nirmala called and said that she would call back immediately after she finished, which she did
She would invite four people from her class over to her house for dinner	None of them will say yes	Three quarters of people accepted her invitation and the fourth said she could not come because it was her mum's birthday and the family was going out on that day

She came out of this period much more confident that she was a likeable person and if people did not accept her invitations or attempts to contact them it was probably because they had prior commitments.

DEVELOPING A POSITIVE CORE BELIEF LOG

Keeping a log of your new positive core beliefs is a good way of letting information permeate from your conscious mind into the deeper layers of your personality. Write down your new core belief in the second column. Then when you have some evidence for it, write it down immediately or else you are likely to forget and you would have lost valuable information. Then rate your current level of belief in your new positive core belief. Standing on the shoulders of the masters (Beck, 1992), I have created a core belief log for you.

Exercise 3.8: Your Positive Core Belief Log

Date	Positive Core Belief	Evidence	Level of Belief (0–100 per cent)
20/01/2017	For e.g., I am likeable		

Do not be dismayed if you find that it is difficult for you to access your underlying assumptions and your core beliefs. Many people find these difficult to uncover. You might be able to work with these more usefully with the help of a cognitive behaviour therapist.

Key Points from this Chapter

— Our thinking plays a pivotal role in creating our emotions, physiological sensations and our behaviours. The Hot Cross Bun is useful to understand this

— We can learn to catch our NATs and become aware of our unhelpful thinking styles in order to challenge our thoughts and develop new and more helpful styles of thinking. The thought record is useful for this

- Our underlying assumptions take the form of 'If... then...' statements and our negative underlying assumptions can be tested in behavioural experiments
- Our negative core beliefs seem 100 per cent true to us. We can learn to develop flexibility about this by seeking evidence that they are not 100 per cent true and by developing a positive core belief log

REFERENCES

1. A.T. Beck, A.J. Rush, B.F. Shaw, and G. Emery, *Cognitive Therapy of Depression*, New York: Guildford Press, 1979.

2. J.S. Beck, *Cognitive Therapy: Basics and Beyond*, New York: Guildford Press, 1995.

3. J. Bennett-Levy, G. Butler, M. Fennel, A. Hackman, M. Mueller, and D. Westbrook, *Oxford Guide to Behavioural Experiments in Cognitive Therapy*, Oxford: Oxford University Press, 2004.

4. D. Chopra, *Magical Mind, Magical Body: Mastering the Mind/Body Connection for Perfect Health and Total Well-being*, Illinois: Nightingale Conant, 1995.

5. A. Ellis, and R. Greiger, *Handbook of Rational-Emotive Therapy*, New York: Springer Publishing, 1977.

6. C. Fernyhough, 'The voices within', http://www.psychologytoday.com/blog/the-child-in-time/201008/what-do-we-mean-thinking, 2010. (Last accessed on 17 October 2016)

7. M. Gladwell, *Blink: The Power of Thinking Without Thinking*, London: Penguin Books, 2005.

8. D. Greenberger, and C. Padesky, *Mind Over Mood: Change How You Feel by Changing the Way You Think*, 2nd Edition, New York: Guildford Press, 2015.

9. J. Krishnamurti, *The Observer Is the Observed*, Ojai, California, 1946.

10. M. Neenan, *Developing Resilience: A Cognitive-Behavioural Approach*, London: Routledge, 2009.

11. National Institute for Health and Care Excellence Guidance (NICE), 'Post-traumatic Stress Disorder (PTSD): Management, http://www.nice.

org.uk/guidance/cg26/chapter/key-priorities-for-implementation, March 2005. (Last accessed on 08/08/2016)

12. NICE Guidelines 'Obsessive- compulsive disorder and body dysmorphic disorder: treatment', https://www.nice.org.uk/Guidance/cg31, November 2005. (Last accessed on 8 August 2016)

13. NICE Guidelines, 'Depression in Adults: Recognition and Management', https://www.nice.org.uk/guidance/cg90, published October 2009. (Last accessed on 8 August 2016)

14. NICE Guidelines, 'Anxiety Disorders', https://www.nice.org.uk/guidance/qs53, February 2014. (Last accessed on 08/08/2016)

15. C. Padesky, and D. Greenberger, *Clinician's Guide to Mind Over Mood*, London: Guildford Press, 1995.

16. R. Rohr, *The Naked Now: Learning to See as the Mystics See*, New York: Crossroad Publishing Company, 2009.

17. R. Rohr, *Yes, and … Daily Meditations*, Cincinnati: Franciscan Media, 2013.

18. N. Sage, M. Sowden, E. Chorlton, and A. Edelaneau, *CBT for Chronic Illness and Palliative Care: A Workbook and Toolkit*, Chichester: John Wiley and Sons Ltd, 2008.

19. N. Wills, L. Thomas, A. Abel, M. Barnes, F. Carroll, N. Ridgway, S. Sherlock, N. Turner, K. Button, L. Odondi, C. Metcalfe, A. Owen-Smith, J. Campbell, A. Garland, S. Hollinghurst, B. Jerrom, D. Kessler, W. Kuyken, J. Morrison, K. Turner, C. Williams, T. Peters, and G. Lewis, 'Clinical Effectiveness and Cost-effectiveness of Cognitive Behavioural Therapy as an Adjunct to Pharmacotherapy for Treatment-resistant Depression in Primary Care: The CoBalT Randomized Controlled Trial, *Health Technology Assessment, 18*(31), 1-167, doi:10.3310/hta18310, 2014.

A USEFUL WEBSITE:

www.livinglifetothefull.com

4

Applying CBT to Depression

'Our greatness lies not so much in being able to remake the world as being able to remake ourselves.'

– Gandhi

'Let me not pray to be sheltered from dangers,
But to be fearless in facing them.
Let me not beg for the stilling of my pain, but
For the heart to conquer it.'

– Rabindranath Tagore

In this chapter:

— The vicious cycle of depression
— Act your way into feeling – behavioural activation
— Working with thoughts: cognitive restructuring
— Relapse prevention

Sunita was a young woman who had struggled with depression for as long as she could remember. She was very tearful and had reached the stage where she felt unable to get out of bed, brush her teeth and get dressed in the morning. She had withdrawn from activities that had previously given her pleasure. She basically felt as if she was no good and that her father did not appreciate her, giving all of his attention to her two beautiful sisters.

Sunita and many people like her have used CBT to overcome and recover from depression. Even though depression has many causes and triggers which can be biological, psychological or social, people stay depressed due to their thoughts and their behaviours. Changing day-to-day behaviour, and challenging or defusing from these thoughts can bring you out of depression.

Chapter 1 introduced a few different terms for various types of depression and explained their treatment options. This chapter focuses on cognitive behaviour treatment for depression since it has been one of the most effective treatments in my clinical experience.

If you are having serious suicidal thoughts, you must tell someone immediately. Most of us have some suicidal thoughts occasionally. However, if you find yourself thinking about how to put this into action and you cannot find any reason for living, you should seek professional help.

If your score on the questionnaire in Chapter 1 indicates that you are severely depressed and there is no psychotherapy available in your area, then try to treat yourself by becoming active, do some good quality heart pumping exercises so that the endorphins are released in your body which will make you feel good for a short period of time and talk with your friends and significant others rather than withdraw from them. Because your depression is severe, it is likely that you will be unable to concentrate long enough to reap much benefit from this book. However, if you cannot locate a cognitive behaviour therapist or any other therapist and if you can find the energy and motivation to do the exercises in this book, you will find some relief. I recommend that you see a psychiatrist. They may advise you to go on a course of anti-depressants, which can be useful in jump-starting you to a more even keel from where you can begin to look at some of the difficult issues in your life.

This book is for people who suffer from mild to moderate depression.

BECK'S THEORY OF DEPRESSION

Aaron Beck, the founding father of CBT began his work with the study of depression (Beck, 1979). In his understanding, we may have suffered some kind of loss early in our lives, usually childhood, which then makes us vulnerable to depression. This early loss causes us to form depressive **core beliefs** about ourselves (for example, I am rubbish/ inadequate/helpless/a failure/deficient), the world (for example, the world is a harsh place/the world will treat me badly) and the future (for example, I have no future/the future is hopeless). We will develop **underlying assumptions** in line with our core beliefs, for example, 'If I trust others, then I will be taken for a ride or if I get my hopes up too high, then I will inevitably be disappointed.' Something in our current life (like the loss of a job, the partiality of a parent towards others in the family) triggers or sets off the core beliefs that we have formed, thereby activating all our underlying assumptions. This leads us to having many negative automatic **thoughts** about ourselves, other people and our future. These thoughts create the **feeling** of depression which manifests itself in **physical sensations** in our body such as tiredness, tearfulness, lack of concentration and motivation, all of which tend to make us **behave** in such a way so as to withdraw from everybody and to disappear into our bedrooms.

THE VICIOUS CYCLE OF DEPRESSION

Psychologist Stirling Moorey (Moorey, 2010) has taken Beck's theory further saying that once depression is triggered by some life event or internal thoughts, we tend to develop a 'depressive mode', which is a mode of being similar to a huge negative mental filter through which everything in life is distilled. Moorey talks about the vicious flower of depression at the centre of which is the depressive mode. This mode is best thought of as an 'organizing principle' (Moorey, 2010) which encourages unhelpful behaviours, rumination, negative automatic thoughts (NATs), unpleasant physical symptoms and low mood. A depressive mode leads to constant negative appraisals of everything and everyone. This tends to activate a negative spiral where the different features of the depressive mode, such as rumination and avoidance, become self-perpetuating and ensures that depressive mode is maintained. (See Fig. 4.1)

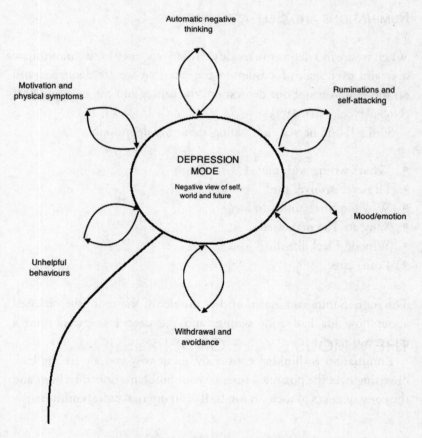

Figure 4.1: The Vicious Flower

AUTOMATIC NEGATIVE THINKING

Automatic negative thinking refers to NATs, the thoughts and images that just pop into your head leaving you feeling bad. They seem to be beyond your control, like gnats buzzing around. Going into a depressive mode creates more NATs and the NATs make you feel more depressed. Since Sunita's depression was linked to her feelings of worthlessness and lack of attention from her father, she had NATs such as, 'I don't exist for my father' and 'He doesn't notice me'.

RUMINATIONS AND SELF-ATTACKING

When we are in a depressive mode there is a tendency for us to ruminate over and over again, focusing on the fact that we are depressed and on the symptoms of our depression, the causes and the meaning of it (Nolen-Hoeksema, 1991).

Sunita found herself ruminating about her depression.

- What's wrong with me?
- I'll never get over this!
- Why did this happen to me?
- Why am I so depressed?
- Why do I feel like this?
- I can't cope

The more Sunita ruminated on her problems, the more she obsessed about how life had gone wrong, and the deeper she went into a depressive mode.

Rumination is thinking constantly about why you are feeling bad, obsessing over the possible causes of your problems or bad feelings and the consequences of them. It can be like an internal radio, continuously transmitting negativity. Rumination is passive and does not involve active problem solving.

When we ruminate we also tend to attack ourselves. Self-attacking is the opposite of inner compassion for the self (Gilbert, 2000). Sunita began to berate herself for being depressed, calling herself 'mad', 'an idiot', 'totally useless' and 'a burden to my family'. This self-attacking made her depression worse.

MOOD/EMOTION

It is interesting to note that emotions and mood are just one part of the vicious flower and again, the lower we feel, the deeper we sink into depression. However, not everyone who is depressed feels sad. Some people report emotional flatness and irritability as key affective aspects of their depressive episodes.

WITHDRAWAL AND AVOIDANCE

Sunita had a group of friends she used to go shopping with and drink coffee with, activities that she really used to like. Since Sunita had been depressed, she no longer became excited by the prospect of going out to the mall, so she stayed at home in bed instead. However, this pushed her further into a depressive mode because she stopped any possibility of having a good time since she was in bed all day.

The next two petals of the flower are to do with behaviour. We are particularly interested in these because behaviour and daily activity is the first thing to deal with when tackling depression. When we are deeply depressed we tend to withdraw and avoid things and no longer engage in activities that we used to enjoy. When withdrawal and avoidance become key elements in our life and are perpetuating the depressive mode, we find ourselves in a vicious cycle of depression from which it seems there is no relief.

UNHELPFUL BEHAVIOURS

Unhelpful behaviours specifically refer to activities like moaning and whining, constantly seeking reassurance, over-eating and drug and alcohol abuse. These behaviours allow us to escape feeling bad in the short term but in the long term they maintain us in our depressive mode.

MOTIVATION AND PHYSICAL SYMPTOMS

People in a depressive mode often experience a lack of motivation to even get out of bed. You may not be able to motivate yourself to do what you used to do, for example, pursue your favourite activities, sports, meeting friends or go to work. Physical effects such as sleeplessness, apathy and tiredness can push you further into a depressive mode because they prompt you to stop doing what you used to enjoy.

Sunita's twin brother died when both of them were born. The parents were grieving the death of their son rather than celebrating Sunita's birth, leaving Sunita with the thought, 'I should have died instead of him.' Sunita had two beautiful sisters, one older and one younger than her. It seemed to her that her dad paid far more attention to these sisters than he did to her, ignoring her a lot of the time. Sunita always saw herself as plain compared to her sisters. According to Beck's model, this was her early experience that made her vulnerable to depression. Early loss meant that Sunita developed core beliefs about her worth (or lack of it). When later on, Sunita felt systematically ignored by her parents, particularly at important family events such as Christmas, the core beliefs and underlying assumptions were activated. NATs such as 'I don't exist for my dad' and 'My dad never notices me', started buzzing around Sunita's head. This led to her becoming very depressed.

Here we have combined Beck's model of how depression develops with Moorey's model of how depression is maintained. It is then applied to the example of Sunita's life as she presented it to me.

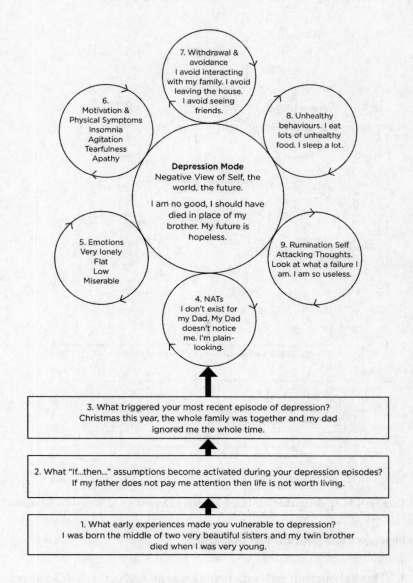

Fig. 4.2: Combined Model of Depression as Applied to Sunita

You might like to use our adapted version of Beck's and Moorey's models of depression with your own examples.

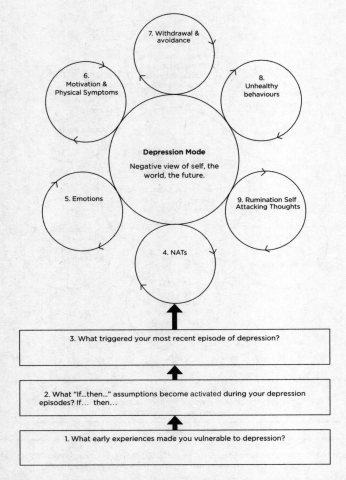

Exercise 4.1: Applying the Combined Model of Depression to Your own Situation

Here are some steps for you to follow:

1. Think about your early experiences as a child. What early experiences
   made you vulnerable to depression? Write a snap shot version of
   these in the box labelled 1.
2. What 'if… then…' assumptions become activated during your
   depressive episodes? See Chapter 3 for an explanation of 'If…
   then…' assumptions. Write these in Box 2.

3. What triggered your most recent episode of depression?
4. What negative automatic thoughts came into you mind when you were triggered?
5. What emotions did these thoughts produce in you?
6. What level of motivation did you experience and what physical symptoms occurred in your body?
7. What were your withdrawal and avoidance patterns?
8. What unhelpful behaviours do you engage in as a result?
9. What ruminations and self-attacking thoughts do you have?

Do not worry if this is too complex at the moment. Just carry on doing the exercises in the remaining part of the chapter.

MAINTENANCE CYCLE OF DEPRESSION

Here is a simple diagram that encapsulates how you keep your depression going.

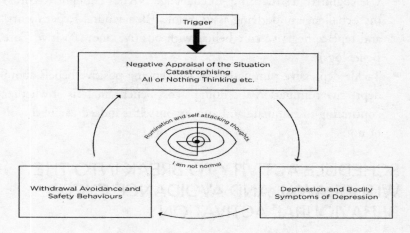

Fig. 4.3 Maintenance Cycle of Depression

Something or someone or even your own internal dialogue acts as a trigger. This then leads you to judge the situation and because of habits of unhelpful thinking you do so in a negative way, filtering out the positives and perhaps catastrophising the situation. Your negative appraisal of the trigger then produces your low mood with all its symptoms (tearfulness, lethargy or agitation). This then causes you to withdraw from social situations and you begin to avoid these and avoid doing things that used to bring you pleasure. When you use your Third Eye to reflect upon yourself, you attack yourself with self-critical thoughts such as, 'I am such a failure.' Such rumination and self-attacking then feeds into your already negative appraisal of the situation which then produces a new cycle, causing your depression to go round and round, indeed causing you to spiral downward to a very low place.

TACKLING DEPRESSION WITH CBT

We need to break the power of this vicious cycle!
    There are three ways to do this:
- Schedule activities to break into the withdrawal and avoidance cycle (Behavioural Activation)
- Use cognitive restructuring to challenge NATs (Thought Records) then challenge underlying assumptions (Behavioural Experiments) and replace negative core beliefs with positive ones (Positive Core Belief logs)
- Tackle depressive rumination by challenging positive beliefs about depressive rumination and doing a cost-benefit analysis of whether continuing to ruminate and attack yourself is indeed useful to you or not.

SCHEDULE ACTIVITY TO BREAK INTO THE WITHDRAWAL AND AVOIDANCE CYCLE: BEHAVIOURAL ACTIVATION

'It is easier to act your way into feeling than feel your way into acting.'

– Dave Andrews

'Have a bias toward action – let's see something happen now. You can break that big plan into small steps and take the first step right away.'

– Indira Gandhi

The first thing to do in order to respond in a resilient way to depression is to increase your daily activities. This is known as behavioural activation. It was developed in the 1970s in a climate of behaviourism. Behavioural activation became less fashionable in the 1980s due to the growth of cognitive therapy, but then regained popularity and scientific credibility as studies revealed that the behavioural component of cognitive therapy was highly effective (Jacobson et al., 1996). Recent studies have shown that behavioural activation leads to improvements in depression and overall functioning, even when it is not guided by an experienced therapist (Ekers et al., 2011). Even in severe depression, behavioural activation has been found to be as effective as antidepressants and more so than cognitive therapy on its own (Dimidjan et al., 2006).

Since depression makes us feel tired, apathetic, low and physically unwell, avoiding activity seemingly makes us feel better in the immediate moment. We often stop socializing and going out. We drop our levels of physical activity and no longer take part in activities that we used to enjoy. Since we no longer do these things, we unintentionally deprive ourselves of the positive effects of these activities.

To explain this a little bit more: one of the essential features of learning theory upon which CBT is based is that we repeat actions that are positively rewarded and avoid actions that bring unpleasant consequences. For example, eating a chocolate biscuit gives us an immediate positive reward. The sweet taste of the chocolate, the crunch of the biscuit and satiation of our hunger make us feel good. We are receiving a positive reward for the behaviour, making us more likely to repeat that behaviour in the future. Whatever is positively rewarded is repeated and whatever is negatively rewarded is not repeated or actively avoided.

Avoiding physical exercise brings us a positive reward in the immediate moment. It enables us to escape the hassles of being with other people in a gym or a park, but in the long run it is negatively rewarding because gradually our bodies run low on the endorphins that are its natural opium, preventing us from feeling good.

You know that you had planned to go for a run with a friend. However, you are still in bed and are tired. Avoiding the exercise gives you immediate positive reward – the bed is comfortable and by staying in you avoid the discomfort of getting up and having to face the world, but in the long term it prevents you from getting the benefits of physical exercise. However, if you cajole yourself to go out, put on your favourite music, push through the discomfort barrier and enjoy the sensation of physical exercise, you will eventually receive the much greater positive reward of feeling fit and flushed with energy.

In depression, avoidance of many different activities is positively rewarded in the immediate moment but in the long run produces a negative reward like in the case study below. *Safyan used to enjoy seeing his friends. However, over the last few months, seeing them has made him feel miserable as he compares his own lack of success in life to their achievements. Therefore, he now avoids seeing his friends, which stops him feeling miserable in the immediate short term. This encourages Safyan to continue avoiding social situations. Additionally, when Safyan used to play cricket with them, he experienced the positive reinforcement of good quality exercise. The enjoyment of the activity encouraged him to repeat it. However, now that he has withdrawn from that activity, he does not experience the same positive reinforcement any more.*

This turns into a cycle of depression, inactivity, avoidance and then even lower mood. People who are depressed avoid many types of activities: routine, pleasurable and necessary activities (Richards and Whyte, 2010).

Routine activities include:

- Cleaning
- Tidying
- Cooking
- Bathing and other hygiene activities
- Regular eating
- Going to bed and waking up at a regular time

Pleasurable activities include:

- Seeing family and friends
- Going out for walks
- Physical exercise
- Art and creative work
- Playing games

Necessary activities could include:

- Work tasks
- Paying bills
- Attending appointments

THE ACTIVITY MONITORING DIARY

On the advice of a therapist trained in CBT, Safyan started by looking at the activities he was doing on a daily basis. Over the course of a week, he monitored his activities using a diary (see next page). He wrote down everything he did. Additionally, he monitored how he felt on each day, using a rating on a scale of 0–10 for how pleasurable the day was to him, where 10 was the most pleasurable and 0 was the least pleasurable.

Safyan's Activity Monitoring Diary

		Mon	Tues	Wed	Thurs	Fri	Sat	Sun
MORNING		10 a.m.- woke up	9 a.m. - woke up	7 a.m. - woke up early with a headache	asleep	11 a.m. - woke up with headache again	12 noon - woke up	10.30 a.m. - woke up
		10.30 a.m.- lay in bed feeling miserable	9.30 a.m. - lay in bed feeing miserable, tried to get back to sleep	7-11 a.m. - tried to get back to sleep but felt unwell				11 a.m. - lay in bed feeing miserable, tried to get back to sleep
		11 a.m. - lay in bed to get back to sleep	10 a.m. - went downstairs to get breakfast and then back to bed					

	Mon	Tues	Wed	Thurs	Fri	Sat	Sun
AFTERNOON	12 noon - played computer game	12 noon - watched TV	12 noon - walked to pharmacy to get headache tablets		12 noon - watched TV and took headache tablets	12 noon - went shopping with mother to buy food and felt embarrassed when bumped into neighbours and they asked me about my life	12 noon - played computer game
	1 p.m. - played computer game	1 p.m. - watched TV	1 p.m. - took headache tablets and went back to bed. Ate lunch in bed	1 p.m. - woke up	1 p.m. - played computer game		1 p.m. - played computer game
	2 p.m. - had lunch alone	2 p.m. - watched TV	2-5 p.m. - played computer game	1.30 p.m. - watched TV and ate lunch	2 p.m. - had lunch alone	2 p.m. - felt tired so went to bed	2 p.m. - played computer game
	3 p.m. - watched TV	3 p.m. - watched TV		2 p.m. - watched TV	3 p.m. - watched TV	3 p.m. - asleep	3 p.m. - watched TV
	4 p.m. - watched TV	4 p.m. - watched TV		3 p.m. - watched TV	4 p.m. - watched TV	4 p.m. - played computer game in bed	4 p.m. - watched TV
		5 p.m. - watched TV		4 p.m. - watched TV			
				5 p.m. - watched TV			

	Mon	Tues	Wed	Thurs	Fri	Sat	Sun
EVENING	6 p.m. - drank beer and watched TV	6 p.m. - went to shop to buy beer	6 p.m. - headache felt a bit better, came downstairs to watch TV. Sister is there with her friends so went back up to bedroom.	6 p.m. - played computer game	6 p.m. - watched TV	5 p.m. - watched TV	5 p.m. - rest of family went to aunt's house. Stayed at home
	7 p.m. - had dinner with mother and sister. Feel very miserable as sister talks about her new job	7 p.m. - drank beer and watched TV		7 p.m. - dinner with mother and sister. After dinner, mother forced me to look on Internet for jobs. Feel overwhelmed and inadequate	7 p.m. - had dinner alone in front of TV	6 p.m. - watched TV	7 p.m. - had dinner alone but thought about how family must be talking about me and how pathetic I am
		7.30 p.m. - ate dinner alone today to avoid uncomfortable conversation with family	7 p.m. - awkward conversation with sister downstairs			7 p.m. - watched TV	
	8 p.m. - lay in bed playing computer game	8 p.m. - lay in bed playing computer game	8 p.m. - played computer game	8 p.m. - argument with mother, end up shouting at each other	8 p.m. - lay in bed playing computer game	8 p.m. - had dinner	8 p.m. - lay in bed playing computer game
	9 p.m. - played computer game	9 p.m. - played computer game	9 p.m. - played computer game	9 p.m. - went to bed, played computer game in bed	9 p.m. - played computer game	9-11 p.m. - played computer game in bed and then fell asleep	9 p.m. - played computer game
	10 p.m. - tried to sleep	10 p.m. - went back downstairs to watch TV	12 midnight - played computer game	10 p.m. - played computer game in bed	10 p.m. - tried to sleep		10 p.m. - went back downstairs and watched TV
		11 p.m. - went to bed	1.30 a.m. - went to bed	11 p.m. - tried to sleep			11 p.m. - watched TV
							12 midnight - went to bed
	0	1	2	3	2	3	1

At the end of the week, Safyan realized that his life had become restricted to watching TV and playing computer games. His therapist asked him a number of questions, Safyan's answers are given below:

1. Are there activities that you used to do that you do no longer? What are they?

Safyan: I've stopped going to family gatherings even though they're not really my favourite activity but I know how important they are to my mother. Before I was a student at university so I would go out to my lectures and then complete my assignments.

2. What are you doing that you didn't do before?

Safyan: I spend a lot more time playing computer games and watching TV. I also argue with my mother more. But despite this I notice that some contact with my mother is better than no contact and I feel a little less depressed than before.

3. What are you avoiding that brings you too much stress?

Safyan: Socializing. Seeing friends. Seeing relatives. Having meals with the family (most of the time). Looking for a job.

4. What behaviours have you developed that help you feel safe?

Safyan: I'm not sure about this one. Not seeing people face to face? Not looking at the newspaper because I would have to look at the job ads? Is this what you mean?

5. Yes. We want to look at what you are avoiding doing because of your depression. Do you see any link between your level of activity and your mood?

Safyan: I felt a bit better the day I went out shopping with my mother. The days that I felt the worst were when I avoided spending any time with other people. However, when I had an argument with my mother

I also felt very low afterwards. But some contact seems to be better than no contact at all. This is a surprise to me.

6. Is there anything you notice about routine, necessary and pleasurable activities?

Safyan: I don't carry out the routine activities that I used to. I don't get up at a regular time or go to bed at a regular time. I don't do many necessary activities – my mother and sister look after me and buy and cook all the food. I haven't been looking for a job recently, which I suppose is a necessary activity. As for pleasurable activities, I do enjoy playing games on the computer but I don't play cricket like I used to.

Then Safyan made lists of routine, pleasurable and necessary activities that he wanted to or felt he needed to include in his week. He included some things that he already did as well as some that he avoided.

ROUTINE:

- Getting up at 9 a.m. every morning
- Getting dressed
- Going shopping
- Going to family events
- Going to the mosque

PLEASURABLE:

- Seeing friends
- Playing cricket
- Going for walks in the park

NECESSARY:

- Looking for a job

Safyan thought about which activities were the easiest and which were the most difficult. He sorted them into three categories:

Easiest – going to shops, getting dressed.

Medium difficulty – going for walks in the park, getting up at 9 a.m., playing cricket.

Hardest – going to family events, looking for a job, going to the mosque, seeing friends.

Then Safyan planned out his next week, fitting the easiest activities into his schedule and some routine, pleasurable and necessary activities too.

	Mon	Tues	Wed	Thurs	Fri	Sat	Sun
MORNING	9 a.m. - wake up and get dressed 10 a.m. - go to shops, buy a newspaper 11 a.m. - watch TV or play computer games if I want to	9 a.m. - get dressed as soon as wake up 11 a.m. - go for a walk in the park	9 a.m. - wake up and get dressed 10 a.m. - go to shops, buy a newspaper and look at ads for jobs	9 a.m. - get dressed as soon as I wake up 11 a.m. - go for a walk in the park	9 a.m. - wake up and get dressed 10 a.m. - go to shops and buy a newspaper and look at ads for jobs	get dressed at some point during the day	get dressed at some point during the day
AFTERNOON	2 p.m. - have lunch with mother and sister even if I don't feel like it 3-5 p.m. - can watch TV or play computer games if I want 4 p.m. - look at newspapers and start working on my CV in relation to some job	2 p.m. - have lunch with mother and sister	2 p.m. - have lunch either with mother and sister or alone	2 p.m. - have lunch with mother and sister	2 p.m. - have lunch either with mother and sister or alone. 3 p.m. - work on CV again. Send it off somewhere	2 p.m. - send message to my friend Hussain, asking him if he wants to meet up soon then have lunch with mother and sister 3 p.m. - go for a walk in the park	2 p.m. - send message to another friend asking about meeting up soon then have lunch with mother and sister

	Mon	Tues	Wed	Thurs	Fri	Sat	Sun
EVENING	Evening - relax/ free time	Evening - relax/free time	Evening - relax/free time Call Sanjit to see if people are still playing cricket. Just chat with him	Evening - relax/free time Go for a short run	Evening - relax/free time	Evening - relax/free time	Evening - relax/ free time Meet with either Hussain or Sanjit

THE ACTIVITY MONITORING DIARY – OVER TO YOU

In order for CBT to be as helpful as it can for you in tackling your depression, you need to think about what triggers your depression and what you are avoiding in your own life. You need to consider what you do to avoid completing the routine, pleasurable and necessary tasks in your life, what the consequences of this are and how you can choose to complete activities in line with your own values. Use Exercise 4.2 to do this.

In Exercise 4.2 like Safyan did, I encourage you to spend a week monitoring your daily activities. This will give you information about what you do currently so that you have a baseline to increase your level of activity from. Remember to write the time at which each activity takes place into the table and be as specific as possible. You might also like to monitor how you felt on each day. Ask yourself whether there is a link between your level of activity and your mood. At the end of each day, rate your mood from 0 (very depressed, i.e., low mood) to 10 (not at all depressed, i.e., high mood).

Exercise 4.1: Activity Monitoring Diary

	Mon	Tues	Wed	Thurs	Fri	Sat	Sun
MORNING							
AFTERNOON							
EVENING							

Exercise 4.2: Activity Monitoring Diary

Now that you have a map of your current activity levels, ask yourself the following questions:

1. What am I doing that I didn't used to do before, for example, not getting out of bed/pyjamas, not bothering to brush my teeth, not cooking for family, etc?

    _____

    _____

    _____

    _____

    _____

2. What am I not doing that I used to do before, for example, going to the gym, meditating, not doing puja, not going to the temple?

    _____

    _____

    _____

    _____

3. What am I avoiding doing because it brings me too much stress, for example, seeing friends, meeting my boss, calling in sick to work?

    _____

    _____

4. What safety behaviours have I developed to help me feel secure, for example, giving excuses to boss for not being

able to meet deadlines, always carrying my aspirins with me?

_____

_____

_____

5. Is there a link between your level of activity and your mood?

_____

_____

_____

_____

6. Once you have done this, you now need to think about increasing your activity levels. Depending on how you deal with depression personally, this might mean increasing all three kinds of activities or you may be managing to do most of the necessary tasks but the pleasurable ones are lacking from your life.

    Make a list of routine, pleasurable and necessary activities in your own life. These should be a mixture of things that you still manage to accomplish despite your depression or tasks that you currently find too difficult. Don't only think about the most common activities but really consider what used to give you joy, pleasure and dignity.

    Routine: (for example, going to bed at a certain time, health and cleanliness routines)

-
-
-
-
-
-

-
-

Pleasurable: (for example, going for walks, seeing friends, playing music)

-
-
-
-
-
-

Necessary: (for example, paying bills, going to work, looking after family)

-
-
-
-
-
-

Now use the activity diary provided to schedule some of these activities into your week. Schedule the easiest activities first, but make sure you get a mixture of routine, pleasurable and necessary activities. Make sure that you fill in where, when and what you are going to do as well as who you are going to do it with; the more specific the better. When it comes to doing the activities, always tick the activities that you have accomplished and cross the activities that you have not.

Exercise 4.3: Behavioural Activation Diary

Here is a behavioural activation diary. It is different to the activity schedule that you have filled out because here you gradually increase the pleasurable, routine and necessary activities that have dropped away during your depression. Remember to GRADUALLY introduce more and more activities. Otherwise you will be in line for BOOM AND BUST!

	Mon	Tues	Wed	Thurs	Fri	Sat	Sun
MORNING							
AFTERNOON							
EVENING							

> ## Hints and tips for creating a behavioural activation diary
>
> - Identify which activities you are avoiding and what you used to do and schedule the easiest ones first
> - Make sure you know WHY you are putting that activity in – how does it help you work towards a valued direction?
> - Start small – go for easy, short-term goals first
> - Monitor how the activities affect your mood
> - After each week, evaluate your activity diary. What are you still avoiding? Do you need to increase or decrease the difficulty level of the tasks?

You may be thinking that all of this is simple common sense. Why go through all of this in such a systematic way? The reality is that behavioural activation works best if it is written down on the forms that are available for it. Just thinking things through in your head does not seem to have the same effect. So I would encourage you to have the patience to write things out for yourself. You may surprise yourself at how powerful the technique is if you follow the steps systematically.

TWO COMMON MISTAKES

There are two common mistakes that people make when they start doing activity diaries:

1. PLANNING TOO MUCH TOO QUICKLY: AVOID BOOM AND BUST

Make sure that you don't make it too difficult to complete the activities. People often get so enthusiastic that they plan too many activities together. It is very important to start off small and then work up to more increasingly challenging activities. Often, you just want to feel better as soon as possible that you 'boom' with activity in the planning stage and then go 'bust' when you can't complete your whole schedule. Foster inner compassion (Gilbert, 2000), make sure that you look after yourself and don't expect yourself to do too much in the first few weeks.

2.   PLANNING ACTIVITIES THAT DO NOT RELATE TO WHAT YOU HAVE BEEN AVOIDING OR DO NOT RELATE TO YOUR DEEPLY HELD VALUES

If you have been avoiding a necessary activity, such as starting a piece of work like a university assignment, there is little use in scheduling only physical exercise and social occasions into your activity diary for the next few weeks. By all means, start small with the easier activities. However, if it is of great importance to you that you will complete the assignment by the deadline, you will have to tackle it as soon as you can. Break the avoided activity down into little steps. For example, you might say that on Monday you will turn your computer on and spend five minutes writing a very rough plan for the assignment. On Tuesday, you could spend five minutes doing an Internet search for relevant articles.

Similarly, the activity needs to be related to your values. One of your values might be to keep your body and mind healthy. If you hate exercise, don't force yourself to go to the gym, scheduling it in three times per week. Think of creative ways related to activities you used to enjoy in order to move towards your values.

For example, I really enjoy listening to music as well as being in green spaces so I schedule in walks or runs in the park with my MP3 player on. Another one of my values is to lovingly look after my family. I plan small actions that help me move towards my values, such as phoning or texting my daughter when I know she's been having a hard week. I do feel better when I have done these things, since I know that they help me move in valued directions. And normally, I get a lot of enjoyment and pleasure out of being in touch with my family.

BUT WHAT IF I DON'T FEEL LIKE IT . . . THE FIVE-MINUTE RULE

Depression makes people feel low and apathetic. What if you wake up in the morning with all of these activities scheduled and you just don't feel up to it? Well, just as the quotation at the beginning of this section states, you need to 'act your way into feeling', not 'feel your way into acting'. You may never feel like doing these activities but inactivity will only make it worse and feed the vicious cycle. Christine Padesky always says that if you have done the activity for five minutes, you can tick it off your list as 'done'. Even if the activity looks very daunting, tell yourself that you only need to do it for five minutes. You might find that once you have started it, you want to continue. However, even if not, you can work up to doing it for longer periods of time as you go on.

As you progress in increasing your levels of activity, try scheduling harder, often avoided and more important activities into your week.

Behavioural activation is a very powerful way of cutting into depressive cycles, particularly if you have become significantly inactive due to the fact that you are depressed. Another powerful way of breaking through depression is to tackle the thoughts through what is commonly known as Cognitive Restructuring.

Use Cognitive Restructuring to Challenge Your NATs

In Chapter 3 we have already learnt how to deal with our NATs by challenging them using thought records. We have learnt to identify our underlying assumptions and devise behavioural experiments to test these and to form new ones. We have also looked at our core beliefs and how we can form new ones to replace old, negative ones using positive core belief logs. If you have not read this chapter, please go back to it now and teach yourself how to deal with the cognitive aspects of depression. The cognitions that support depression can be disastrous and can wreck our lives and so it is important to know how to do battle with them.

Here, we will look at Sunita's thought record and how she came to a balanced belief about a very difficult situation. She was feeling marginalized by her dad when her vivacious sister and family came over for dinner the previous week. This left her feeling low and very depressed because she thought of herself as an uninteresting person. Because she had been doing some CBT on herself, Sunita decided to look for the evidence for this very hot thought. Then she collected data, which constituted the evidence against the hot thought. After she collected this factual evidence, she created a more balanced perspective on the hot thought, which significantly reduced her feelings of being low.

Below Sunita's thought record is a box containing a blank thought record for you to use on yourself and below that are some hints and tips that might help you as you use the thought record.

Sunita's thought record

Think of a recent situation that made you mildly upset.

1. **Situation:** Describe what you were doing, who you were with, and the time and place the situation occurred.
Having dinner with family on a Thursday night – one of my sisters was getting all my father's attention

2. **Mood:** Describe the mood or moods you were feeling at the time, rate their intensity on a scale of 0–100 per cent.
Depressed 90 per cent

3. **Negative automatic thoughts:** What was going through your mind, who were you thinking about, how do you feel about yourself, what made you feel that way, what does this mean, what memories went through your mind, and anything else you may have been thinking about at the time.
   Circle one hot thought. This is the thought that has the most emotional energy and is responsible for driving the mood that you have mentioned above.
   How dare she hog his attention!
   Why can't I get his attention?

I am uninteresting and boring. (This is Sunita's hot thought, as it carries the most emotional energy.)

4. Evidence for the hot thought: Write down any factual evidence that supports your hot thought.

My father did not ask me any questions about my day during dinner. My sisters have interesting lives. One is already married with children and the other is training to be a lawyer. I don't have a job and I am not married.

5. Evidence against the hot thought: Write down any evidence that does not support your hot thought.

Other people find me interesting – my friend Jasminder always wants to talk to me and hear what I've been doing.

I'm always at home and my father has all day to ask me questions. My sister was visiting with her family so it is normal that the attention would be on her.

6. Alternative/balanced thought: Write an alternative or balanced thought.

I am interesting sometimes. Just because one person is not paying attention to me, it doesn't mean that I am completely uninteresting.

7. Re-rate your Mood: Copy your feelings from #2. Take your alternative balanced thought into the situation and think it. How would you feel if you thought this thought instead of your hot thought? Re-rate the intensity of each feeling.

Depressed 40 per cent

Exercise 4.4: My Thought Record

Think of a recent situation that made you mildly upset.

1. Situation: Describe what you were doing, who you were with, time and place the situation occurred.

_____

_____

_____

_____

2. Mood: Describe the mood or moods you were feeling at the time, rate their intensity on a scale of 0–100 per cent.

_____

_____

3. Automatic thoughts: What was going through your mind, who were you thinking about, how do you feel about yourself, what made you feel that way, what does this mean, what memories went through your mind, and anything else you may have been thinking about at the time. Circle one hot thought. This is the thought that has the most emotional energy and is responsible for driving the mood that you have mentioned above.

_____

_____

_____

_____

_____

_____

4. **Evidence for the hot thought:** Write down any factual evidence that supports your hot thought.

_____

_____

_____

_____

_____

_____

_____

5. **Evidence against the hot thought:** Write down any evidence that does not support your hot thought.

_____

_____

_____

_____

_____

_____

6. **Alternative/balanced thought:** Write an alternative or balanced thought.

_____

_____

_____

_____

_____

_____

7. Re-rate your mood: Copy your feelings from #2. Take your alternative balanced thought into the situation and think it. How would you feel if you thought this thought instead of your hot thought? Re-rate the intensity of each feeling. What is your conclusion?

_____

_____

Hints and tips

- Fill the thought record in as soon as possible after you felt upset about something. Ask a trusted friend or relative to help if you are struggling
- The thought record will take a long time at first but it will become easier as you get used to using it
- Many of your thoughts will repeat themselves. This makes the thought record easier, since after you have tackled a difficult thought once, you will know how to reassess it and come up with alternatives
- If you have suicidal thoughts, get professional help immediately
- If you are having specific difficulties in challenging your thoughts, an approach based on mindfulness and ACT might be better for you at first so you can defuse from your thoughts instead of challenging them directly
- Consider using an antidepressant medicine if you have tried behavioural activation and the thought record feels completely impossible for you. Once you are on the antidepressant for three to four weeks, consider trying behavioural activation and the thought record again

TACKLING DEPRESSIVE RUMINATION

Depressive rumination is not easy to tackle. This is because many people who ruminate about their depression hold positive beliefs about the usefulness of their rumination (Papageorgiou & Wells, 2004). What is a positive belief about rumination? Here are some:

- If I think about my depression, then I might come up with solutions about how not to be depressed
- If I think about why certain events happened to me, I might be able to prevent them from happening again

If you notice, these positive beliefs take the form of 'If... then' statements. They can be tested in the same way as 'If... then...' statements are tested using behavioural experiments. Cognitive restructuring is also useful in tackling depressive rumination. For instance, you could ask yourself what is the factual evidence for and against the thought that if I ruminate about my depression I will come up with solutions of how not to be depressed.

Some people have suggested that suppressing thoughts (thought stopping) about being depressed might stop the rumination from happening. But the research shows that thought stopping only makes things worse (Purdon, 2004).

The cost of rumination is very high. It maintains the cycle of depression and feeds it causing more depression. One way of breaking into your depressive rumination is to do a cost benefit analysis (Papageorgiou & Wells, 2004).

A cost benefit analysis is an empirical way of working out whether the price one is paying for a particular activity or mental act reaps benefits or advantages for our well-being or whether the cost is too high. When we do a cost benefit analysis, we look at the relative advantages of ruminating and compare these with the relative disadvantages of ruminating on our depression. We shift our focus of attention from asking ourselves why we are depressed, why this has happened to me, etc., to how is ruminating about it all useful to me? Shifting from 'why' to 'how' is a good way of working out whether ruminating is useful or not. Here is how Sunita worked out her cost benefit analysis:

Benefits of Ruminating about my Depression	Costs of Ruminating about my Depression
I might come up with a solution	Worrying about being depressed makes me feel neurotic
Worrying about my depression may enable me to prevent it in future	Worrying about my depression seems to create more by adding worry on top of the depression
I might discover what is wrong with me	Worrying about my depression has not yet led to a solution or me knowing how to prevent it
	Worrying about my depression leaves me feeling even more tired and exhausted than I did before
	It focuses on the negative parts of myself
	Makes me withdraw from socializing even more
	I am unable to concentrate on anything
	My friends are fed up with hearing my ruminations and do not really want to talk with me any more
	I lose sleep because I ruminate so much
	My habit of ruminating interferes with my work

If you are a depressive ruminator, it is really important that you break this habit and it would be useful for you to do your own cost benefit analysis. Draw a table similar to the one before and use it to break into your ruminative cycle. It is really important that you see the pointlessness of rumination.

Depressive rumination is significantly helped through behavioural activation described earlier in this chapter. It is also useful to use mindfulness when you catch yourself ruminating about your depression. This technique will enable you to bring your Self into the present moment and will be described in Chapter 6.

RELAPSE PREVENTION

CBT in the form of a self-help book such as this one can help you recover from a mild to moderate depressive episode and teach you skills that will be of use to you throughout your life. It is important that you do not slip back into depression once you are out of it. In order to build resilience and for protection against future depressive episodes, forming a relapse prevention plan will help you keep on the road to well-being (Hollon, 2005).

Sunita made a plan for herself using Hollon's template. Here it is:

1. What are the most useful ideas I have learnt from CBT for depression?

   • That your thoughts don't have to determine how you feel
   • Thought distortions are common
   • Act your way into feeling

2. What are the most useful exercises for me?

   • Behavioural activation
   • Thought record
   • Identifying my thought distortions
   • Keeping a positive core belief log

3. What are my goals for next year?

   • See my job through to the end of my contract

- Spend more time with my closest friends
- Learn to cook

4. What events might trigger another episode of depression?

- Losing my job or doing badly at it
- Not getting into the university course that I want to
- My boyfriend leaves me for someone else

5. What are the signs that I am becoming depressed?

- Stopping socializing or coming home early alone from social events
- Thinking obsessively about death
- Thinking obsessively about my depression
- Feeling tired all the time
- Having a sinking feeling in my tummy

6. If I see these signs, what should I do?

- Re-read this book and especially the exercises that I have filled out
- Do the exercises again with the current situation in mind
- Spend quality time with loved ones who care about me
- Make sure I am doing some pleasurable activities
- Find a therapist or call one that I used to see and make an appointment

7. What will I do regularly to keep myself feeling mentally well?

- Eat healthily
- Exercise regularly
- Spend time with people I love
- Manage my thoughts so that I perceive my reality in a flexible and positive frame

Exercise 4.5: Relapse Prevention

Now, try the relapse prevention plan for yourself:

1. What are the most useful ideas I have learnt from CBT for depression?

1.

2.

3.

2. What are the most useful exercises for me?

1.

2.

3.

3. What are my goals for next year?

1.

2.

3.

4. What events might trigger another episode of depression?

1.

2.

3.

5. What are the signs that I am becoming depressed?

1.

2.

3.

6. If I see these signs, what should I do?

1.
2.
3.

7. What should I do regularly to keep myself feeling mentally well?

1.
2.
3.

Key Points from this Chapter

— We can overcome depression and become resilient
— Getting a baseline of our depressive patterns of activity is important – so using an activity diary is a starting point for tackling depression
— There is an important link between depression and activity: the more depressed you are the less active you become
— Treatment for depression seeks to gradually reintroduce avoided activities such as socializing with friends and family, exercising, etc. Use the behavioural activation table to reintroduce pleasurable, routine and necessary activities
— Challenging our negative automatic thoughts is a very important route to feeling better. Use the thought record fifteen to twenty times at least to do this
— Getting out of the cycle of depressive rumination is key to furthering our treatment of depression. Use a cost-benefit analysis to do this.
— Putting a relapse prevention plan in place in advance will help to stay on track towards increased resilience

REFERENCES

1. A.T. Beck, A.J. Rush, B.F. Shaw, and G. Emery, *Cognitive Therapy of Depression*, New York: Guilford Press, 1979.

2. T. Borchard, How Does Mindfulness Reduce Depression? An Interview with John Teasdale, Ph.D., PsychCentral, http://psychcentral.com/blog/archives/2014/01/19/how-does-mindfulness-reduce-depression-an-interview-with-john-teasdale-ph-d/ accessed on 17 October 2014.

3. S. Dimidjian, S.D. Hollon, K.S. Dobson, K.B. Schmaling, R.J. Kohlenberg, M.E. Addis, R. Gallop, S.L. Rizvi, J.K. Gollan, D.L. Dunner, and N.S. Jacobson, 'Randomized Trial of Behavioural Activation, Cognitive Therapy, and Antidepressant Medication in the Acute Treatment of Adults with Major Depression', *Journal of Consulting and Clinical Psychology*,74:658, 2006.

4. D. Ekers, C. Godfrey, S. Gilbody, S. Parrott, D.A. Richards, D. Hammond, and A. Hayes, 'Cost Utility of Behavioural Activation Delivered by the Non-Specialist', *British Journal of Psychiatry*, 199:510y, 2011.

5. P. Gilbert, *Overcoming Depression*, Audio CD, 2000.

6. S. Hollon, 'Cognitive Behaviour Therapy: From Action to Insight (and Back Again), Institute for the Training of Professionals Interested in Cognitive Therapy.

7. S.D. Hollon, R.J. DeRubeis, R.C. Shelton, J.D. Amsterdam, R.M. Salomon, J.P. O'Reardon, M.L. Lovett, P.R. Young, K.L. Haman, B.B. Freeman, and R. Gallop, 'Prevention of Relapse Following Cognitive Therapy vs Medications in Moderate to Severe Depression', *Archives of General Psychiatry*, 62(4):417–422, 2005.

8. N.S. Jacobson, K.S. Dobson, P.A. Truax, M.E. Addis, K. Koerner, J.K. Gollan, E. Gortner, and S.E. Prince, 'A Component Analysis of Cognitive Behavioural Treatment for Depression', *Journal of Consulting and Clinical Psychology*, 64:295, 1996.

9. J.W. Kanter, A.J. Puspitasari, M.M. Santos, and G.A. Nagy, 'Behavioural Activation: History, Evidence and Promise', *The British Journal of Psychiatry*, 200:361–363, 2012.

10. C. Padesky, and K. Mooney, 'Strengths-based Cognitive-behavioural Therapy: A Four-step Model to Build Resilience', *Clinical Psychology and Psychotherapy*, 19(4):283–290, 2012.

11. C. Padesky, Five-minute rule in Behavioural Activation (personal communication)

12. C. Papageorgiou, and A. Wells, *Depressive Rumination: Nature, Theory and Treatment*, Chichester: John Wiley & Sons Inc., 2004.

13. C. Purdon, 'Psychological Treatment of Rumination', *Depressive Rumination: Nature, Theory and Treatment*, (edited by) C. Papageorgiou, and A. Wells, Chichester: John Wiley & Sons Inc., 2004.

14. S. Moorey, 'The Six Cycles Maintenance Model: Growing a "Vicious flower" for Depression', *Behavioural and Cognitive Psychotherapy*, 38(2):173–184, 2010.

15. S. Nolen-Hoeksema, 'Responses to Depression and Their Effects on the Duration of Depressive Episodes', *Journal of Abnormal Psychology*, 100:569–582, 1991.

16. D. Richards, and M. Whyte, 'Reach Out – National Programme Educator Materials to Support the Delivery of Training for Psychological Wellbeing Practitioners Delivering Low Intensity Interventions', http://www.iapt.nhs.uk/silo/files/reach-out-educator-manual.pdf, 2010.

17. M.E.P. Seligman, and S.F. Maier, 'Failure to Escape Traumatic Shock', *Journal of Experimental Psychology* 74:1–9, 1967, doi:10.1037/h0024514.

18. J.B. Overmier, and M.E.P. Seligman, 'Effects of Inescapable Shock upon Subsequent Escape and Avoidance Responding', *Journal of Comparative and Physiological Psychology* 63:28–33, 1967, doi:10.1037/h0024166. PMID 6029715.

19. M.E.P. Seligman, 'Learned Helplessness', *Annual Review of Medicine*, 23(1):407–412, 1972, doi:10.1146/annurev.me.23.020172.002203.

20. R. Tagore, *The English Writings of Rabindranath Tagore: Poems*, New Delhi: Sahitya Akademi, 2004.

21. M. Williams, J.D. Teasdale, Z. Segal, and J. Kabat-Zinn, *The Mindful Way Through Depression: Freeing Yourself from Chronic Unhappiness*, New York: Guilford Press, 2007.

22. T.N. Hanh, *The Pocket Thich Nhat Hanh*, (edited by) M. McLeod, Boston and London: Shambhala, 2012.

5

Applying CBT to Anxiety

'Through training, we can change; we can transform ourselves.'
– Dalai Lama

'You may never know what results come of your action, but if you do nothing there will be no result.'
– Gandhi

In this chapter:

— Exposure: Theory and Therapy
— The Danger Disorders
   o CBT for Panic Disorder
   o CBT for Obsessive Compulsive Disorder (OCD)
   o CBT for Illness Anxiety
— The Coping Disorders
   o CBT for Generalized Anxiety Disorder (GAD)
   o CBT for Specific Phobias
   o CBT for Social Anxiety
   o CBT for Post-Traumatic Stress Disorder
   o Relapse Prevention

---

*A*mit was an academic at the Indian Institute of Technology, Delhi. He was a very capable engineer and researcher and was proud to have just received a promotion. However, reading through his new contract, Amit was horrified to see that he would have to give lectures to big groups of undergraduate students for the first time in his life. Before Amit's first lecture, he felt nauseous, his heart was pounding and he was sure that he would mess up. His body was going into full fight or flight mode! The first lecture went okay and Amit had to prepare for the second one the following week. The date of the lecture came and Amit was anxious again. However, he did not feel anywhere near as bad as the first time. As the term progressed, Amit felt better and better about his lectures until a day came when he found himself enjoying teaching.

This chapter will provide you with practical ideas and resources for applying the wisdom of CBT in your life in order to combat anxiety. To do this effectively, we will need to delve deeper into some of the theories behind CBT. You may like to think of this as collecting tools to add to your resilience toolkit. The more you practice these exercises, the more you will build up your mental and emotional resilience.

The people I describe in this chapter are real people who I have treated in therapy. Since I have practiced in England for some years now, most of them are English. However, I have treated many people in India too and the problems that the English suffer are universal and as relevant to the Indian context as anywhere in the world. I have changed their names and details to protect them and I also have their permission to write their stories. I am indebted to them for sharing their lives with me.

There are two key elements of CBT for anxiety: fact-finding and exposure. Fact-finding means educating yourself about the particular type of anxiety you are experiencing and getting true factual information. For example, it will help you to cope with panic disorder if you understand the body's fight or flight response (see Chapter 2). Chapter 2 also gives factual information about different anxiety disorders so that you understand why you are thinking and feeling the way you do. Exposure refers to the fact that the more we allow ourselves to get into the very situations that make us feel anxious, the less anxious we will feel.

EXPOSURE: THEORY AND THERAPY

Amit's example shows how the more you are exposed to an anxiety-provoking situation, the less anxious you feel. Exposure is the opposite of avoidance. Anxiety disorders tend to feed off avoidance. When you expose yourself to the feared situation/object/animal/person, you learn how to cope with your anxiety in the long-term. Exposure is the key to managing many anxiety disorders, such as specific phobias, panic and agoraphobia, social anxiety, OCD and PTSD. We will now discuss the anxiety disorders from Chapter 2 and how to apply CBT to them effectively.

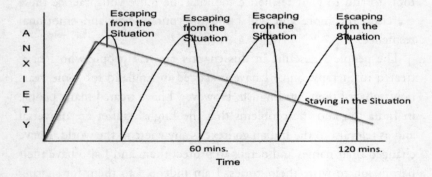

Fig. 5.1: Exposure and Avoidance (adapted from Richards and Whyte, 2010)

The graph above demonstrates the difference between exposure and avoidance. Let us first look at the inverted U shaped curves. Person A finds herself in the middle of an anxiety provoking situation and her percentage level of anxiety shoots up to almost 100 per cent. She then engages in her favourite safety behaviour (usually this is to escape from the anxiety-provoking situation) and this brings her anxiety down. But the next time she finds herself in the anxiety-provoking situation, her anxiety shoots up again to almost 100 per cent. Person A is on an emotional roller coaster of trigger-anxiety-escape-temporary relief … trigger-anxiety-escape-temporary relief …

When you avoid or escape your feared situation, arousal levels drop immediately. However, when you come in contact with the feared situation again, your arousal levels will peak again and the anxiety response will return.

Exposure is different from avoidance. If you allow yourself to be exposed to your anxiety-provoking situation, gradually your anxiety will drop as you realize that the stimulus is not harming you. This is represented by the solid line. In exposure therapy, you plan how you will face your fears. When you stay in the feared situation over a long period of time, your body naturally reduces its level of arousal. Staying in contact with the feared object, animal or situation over time gradually decreases your fear response. This is known as habituation.

According to Richards and Whyte (2010), exposure treatment must fulfill the following four conditions if it is to be successful:

1. Gradual: You should gradually confront the feared object, animal or situation. This might mean looking at a picture of the feared situation or stimulus in the first session and then working up to touching or using it in the last session. For example, if you have a fear of spiders, a therapist might ask you to spend the first session in the presence of a picture of a spider and by the last session, it is likely that you will be able to allow a real one to crawl across your hand. Or you may have a fear of heights and your therapist encourages you to practice standing on a stepladder in the first session and in the last session, you find you are able to stand on your terrace and look down without feeling the intense anxiety that you used.

2. Prolonged: The session has to be long enough for the body's arousal levels to drop and for habituation to take place. This should be for around one or two hours, although some therapists recommend a three-hour session (Öst, 1989). Anxiety levels should have dropped by at least 50 per cent by the end of the session.

3. Repeated: Once exposure has started to take effect and your anxiety begins to decrease, you need to stay in contact with the feared object, animal or situation in order to continue to improve. Richards and Whyte (2010) recommend four or five sessions of one to two hours each, every week.

4. Undistracted: In order to reduce your anxiety, you need to really 'feel the fear'! This means that you don't distract yourself by thinking of other things while you are doing exposure therapy. You should not take tranquilizers whilst doing exposure either, although consult a doctor before stopping any prescribed medication.

Exposure is often the last thing you want to do if you are scared about a particular situation. It can almost seem counterintuitive. 'If this situation, object, person or animal is so threatening, why on earth would I want to spend more time in its presence?' However, exposure has been proven to be effective over and over again. It is difficult initially but if you set your mind to it you may surprise yourself with how quickly you get over your fear.

THE DANGER DISORDERS

As mentioned in Chapter 2, the syndromes classified under anxiety generally fall into one of two categories, according to Padesky (2013): danger disorders and coping disorders. Danger disorders are syndromes in which threat is experienced as external to the self. Thus, panic disorder, obsessive compulsive disorder and illness anxiety are danger disorders because people who experience it overestimate the level of danger in their lives, while generalized anxiety, phobias and social anxiety are examples of coping disorders because people underestimate their abilities to cope with the situations they find themselves in. PTSD is classified by Padesky as both a danger and a coping disorder.

CBT FOR PANIC DISORDER

Panic attacks are very common and occur in many anxiety disorders. People who do not normally have anxiety disorders can have panic attacks too. The symptoms of a panic attack are listed in Chapter 2 as are the symptoms of panic disorders. The most useful action you can take against panic attacks is to educate yourself about what a panic attack really is. It is not necessarily 'panic disorder'.

A person is classified as having a panic disorder when they have recurring panic attacks and *interpret* the symptoms of their panic attack *in a catastrophic way*. We would diagnose panic disorder if the person having a panic attack sees their elevated heart rate and thinks that they are going to die or are having a heart attack. They then develop anxiety about having further attacks. This catastrophic misinterpretation of symptoms normally results in avoidance and safety behaviours. Thus, for example, people will often take long, round about routes from A to B so that they can always be near a hospital just in case they have a heart attack. If the individual associates their panic attack with particular places and avoids those places for that reason, it is known as panic disorder with agoraphobia. Other people feel that their panic attacks happen randomly and they are not associated with particular situations. This is panic disorder without agoraphobia.

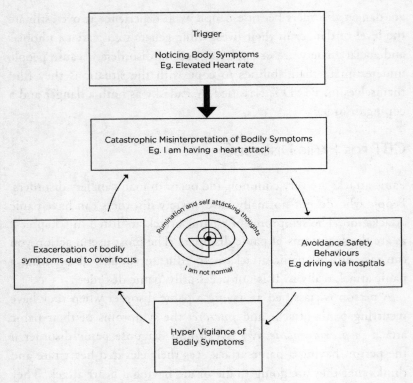

Figure 5.2: A Maintenance Cycle of Panic Disorder

This diagram models how panic disorder is maintained. Very small things can trigger bodily symptoms like drinking too much coffee or liquorice tea can elevate your blood pressure and increase your heart rate. Or stress may cause symptoms of anxiety such as sweating, breathlessness etc. A person with panic disorder looks at these bodily symptoms and misinterprets them as something more serious than they are. They might then go to a doctor who will do a series of tests on them and find that there is nothing wrong with them. Despite having this information, a person suffering from panic disorder will continue to misinterpret their bodily symptoms catastrophically. They will then engage in complex avoidance and safety behaviours 'just in case'. I gave the example of driving past several hospitals on the way to work in case the person has a heart attack. This is a safety behaviour. Ultimately, as they watch themselves, using their unhelpful Third Eye, the person develops a morbid fear of having panic attacks, which to them means a heart attack. Focusing upon the anxiety symptoms such as a racing heart causes those symptoms to increase in intensity, i.e., excessive focus actually exacerbates those symptoms. They therefore engage in elaborate avoidance and safety behaviours to prevent the feared catastrophe from happening, leading to more anxiety symptoms which then feeds the panic cycle.

Karl was forty-six and came to me because he was suffering panic disorder; up to sixty to seventy panic attacks in any one week. After an initial assessment it was clear that Karl was suffering from panic disorder with agoraphobia. He felt utterly miserable and couldn't go anywhere because of his fear of having another panic attack. His doctor had put him on a cocktail of antidepressants and antianxiety drugs. He had been on these drugs for years. When he felt his breathing rate going up, his thoughts were that he was going to die or suffocate. He was also fearful that other people would see him having a panic attack and he would embarrass himself.

We collaboratively formed an anxiety hierarchy. Some of the things that he could no longer do because of his panic disorder were: leave the vicinity of his house and garden, go to the shops, ride his cycle, walk in the woods and drive long distances. This meant that he could no longer do some of the things that used to give him real joy, like photography. His life had become very limited and his relationship was under strain.

The first step was to help Karl taper off the drugs that prevented him from feeling the full blast of his anxiety and created a zombie-like feeling in him.

I then talked to him about his catastrophic misinterpretation of his anxiety symptoms. I had to show him that even though his breathing rate was high, he was not going to die. Even though rationally he knew that dying involved oxygen leaving the body, and not more and more coming in because of his rapid breathing, in his heart he still did not trust that he would not die. So, I brought my gym bike into the therapy room and got him to raise his breathing rate and heart rate. At the end of this behavioural experiment, he learnt that rapid breathing and a racing heart were not symptoms of suffocation or death. He was more easily able to classify his rapid breathing as merely symptoms of anxiety rather than as an indication that he was about to die.

The next step was to get him out of his house and into the wider world. Part of the problem involving agoraphobia is the social embarrassment of having a panic attack in public and being seen by other people as having an attack. So we planned another behavioural experiment that we would carry out together. I asked Karl what he looked like to others when he was having a panic attack. He told me he always took out his cell phone and started typing on it to hide the fact that he was having a panic attack and if people looked closely they would see that his lip was trembling. I practiced acting like Karl in the middle of an attack. I took out my cell phone and began typing on it and let my lip tremble. When Karl was satisfied that I looked like he would look if he was having a panic attack. I drove him to the local grocery store. I was going to act like I was having a panic attack in the aisles and his instructions were to look at how other people reacted to my acted panic attack. I went up close to a woman, took out my mobile and typed furiously on it and let my lips tremble. The woman merely moved away. I did this at least five times with Karl noticing what people did. He was utterly amazed to find that nobody noticed me having a panic attack. This experiment seemed to release him from his agoraphobia and Karl started walking to the shops without anxiety.

Then we tackled some of the behaviours on his anxiety hierarchy. First, he took his long forsaken camera into the woods near his house and used it to photograph pictures of trees, branches and berries. He reclaimed this part of his life.

I took him out in my car with Karl in the passenger seat. He had an anxiety attack, but was able to soothe himself by telling himself that he was not going to die and this was just a panic attack. We drove for about forty-five minutes until his anxiety had quietened down. The next step was getting Karl to sit behind the wheel himself, which we did in a graded fashion. Towards the end of therapy he was driving locally in his neighbourhood and had plans to take a long drive with his partner and mother for a holiday.

In order to manage your panic attacks and stop them from becoming a problem, you need to de-catastrophise your thoughts about the situation. This means learning that the symptoms of a panic attack are the symptoms of anxiety and do not mean that you are having a major catastrophe. Panic attacks are horrible but not life-threatening.

Just like catastrophic thinking, another key element of panic disorders is hyper-vigilance for bodily symptoms. This means that small things such as an increase in heart rate are misinterpreted as the beginnings of a panic attack. For many people, understanding the symptoms of a panic attack and challenging their own catastrophic misinterpretations of those symptoms is enough to manage their panic disorder.

Here are several common misinterpretations that are characteristic of panic disorder:

Symptom	Common Misinterpretation	What Is Really Happening
Chest pain	Heart attack	When the muscles between your ribs become tense, they can cause chest pain. Over-breathing in panic attacks can make this worse
Difficulties in breathing	I'm going to stop breathing	The tensing of your rib muscles during anxiety makes your breathing harder Breathing is an automatic reflex and you cannot stop yourself from breathing
Feeling wobbly and dizzy	I'm going to faint	You feel dizzy because your breathing has become shallow You are extremely unlikely to faint during a panic attack. That is because fainting happens when blood pressure is low. In a panic attack, your blood pressure increases

| Extreme anxiety, feeling like you are losing control | I'm going crazy | Panic attacks are physical reactions to fear. Your body is preparing itself for danger. This is completely natural |
| | | Anxiety does not turn into psychosis no matter how many panic attacks you have |

Normally a CBT therapist would collaboratively design a behavioural experiment to help the person de-link the symptom from its catastrophic misinterpretation. This can be done by artificially inducing the symptoms and showing the person that nothing catastrophic actually occurs. For example, a person who fears that breathlessness means that they are going to suffocate and die can be asked to make themselves breathless by running up and down the stairs. They can then observe that they did not suffocate or die.

Exercise 5.1: Behavioural Experiments for Panic

You may need to design a behavioural experiment, choosing a trigger that normally causes you to panic. You could either purposefully induce one of the physical symptoms of a panic attack or visit the place that triggers the attacks (if you have panic disorder with agoraphobia).

If the fear of fainting perpetuates your panic attacks, you could design an experiment where you spin round and round in circles to make yourself dizzy on purpose. People with agoraphobia design experiments around going to shops, parks or theatres.

Following is a sample behavioural experiment record sheet. It is important that you write this out so that you record your findings and observations.

Date	Friday, 20 July
Situation or trigger	Heart going faster and breathing changing
Experiment I will carry out	I will run up the stairs
Specific prediction of what I think will happen with per cent of how likely it is	I will have a panic attack I will have a heart attack – 90 per cent I will suffocate – 90 per cent I will die – 80 per cent
What I did	I ran up the stairs
What happened? Did it confirm my prediction?	Immediately felt my breathing became difficult, I felt my heart beating faster and this made me anxious. I felt panic. However, I did not suffocate, have a heart attack or die.
Learning and new strength of conviction (0–100 per cent)	Just because my heart is beating faster, this does not mean that I am going to have a heart attack. I will have a heart attack – 40 per cent I will suffocate – 40 per cent I will die – 20 per cent

PANIC DIARY

Date	Situation Where? When? Who? With?	Physical symptoms	Feared consequences What did I think the symptoms meant?	Behaviour What did I do?	Alternative explanation for symptoms
14/5/2015	Walking to the bus stop in the morning on my own	Raised heartbeat, hard to breathe, sweaty	I can't breathe, I am having a heart attack, I will die	I sat down and it passed	I was not having a heart attack. These were just symptoms of anxiety

On the previous page is a template for a panic diary. The panic diary is a very useful tool to help you watch your panic. It enables you to get a handle on your anxiety and to test it out in your psychological laboratory. It is similar to the thought record and can be used in the same way.

CBT FOR OBSESSIVE COMPULSIVE DISORDER (OCD)

When people with OCD experience a trigger like touching something dirty, they interpret the situation as more dangerous than it actually is. Everyone has strange, intrusive and upsetting thoughts but most people just discard them and don't think any more about them. However, people who have OCD place personal significance on those thoughts. It is the interpretation of thoughts and associated behaviours that is a problem, not the thoughts themselves. People with OCD develop compulsive behaviours in order to reduce the anxiety that these intrusive thoughts produce. These compulsive behaviours serve as a 'neutralizing' activity that temporarily reduce anxiety.

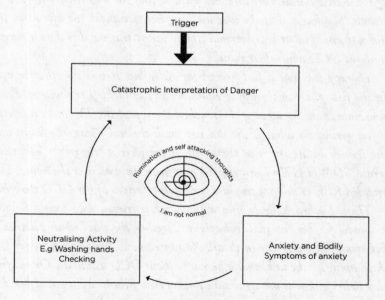

Figure 5.3: A Maintenance Cycle for OCD

Kelly, sixty-five, had suffered from OCD for over thirty years. She had a fear of contamination and saw germs and bacteria everywhere. This produced a huge amount of anxiety in her and she washed her hands up to seventy times a day, after which she felt immediate relief for a couple of minutes. Because she felt relief from anxiety, she washed her hands again and again and again. Washing her hands served to 'neutralize' her anxiety — for a few moments. When the postman came to the door, Kelly would put on gloves to receive her mail. Every time she filled petrol in her car, she carried her gloves with her. She would only go to certain restaurants because she was scared that she would be contaminated by germs and she would send her daughter ahead of her to check the toilets. She never cooked because she was horrified at touching raw meat and even raw vegetables. Nor did she ever go shopping at the market. In the morning she would take two hours to complete her ablutions. She would first clean the whole bathroom before she got into her shower. And then she would spend a lot of time putting cream solutions on her body to protect herself from germs. If when doing the laundry a sleeve of her husband's shirt fell onto the floor, she would have it back to be washed again. Kelly's hands were sore and painful and she was tired out by these rituals. She knew that she was washing her hands far too often but she did not know what was 'normal'. How many times a day does a person without OCD wash their hands?

Therapy was not a fast process for Kelly but it was an effective one. In the first phase of therapy, I enabled Kelly to tackle her thoughts about contamination. So what if she touched the top of the TV and contracted a few germs? So what if she did not wash the toilet seat, the basin and the shower before she used them, and there were a few germs left? Kelly wrote 'SO WHAT?' on post-it notes and stuck them all over the house. This enabled Kelly to de-catastrophise her interpretations of her OCD thoughts.

Then, I asked Kelly to find a supporter, a friend, who would be able to model for her 'normal' behaviour. Together the three of us planned a behavioural experiment in detail. Kaushi came to live with Kelly for two days, doing all the tasks that a person without OCD would do. On the first day Kelly's task was merely to take note of how Kaushi went about her day, how many times she washed her hands, how she did the laundry, how she bought vegetables at the supermarket, how she did the cooking and how she filled in petrol. In the evening we planned that she would go with Kaushi to a restaurant and Kelly would observe Kaushi there as well. On the second day, Kelly would do the tasks as Kaushi had done them the day before. Kaushi's role was to affirm and positively reinforce Kelly whenever she refrained from washing her hands unnecessarily. These two days were immensely useful to Kelly as they modelled norms for her that she could live by.

I used a combination of two techniques here. The first was modelling, where Kaushi showed Kelly how to live her day. This enabled Kelly to determine a 'normal' level of hand washing. The second was exposure and response prevention (ERP). Exposure refers to the exposure therapy that I described in the first part of this chapter. Kelly needed a direct exposure to germs so as to prove to herself that she would not be contaminated by them, get ill and die, and so that she could learn that anxiety dissipates if you sit with it long enough. The second part of ERP is the part where Kelly was asked to refrain from washing her hands so many times. Because she had a model to imitate, she now knew how to do this without prompting.

In the third phase of therapy for Kelly, I taught her some mindfulness skills and encouraged her to develop a daily meditation practice. I also asked her about activities that she could engage in that would leave less room for her OCD behaviours. She identified Sudoku and bridge, both of which got her into a state of 'flow'. Finally I constructed for her a meditation on the acceptance of death (see in Chapter 9). As she accepted her mortality and stopped resisting it, she found real liberation and was finally able to drop her OCD behaviours and thoughts.

If you think you may have OCD, read the section on it in Chapter 2 and fill out the OCI questionnaire to assess your symptoms.

To treat OCD, you will need evidence that your thoughts and behaviours are not really dangerous. In tackling and managing OCD, it is very helpful to have a trusted friend, relative or therapist to support you. This is because you will find it useful to have someone to model normal, healthy behaviour.

Exercise 5.3: Monitoring

Firstly, you will need to monitor your OCD behaviours. When you completed the OCD questionnaire in Chapter 2, you should have received a score for different kinds of OCD behaviours, for example, washing, checking, doubting, obsessions, hoarding and neutralizing. This chapter will mostly focus on contamination OCD, i.e., OCD that compels the person experiencing it to engage in excessive washing. However, the exercises and forms should allow for adaption to other forms of OCD. Over the course of a day, monitor the compulsive behaviour that you are having problems with. You may experience several different kinds of compulsive behaviours. You could either decide to just focus on one of those like hand washing, or you might want to look at several at once. Here is an example of a monitoring sheet:

Date	Time	Situation	Response
Monday, August 20	10 a.m.	Waking up	Washed hands
Monday, August 20	10.15 a.m.	Before making a cup of coffee	Washed hands
Monday, August 20	10.17 a.m.	After making cup of coffee	Washed hands

Date	Time	Situation	Response

Now count up the number of times you carried out each behaviour:

Behaviour 1 _____: _____ times a day
Behaviour 2 _____: _____ times a day
Behaviour 3 _____: _____ times a day

This is where it is useful to have a supporter helping you. It should be someone you trust because you are going to have to either show them your monitoring sheet or at least tell them how many times a day you have been performing that behaviour. Ask them to also fill out a monitoring sheet over the course of a day, documenting how many times a day they perform that behaviour. If you do not feel comfortable doing this, simply ask them how many times a day they perform that behaviour.

Review all of your monitoring sheets with your supporter if possible. Is there a big difference between the number of times you are carrying out the behaviour and the number of times your supporter does it? With your supporter, discuss how many times a day would be reasonable. Compare that number with the number of times you are currently carrying out that activity. Together with your supporter, set yourself a goal of how many times a day you will do this:

Goal for behaviour 1: _____ times a day
Goal for behaviour 2: _____ times a day
Goal for behaviour 3: _____ times a day

You can come back to this exercise as many times as you want. You may feel that for now you can reduce your compulsive behaviour by a small amount but not to what your supporter sees as normal. This is fine – just continue to revisit and reset your goals as you progress in managing your OCD.

Exercise 5.4: Surveys

It is not the content of unwanted thoughts that distinguishes OCD sufferers from people without OCD but the degree to which the thoughts distress you, the number of distressing thoughts you have and how persistent these thoughts are. In order to establish the evidence of this for yourself, you will need to conduct a survey of people you know.

Make a list of distressing and intrusive thoughts that you have. Use your monitoring sheet for this.

Identify people who you can ask if they have ever had these thoughts. You could ask your supporter as well as a few more trusted friends or relatives. To make it less personal, you could say that you are doing research (which, of course, you are!)

or that it is part of a psychology project (which it is). Make sure that these people take the survey seriously and answer honestly.

Here is a list of questions that you could include in your survey:

- Do you ever have the thought that (put your own intrusive thought down. Here is an example: 'If I do not touch wood many times in the day harm will come to my family')_____?
- How does this thought make you feel?
- How often do you have this thought?
- What do you do when you have this thought?
- What is the significance of this thought to you?

You should find that other people have similar thoughts to you but that they do not attach the same personal significance to them as you do.

BEHAVIOURAL EXPERIMENTS FOR OCD

Once you have established that everyone has intrusive and strange thoughts, it is time to try out a behavioural experiment. It would be very helpful to have your supporter carry out the behavioural experiment before you do or to carry it out together. Behavioural experiments are another way of exposing yourself to your anxiety and facing your fears.

Just like the goal-setting, you can start your behavioural experiments with easy tasks and then work up to harder ones. It might be useful to photocopy the table below so that you can try many different behavioural experiments.

First, you need to have already identified the thoughts that come with your OCD. This is done through the thought monitoring form.

Here are some examples of thoughts and behavioural experiments that real people with OCD have carried out:

Thought or belief and strength of conviction (0 per cent = do not believe at all, 100 per cent = believe this wholeheartedly)	If I do not keep checking if the taps are all closed in my house before I leave, I will become so anxious that I will go mad. Believe 100 per cent
Experiment I will carry out	Leave tap open on purpose
Specific prediction of what I think will happen	I will feel so anxious that I will go mad or I will go back home and turn it off since I cannot control my actions
What I did	I continued to work, felt very anxious and tearful and could not concentrate on what I was doing that day. Arrived back home at regular time and tap was still running
What happened? Did it confirm my prediction?	Only partly. I did feel very anxious but I certainly did not 'go mad'
Revised strength of conviction (0–100 per cent)	60 per cent
Revised thought that I can test	If I do not check all the taps in the house, I will feel anxious but I will not go mad and the anxiety will go down with time

Thought or belief and strength of conviction (0 per cent = do not believe at all, 100 per cent = believe this wholeheartedly)	If I do not wear gloves to put petrol into my car, I will get a horrible disease. Believe 80 per cent

Experiment I will carry out	Put petrol in car without wearing gloves
Specific prediction of what I think will happen	I will get very ill
What I did	I put petrol on without wearing gloves but then did wash my hands several times afterwards
What happened? Did it confirm my prediction?	Nothing bad happened except I felt very anxious. I felt like my hands were very dirty
Revised strength of conviction (0–100 per cent)	40 per cent
Revised thought that I can test	If I do not wear gloves to put petrol in my car I will feel anxious but nothing bad is likely to happen

Below is a behavioural experiment template adapted specifically for OCD. It is adapted from Shafran and Radomsky (2013).

BEHAVIOURAL EXPERIMENTS TEMPLATE FOR OCD

Thought or belief and strength of conviction (0 per cent = do not believe at all, 100 per cent = believe this wholeheartedly)	
Experiment I will carry out	

Specific prediction of what I think will happen	
What I did	
What happened? Did it confirm my prediction?	
Revised strength of conviction (0–100 per cent)	
Revised thought that I can test	
My conclusions:	

People with OCD suffer a great deal and the treatment outlined asks you to take risks. So I would not be surprised if it is difficult for you to apply the treatment without some outside help. If the table has not helped you enough and you find you are still plagued with your OCD thoughts and compulsions, then perhaps it is time for you to find a therapist who can help you get over the hurdles.

CBT FOR ILLNESS ANXIETY

In illness anxiety, a person becomes hyper vigilant to possible symptoms of disease. Triggers could be aches and pains, increase in heart rate or just a particular body part feeling a bit different. They could also be reading reports of epidemics or scares in the news or talking to someone with a serious health condition. It is also common to develop anxiety over visiting doctors or hospitals.

People with illness anxiety hold problematic beliefs about health and illness, and this leads them to misinterpret a small and probably unimportant symptom as a major catastrophe. This precipitates strong feelings of anxiety, which then leads to safety behaviours of checking and scanning their bodies over and over again and seeking reassurance from doctors and loved ones. Despite the fact that medical tests indicate that there is nothing wrong, a person with illness anxiety will believe that the tests were inadequate to pick up the disease or that the doctor was wrong in his/her interpretation. Even when confronted with disconfirming evidence, the person with illness anxiety will hold on to the belief that they are ill or are going to fall ill in the future.

In addition to her OCD, Kelly also suffered from illness anxiety. The reason she put on gloves when receiving the post was that she thought the postman might have HIV/AIDs as he was a black man from Africa. She was also very concerned that the wood furniture in her garden was treated with creosote, which is thought to produce cancer. She got her husband to get rid of all creosote from everywhere in the house. She had a minor fungus on her toes, which she treated diligently with creams and ointments. She spent a lot of time every morning examining her body for lumps and bumps and other abnormalities. She avoided umpteen foods and oils because of their suspected carcinogenic properties. Then she researched all these abnormalities for a number of hours on the Internet.

The first step in therapy was for her to understand that when she spent so much attention on particular symptoms, the symptoms themselves often seem to become worse. Kelly did not realize at first that the body throws up all sorts of sensations at times and that though most people disregard these sensations, the person with illness anxiety focuses on them and misinterprets them to mean illness. The second step was to get Kelly to drop her safety behaviours of checking and seeking reassurance. This meant stopping the habit of scanning her body so acutely and also refraining from using the Internet to find information all the time. It also meant that she was to refrain from asking her husband for reassurance about her various 'illnesses'.

The next step was to get her to take some risks related to all the foods that she was avoiding. Finally, I took Kelly through guided meditation about integrating death as being a part of life. This meditation, which I share with you in Chapter 9, seemed to be a turning point for Kelly. As she grappled with the fact that one day she would die, like the rest of humanity, her illness anxiety became less and less.

See the diagram below for a CBT model of how illness anxiety is perpetuated.

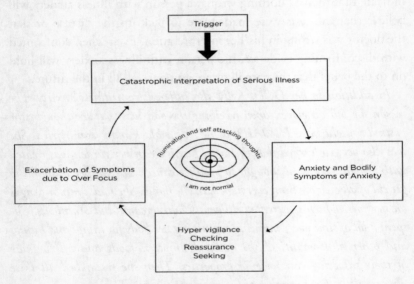

Figure 5.4: A Maintenance Cycle for Illness Anxiety

Date	11 January
Situation or trigger	Headache and feeling under the weather
Experiment I will carry out	I will stay at home and relax rather than going to the doctor as I would usually do. If I still have a headache and am feeling ill after three days, I will visit the doctor

Specific prediction of what I think will happen with per cent of how likely it is	I will get very ill; 90 per cent I will die; 80 per cent
What I did	I stayed at home
What happened? Did it confirm my prediction?	I felt a bit better on the second day and much better on the third day. I did not book a doctor's appointment and I got better on my own
Learning and revised strength of conviction (0–100 per cent)	I've learnt that having a headache does not mean that I am always seriously ill. Next time I will try to go out even if I have a headache and do some normal activities. However, I still feel like a headache is serious and I could get very ill 50 per cent

Since people with illness anxiety overestimate the danger they are in from illness and they adopt certain behaviours to stop themselves becoming sick. People might constantly make medical appointments and require further tests. Conversely, it is also typical of illness anxiety to avoid medical appointments, hospitals and any mention of illness. People with illness anxiety engage in safety behaviours, which could be anything from always bringing a bottle of hand sanitizer out with you to making sure you are never more than a ten-minute drive from a hospital. Since they are hyper-vigilant of bodily symptoms, they tend to notice minor ailments and anything out of the ordinary to do with the body. This often starts with checking the body for signs of illness. This could be checking for lumps, examining saliva, blood and urine, taking their pulse and touching or poking any areas of the body that look a bit different. Reassurance is sought by searching for symptoms on the Internet and asking friends and relatives to tell them that they are not ill. This over-focus on bodily symptoms often leads to an exacerbation of the symptoms themselves. For example, most of the day I am absolutely fine but if I bring my attention to my hip joints, I notice I am uncomfortable there and interpret this as arthritic pain.

Similar to OCD, useful activities for illness anxiety are behavioural experiments to test our thoughts (i.e, interpretations of serious illness) and dropping our hyper vigilance and over-focus on bodily symptoms and letting go of our safety behaviours such as checking and reassurance seeking. Targets can be set of the number of times you check for certain symptoms, for example, looking at a sore on your arm. Experiments can be designed and carried out to see what happens when safety behaviours aren't carried out. See the table for examples of behavioural experiments for illness anxiety.

COPING DISORDERS

You may sometimes feel overwhelmed by the stresses in your life and under-confident about your ability to cope with them. You may find that when problems arise, your mind goes into 'freeze' mode and you find yourself floundering, not knowing what to do and how to do it. Your anxiety rockets sky high and you get caught in a vicious cycle of fear. The three coping disorders that we will consider here are generalized anxiety disorder, phobias and social anxiety.

CBT FOR GENERALIZED ANXIETY DISORDER OR GAD

GAD is characterized by extreme, upsetting levels of worry, which lead you to feeling exhausted and wiped out. You can recognize GAD by the fact that your thoughts often start with the phrase 'What if…'. This thinking sits on a background of intolerance of uncertainty (Dugas and Robichaud, 2007). You think it is important that you worry because you have a number of positive beliefs about worry, for example, 'If I do not worry, I will never get it right', but you also find yourself paralysed by worry. This worry is generalized over many situations and you are unable to feel confident in your ability to solve problems as they arise. Then you attack yourself for worrying too much and ultimately you are exhausted and demoralized about your ability to cope. Below is a diagram of how this may work in your life

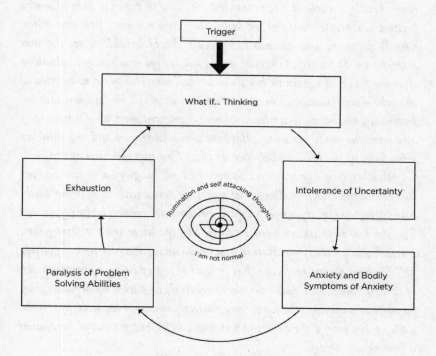

Figure 5.5: A Maintenance Cycle for GAD

For a fuller description of what GAD is, see Chapter 2.

During my practice in the UK, a seventy-seven-year-old woman, who I shall name Barbara, came to me for therapy because her level of worry had spiralled out of control, leaving her exhausted and desperate for help. She completed the diagnostic questionnaires and sure enough, the scores on GAD were very high. In her younger years she had been a teacher and later trained as a lawyer. She showed a good understanding of the five areas diagram and took to the thought record easily. She became aware of the fact that she could not tolerate uncertainty in any measure. If guests were coming over for dinner she would overthink every detail of the meal; the table setting, the menu and the flowers in the room to the point that she was tired before they arrived. Barbara was on the governing body of a large, prestigious school. One morning she came to me in a tizzy of worry because her printer was not working. She could not get a printout of the school's finances, and she was sure people would be able to see she was unprepared. She worried that she would lose her job as a governor. Another time she reported a pain in her shoulder and was 100 per cent convinced that the doctor thought this was cancer even though he had not said so. In therapy, she began to understand how intolerant she was of uncertainty and how this made her worry. Barbara was a Christian and so I used her knowledge of the Bible to help her do this. 'Consider the lilies of the field, they neither spin nor reap, yet Solomon in all his glory was not arrayed like one of these.' She realized that worrying was antithetical to her faith. Slowly, instead of trying to produce greater and greater certainty in her life, she learnt to sit with uncertainty. She learnt to trust a loving God instead, using a daily meditation practice to do so. She gave up her positive beliefs about worry, realizing that instead of worry being a manifestation of care, her near and dear ones were negatively impacted by her worrying. In place of worrying, she learnt to go directly into problem-solving. As she gave up her worry, she began to feel much more energetic and harboured a greater zest for life.

Treatment for GAD occurs in several steps. Quite often, people with GAD don't realize the extent to which they worry. The first step is to realize when you worry, why you worry and what you worry about. This can be achieved by keeping a diary. It is important to note whether the worries you have are hypothetical or current. A hypothetical worry is something that has not yet happened and in most cases never will. In the worry diary mark each one as either H or C.

Exercise 5.6: Keeping a Worry Diary.

Over the course of a week, fill out this diary with your main worries. People with GAD are often unaware of how much they are worrying. This worry diary can help you raise awareness of your worries.

Date	Time	Situation	Worry: Hypothetical/Current

At the end of the week, read through your worry diary and identify your top five worries. Is there a particular theme to them?

Do you worry most at a particular time of the day or in certain situations?

Write down your top five worries below:

1. _____

2. _____

3. _____

4. _____

5. _____

From your worry diary, you should be able to identify that worries are concerns about the future. We worry when we are finding it hard to deal with the uncertainty of a situation. For example, what if my husband is in a car crash? What if I fail my exam? What if my daughter starts drinking too much alcohol? These 'what if' statements always include different future possibilities; in other words, the outcome of each situation is uncertain.

TOLERATING UNCERTAINTY

People who suffer from GAD are unable to tolerate uncertainty. If you are one of these people then you will agree that they only feel relaxed if everything is predictable, controlled and ordered. People who suffer GAD engineer their lives to move in the direction of greater certainty about things. They will avoid situations which are unpredictable or which they cannot control.

However, uncertainty is an unavoidable part of life. We can never be 100 per cent certain of anything in life. Sometimes, the things that we worry about are real and distressing. We do not know for certain if we will develop cancer or whether our children are completely safe.

It is possible that a loved one will be injured in a car accident on their way home and we cannot know in advance if this will happen or not. Although there is always the possibility of horrible things happening, most of us learn to go on with our lives dealing with the uncertainty. We learn to tolerate uncertainty and accept it as part of life.

Everyone gets caught up in excessive worry sometimes. For example, I have just spent a few nights in an isolated house on my own while my family was on holiday. The first night, I kept waking up in the night, thinking that there were burglars trying to break in. I sat in bed worrying. But at the end of the day, worrying cannot solve this problem. I put my problem-solving hat on, fearfully got out of bed and checked if I had locked up everything securely. Then I had to tell myself to go back to sleep and to accept the uncertainty. By the end of the week, my anxiety and worry had completely dissipated. Needless to say, I was not burgled!

People who have GAD worry incessantly about situations that they are uncertain about. Small levels of uncertainty can quickly spiral into large worries. Going to visit the doctor, having an argument, leaving the children at home with a new domestic helper or reading about a car crash in the newspaper generate uncertainty and potentially lead to 'what if' questions and cycles of worry.

It can be very difficult at first to accept uncertainty. However, to recover from GAD, you need to move in the direction of tolerating uncertainty. This means sitting with your anxiety. Uncertainty will continue to make you anxious at first. Try to embrace the 'not knowingness' of it and live with it!

WHAT IF ... THINKING

Exercise 5.7: Practicing embracing uncertainty and 'sitting with' your anxiety

Look back at your worry diary and consider this: in which situations do you find it difficult to tolerate uncertainty? Here are some suggestions for activities that you could do to expose yourself to uncertainty. This exercise is adapted from Meares and Freeston (2013). Try some easy activities first that you don't think will make you feel too anxious. Then work your way up to doing activities that make you feel very anxious due to the uncertainty.

— Order a new kind of food you have never had before in a restaurant
— Go to a different shop for your groceries
— Delegate some small jobs at work to a colleague or employee
— Leave your children with a trusted babysitter or family member for the evening
— Stop checking emails before you send them
— Tell your children/husband/wife NOT to tell you where they are going or what time they will be home
— Try out a new hobby or sport
— Meet new people
— Buy something new
— Make a decision and don't ask others for reassurance that your decision is right

Activities that will help you practice tolerating uncertainty and sit with anxiety:

1. _____

2. _____

3. _____

4. _____

People with GAD do a lot of 'what if ...' thinking. For example, what if the car breaks down, what if I have an accident, what if the police stop me, what if everyone laughs at me? This incessant worrying leads to people going round and round in their heads about umpteen situations. This exacerbates a feeling of anxiety and stress and is extremely exhausting.

Greenberger and Padesky (2015) have developed a problem-solving approach whereby every 'what if' is answered with a 'then what'. Here is an example of this approach:

Sumitra is an anxious mother who constantly worries about her family. She thinks that worrying serves a positive function in that it shows that she really cares about her family. However, her anxiety impacts all the others in the family who get really quite fed up with her constant cycles of worry. She also feels drained by not being able to control her worrying. Below are her worries and nervous thoughts that were focused on her son:

What if ...	Then what?
What if my son gets ill at school?	Then the teacher will send him to the school nurse who is a qualified professional. She will know what to do. If I have to pick him up myself, my boss is very understanding and will let me have the afternoon off
What if his teacher thinks I'm mad and neurotic?	Then I'm probably acting on an unhelpful core belief. Anyway, what other people think of me is none of my business! I don't have to accept what she thinks of me
What if my son eats unhealthy food when I'm not there?	Then that's his choice. I cook him healthy meals at home and he eats plenty of fresh fruit and vegetables at home and gets physical exercise. One or two chocolate bars won't hurt him. I can teach him about how to live healthily and encourage him

What if ...	Then what?
What if my son starts getting bad grades?	Then I will still love him no matter what happens. I could meet with his teacher to check that there are no problems. I could also help him more with homework or pay for him to have a tutor.

CHALLENGING UNHELPFUL THINKING ABOUT THE POSITIVE NATURE OF WORRY

One of the stumbling blocks to getting over GAD is that many sufferers think that worrying is useful and symbolizes care. In other words, they have a number of positive beliefs about worry and these positive beliefs stand in the way of becoming less anxious and shedding unnecessary worry altogether. In Chapter 3 we learnt to use the thought record and behavioural experiments to challenge unhelpful thinking. They are useful here as well.

Sumitra looked at her positive beliefs about worry. She realized that she had an 'If... then...' statement that captured these. 'If I don't worry about my family, then they will think I do not care about them.'

She decided to refrain from worry on Monday, Tuesday and Wednesday, and then worry a lot on Thursday, Friday and Saturday. She then asked her son on which days in the past week did he feel her love and care most. She was surprised to find that he did not notice much difference in her level of love and care for him. This told Sumitra that she could easily drop her worry without it affecting her family.

Teaching ourselves to challenge our unhelpful beliefs about worry is very important in getting ourselves out of GAD.

MOVING FROM 'WHAT IF'-THINKING MODE TO PROBLEM-SOLVING MODE

How can you get out of the cycle of 'what if?' thinking? The key is to put on your problem-solving hat as quickly as you can, so that you don't put yourself in a ruminating cycle of worry. If you can do something about it, you should do it now. If not, schedule a time when you will deal with the issue. Perhaps the problem is one that cannot be solved. If this is the case, there is nothing you can do about it and you need to learn to accept this and perhaps do some mindfulness exercises (see Chapter 6) or you need to distract yourself with another activity.

Work out if the worry is real or hypothetical. Coping with GAD means distinguishing between the two. A real worry is linked to a specific situation that will come to pass. There is an actual time and date linked to it and an outsider would be able to recognize it as a problem that can be solved. A hypothetical worry is one that might happen in the future. Real worries can spiral into hypothetical ones.

EXAMPLES:

Real worry: I haven't cooked enough food for dinner.

Hypothetical worry: my guests will be angry with me and will never come to my house again.

Real worry: I only have five hours until the deadline for this essay and I still haven't finished it.

Hypothetical worry: I will fail this module and then I won't get my degree. Then I will never be able to get a job and have to live at my parents' house forever.

I find the worry tree a useful tool in these circumstances. This has been taken from Butler and Hope (2007).

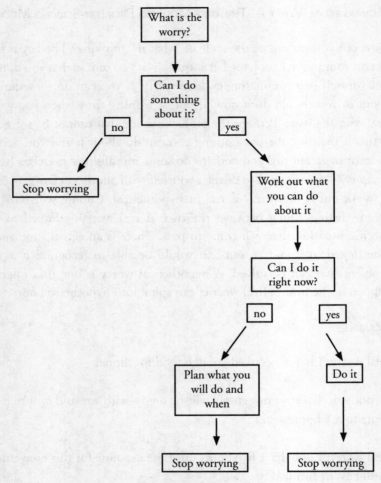

Figure 5.6: The Worry Tree

Perhaps you are not confident of your abilities to solve problems. Evidence suggests that people with GAD are just as good as or better than the general population at solving problems. People with GAD often find their worries so distressing that they feel paralysed and they suppress their problem-solving skills rather than tackling the issue directly. Here is a tool you can use to help you solve real, but not hypothetical, problems before you enter the spiral of worry.

Exercise 5.8: Problem Solving

You can use this table to solve real, not hypothetical, problems instead of continuing to think about them. It can be used in conjunction with the Worry Tree to help you work out how to solve the problems and when you will take steps to work on them.

What is the problem? State in one short sentence.

What solutions are there to this? Write down as many as possible.	What are the pros and cons of each solution?

Problem: I don't have enough money to take my mum out to dinner for her birthday.

What solutions are there to this? Write down as many as possible.	What are the pros and cons of each solution?
Ask my brothers and sisters if they can pay more and I will pay them back later	Pros – we can still take mum out as planned Cons – I might not have enough to pay them back next month, I will feel embarrassed
Offer to cook at home for the family this year	Pros – this will be cheaper and we can still have a nice time together Cons – mum really does enjoy going to restaurants. I'd feel like I was letting her down

Don't mention it and hope nobody asks me about a birthday dinner	Pros – I won't have to tackle the problem head on Cons – I won't be taking responsibility for the situation
Go to a cheaper restaurant	Pros – We can still go out and enjoy ourselves Cons – I don't know if the food will be any good
Take out a small bank loan	Pros – We can continue our tradition of going to the restaurant we like Cons – I might not have enough to pay it back next month
Sell some of my possessions online	Pros – Enough money to take mum to the restaurant she likes Cons – This seems like an extreme solution to the problem. Mum would not want me to do this
Try to work more overtime this month	Pros – I can make more money and take mum to the restaurant she likes Cons – I am already very busy and this would be hard. Also, by the time I am paid for it, mum's birthday will have passed

You should now choose one or more of the solutions and then produce a plan of how you are going to carry them out. In the above example, you might choose solutions 1, 4 and 7.

PLAN:

Explain my financial issues to my brothers and sisters. Have an honest discussion and suggest we take mum to a slightly cheaper restaurant this year. Ask them how much they will be able to pay.

Ask around the neighbourhood for restaurant recommendations. Ring the restaurants and ask them to estimate costs of a meal. Choose a cheaper one and book a table.

Ask the boss if I can work some overtime this month; then I can pay my brothers and sisters back next month with the money I earn.

So that mum isn't disappointed on the day, explain to her that we wanted to save some money and it would be nice to go somewhere else for a change.

After the event, you should then review your solutions thinking about how they played out in real life. How well did the plan work?

CBT FOR SPECIFIC PHOBIAS

People who have specific phobias fear particular things, animals or situations. To be classed as a phobia, the fear has to be excessive and unreasonable and often results in a panic response from an individual. See the section on specific phobias in Chapter 2 for further explanation of this. Luckily, there are clear and well-evidenced CBT techniques for managing and overcoming specific phobias.

Evidence suggests that the best way of tackling specific phobias is exposure therapy. In other words, you need to face your fears.

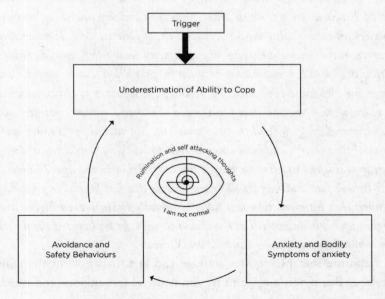

Figure 5.7: A Maintenance Cycle for Phobias

If you have a panic reaction to a feared object or situation, it might be useful to also read the section in Chapter 2 on panic attacks, which explains the signs and symptoms.

Exposure therapy is normally carried out over the course of several sessions, although there is good evidence that even one extended exposure session of around three hours can help reduce phobias permanently (Öst, 1989).

I have already explained this in several places in this chapter. However, I repeat the exercises here.

I have not recently worked with a client suffering from specific phobia. However, I have supervised the training of a student, Camilla, who worked with a client, Brian, suffering from blood and needle phobia. This blood and needle phobia was life limiting in that it prevented him from attending any sort of medical appointment. Brian wanted to get over this phobia because he realized that in the long run it could be life-threatening. Camilla facilitated Brian to form an anxiety hierarchy. The items on the hierarchy, in no particular order, were: watching a video of an operation, seeing pictures of blood, pricking himself with a needle, stabbing a bloody piece of meat with a needle, donating blood to the Red Cross. Camilla asked Brian to rank these in order from least anxiety provoking to most anxiety provoking using the Subjective Units of Distress scale. Together they worked out a series of behavioural experiments in which Camilla enabled Brian to look at the relationship between his prediction that he would faint on seeing blood and the reality. For example, as a first step, Brian watched a video of an operation being conducted. Further along in treatment, he incorporated his girlfriend in an experiment. She was to put a tourniquet around Brian's arm and hold a needle close to his skin. In advance of doing this in real life, Camilla role-played this with Brian in therapy. The blood left Brian's face and he turned green. But he did not faint! He proved to himself that his prediction was false. Gradually Brian moved higher and higher up his hierarchy till at the end of therapy, he had visited the doctor for a blood test. Well done Camilla and Brian!

Exposure therapy requires courage and grit. It is not for the faint hearted. But if you engage in it, you will feel less anxious and much happier in your life.

Before starting your exposure, you should examine your own beliefs about the feared object or situation and look at what you do to protect yourself from your anxieties.

Exercise 5.8: Understanding Beliefs and Determining Safety Behaviours

Ask yourself these questions about your phobia and write your answers below:

1. What is your phobia? (For example, pigeons.)

_____

2. What do you do when you see that object/animal or are in that situation? (For example, I scream and cross the road, every new road I enter I check first to see if there are any pigeons on the wires, or window ledges or on the road itself.)

_____

_____

_____

_____

3. What do you think will happen if you end up in that situation (or with the object or animal) and cannot leave or escape? (For example, the pigeons will swoop down on me, flapping its wings and I will be very scared.)

_____

_____

_____

_____

4. And then what would happen? (For example, I will scream and embarrass myself in public by doing so.)

_____

5. What is the absolute worst thing that could happen in that situation? (For example, they will peck my eyes out.)

_____

_____

_____

_____

6. Imagine you are in that situation now. In the situation, how certain would you be that the worst thing would happen? (Rate from 0–100 per cent) (For example, about 70 per cent.)

_____

_____

_____

_____

7. Sitting in this room now, how certain are you that the worst thing would happen if you confronted your fear? (For example, 20 per cent it is more likely that the pigeons will be scared of me and fly off.)

_____

_____

_____

_____

Look back at your answer to question 2. These are your safety behaviours. A typical safety behaviour is to leave the situation and escape the feared stimulus. Or perhaps you would avoid getting into the situation in the first place, for example, someone with a fear of dogs might avoid going to parks and someone with a fear of flying would not visit an airport. The problem with safety behaviours and avoidance is that they feed your fear. In the short term, avoiding the feared situation lessens your anxiety and makes you feel better. However, in the long term, it does not solve the underlying problem of your anxiety response to that stimulus.

Make a list of your avoidance and safety behaviours:

1. _____
2. _____
3. _____

Exercise 5.9: Forming an Anxiety Hierarchy

Write a list of situations related to the phobia that would cause you to experience anxiety. For example, a person who had a phobia of driving might list sitting in a car when someone else drives, driving around their local area at a quiet time, driving through busy city streets, speeding, etc. It might help to brainstorm ideas first.

Write your list here.

Your list in no particular order	Your rank ordered list 1= least scary, 8 = most scary	SUD Subjective Units of Distress expressed as a percentage
1.		
2.		
3.		
4.		
5.		
6.		
7.		
8.		

Now, give each of the activities a rank in your anxiety hierarchy with 1 being the least scary and 8 being the scariest. Write the number next to the activity above.

Fill in this table with your anxiety hierarchy, with your most feared activity at the top and your least feared at the bottom.

SUD stands for subjective units of distress. Put this as a percentage. How scared are you of this activity or situation? Use the anxiety scale below.

0 per cent No Anxiety	25 per cent Mild Anxiety	50 per cent Moderate Anxiety	75 per cent Severe Anxiety	100 per cent Panic

Of course, never do any activities that are really dangerous and expose you to actual harm. It is best to do exposure activities with a therapist or trusted friend so that they can help you decide whether you fear the situation due to your phobia or whether it is a truly dangerous situation.

Once you have filled out your anxiety hierarchy, it's time to put your work into action! Start at the bottom of the table or if you can, then somewhere in the middle of the hierarchy, gradually exposing yourself to the feared activities, events or situations. Each time you do an activity, fill out the exposure hierarchy sheet on the following page.

Exercise 5.10: Exposure

Date and time	Duration	What I did	Anxiety Rating Before Exposure in SUDs	Anxiety Rating During Exposure in SUDs	Anxiety Rating After Exposure in SUDs	Comments
3/1/2017	15 minutes	I sat in the passenger seat of my wife's car while she drove. I did not try to block out my anxiety.	80 per cent	90 per cent, but this dropped to 40 per cent during exposure	30 per cent	My anxiety dropped during the exercise

The purpose of exposure is that ultimately 'habituation' occurs. Habituation means that you no longer feel the terrible anxiety that you once did in those situations. When exposing yourself to the feared situation, you should stay in the activity until your anxiety reduces by at least 50 per cent. For example, if you started the exercise feeling like your anxiety was at 100 per cent (panic), stay in the situation until it reduces to 50 per cent (moderate anxiety).

Exposure therapy is extremely effective in getting rid of phobias. People are known to have lost their extreme and irrational fear of dogs, spiders, cockroaches, etc. But it is difficult to do. If you stay on the course, you will emerge a free person!

CBT FOR SOCIAL ANXIETY

Social anxiety is a disorder that involves an intense and persistent fear of being around people or in social situations. It is one of the most common anxiety disorders. Socially anxious people do not have to do something embarrassing or humiliating to feel upset and anxious – they just have to think that they might or that they already have, and others have noticed or think they will soon. To read more about what social anxiety is and to do a questionnaire that could tell you if you have social anxiety, turn to Chapter 2.

WHAT KEEPS SOCIAL ANXIETY GOING?

I draw heavily upon the model presented by Clark and Wells (1995) here. There are three key aspects of social anxiety:

- Unhelpful thinking styles and in particular mind-reading
- Over focus on the self, resulting in extreme self-consciousness
- Poor social presence and/or performance

The diagram below shows the main aspects of social anxiety. The arrows represent the cycles that keep the social anxiety going.

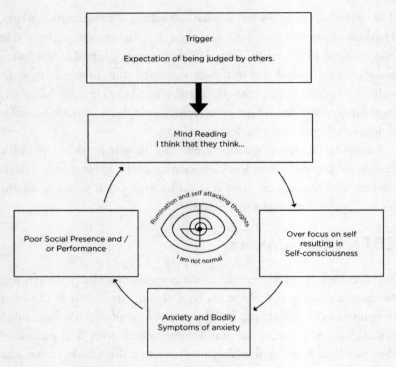

Figure 5.8: A Maintenance Cycle for Social Anxiety

A social situation makes you feel anxious or uncomfortable because you are expecting the others to judge, scrutinize or criticize you. You begin to mind-read, thinking thoughts like, 'I think that they will see I am stupid…' or 'I am sure he finds me boring…'. When this happens you focus on yourself and become increasingly self-aware of the way you think you come across to others. The more you focus on your own perceived shortcomings, the more self-conscious you become and the more socially dangerous the situation seems. This leads you to engage in safety behaviours such as not making eye contact with people who you think may be judging you. Typical safety behaviours for social anxiety are talking a lot in order to avoid awkward or embarrassing silences or keeping quiet in order to avoid saying something wrong.

You may also experience the signs and symptoms of anxiety such as sweaty palms, blushing, shaky hands and sweating and this may embarrass you even further. People with social anxiety are often most concerned with stopping the physical symptoms. However, as you can see from the diagram, the physical symptoms are caused by the beliefs and assumptions you hold. To stop the physical symptoms, you need to tackle your thoughts.

Much of social anxiety is about feeling frightened of negative appraisals from others. People with social anxiety do a lot of 'mind-reading'. They believe that they know what other people think about them. A good piece of advice that I once heard is, 'What other people think about you is none of your business!' However, in social anxiety it is difficult to recognize when you are 'mind-reading' and to stop it. I often ask people who suffer from social anxiety to turn their eyes outward (noticing mindfully things in the environment and people) and rate their level of anxiety and then to turn their eyes inward upon themselves and rate their anxiety again. People who suffer from social anxiety usually discover that when their eyes are turned outward their level of anxiety is less than when they are turned inwards. Their task then is to learn to keep their focus outward rather than inward. Too much self-consciousness is debilitating.

Though not many, there are some disadvantages to having white skin! Teresa, twenty-six, came to me because she was acutely afraid of blushing in public especially when talking to young men whom she was attracted to. She told me that she would go bright red all over her face and neck and this embarrassed her so much because then the young men would know that she was attracted to them. Her safety behaviours were to put on lots of make-up, foundation in particular, to hide her real blush. She also avoided approaching young men whom she liked. This was not very useful in enabling her to find a boyfriend.

Together we designed a behavioural experiment. First, I would put lots of blusher on my cheeks so that it looked like I was red and blushing. Next, we would go out onto the street and I would ask directions to the local pub. Teresa would watch people as they talked with me, how did they behave? Did they seem to mind me blushing? Did they laugh? Did they refuse to give me directions? When we did this together, Teresa observed that nobody even seemed to notice my blush and that all ten people I approached just treated my questions as requests for practical information and gave me directions. They did not laugh and they did not look at me strangely. They just told me where to go. In the second part of the experiment Teresa would put two bright circles of blusher on her cheeks and repeat the experiment. Her findings were the same. People did not seem to notice, and if they did, they gave no indication of thinking badly of it. Thus Teresa learnt that people did not seem to register her blushing as she seemed to think that they did. And if they did, they did not react negatively to it. In the third part of the experiment, Teresa would go out without make-up and approach a young man whom she was attracted to and ask him directions, observing what happened. When she did this, she did blush and she noticed that the young man she approached blushed too! He did not seem to notice her blushing and she was delighted at his blush because it gave her some indication that it was not just she who was attracted to him, he was attracted to her too! This experiment was life changing for Teresa. She dropped her fear of blushing and life opened up for her.

People who are required to give presentations to large groups of people often suffer from social anxiety. When I first started lecturing I think I too suffered from social anxiety. My eyes were turned inward upon myself. My thoughts ran something like this: 'I'm sure they realize I only have a little knowledge about this subject. They will think I am a useless lecturer. They will not respect me.' So, for quite a number of years, lecturing was not a pleasant task for me. Then I discovered this model of social anxiety and started to turn my eyes outward. This really helped and I became a good communicator. Of course, years of practice helped too.

Christine Padesky writes that merely putting yourself into social situations is not enough to manage social anxiety (Padesky, 1997). You also need to learn to deal with criticism and rejection, imagined or real, so that you realize your true ability to cope in a difficult social situation. Social anxiety is much more a 'coping' disorder than a 'danger' disorder. This means that CBT focuses on a person's ability to cope with the situation, rather than their estimation of the situation's risk. In order to realize your ability to cope, you need to develop an 'assertive defence of the self' (Padesky, 1997). What is an assertive defence of the self? According to Padesky people who suffer from social anxiety think that they cannot take the criticism that others may levy at them. And so in therapy she teaches her clients to react assertively (but not aggressively) to criticism. First, she role plays this with her clients and then she sends them out into the world with instructions to 'court' (actively seek) criticism and to practice defending themselves.

Here are some exercises that you can practice to develop an assertive defence of yourself:

Exercise 5.12: The Assertive Defence of the Self

Choose one of your main thoughts which embody your fears about what people think of you. For Lalita, this would be 'people think I am stupid'.

To develop her assertive defence, Lalita imagined she was in her biology class and got a question wrong. The girl sitting next to her says, 'You are stupid.' Lalita wrote a list of assertive responses she could make back to the girl, for example:

- I got that question wrong because it was difficult. Everyone gets questions wrong in class sometimes and that's how they learn! It doesn't mean that they are stupid
- I get good grades in many subjects but biology is tricky. I know that I have many skills and I am intelligent in many ways, for example, I created a beautiful water colour in art class yesterday that the art teacher praised

- If I already knew all the answers, I wouldn't need to take this class! It's good that I got that question wrong because now I know I need to read up on that topic for the exam. That's the clever thing to do

Write down your most feared criticism, things that make you socially anxious and cause you to clam up or avoid the situation, for example, you are stupid, you are weak, you are unfashionable.

Now, just like Lalita, think of six assertive responses to that criticism:

1. _____

2. _____

3. _____

4. _____

5. _____

6. _____

Now comes the interesting part where you put yourself into social situations that you fear and do something that invites criticism. People might outwardly criticize you or they may not. Whether they do or not, you can practice your assertive defence of yourself silently in your head.

Ayesha was really worried that people thought her to be unfashionable. She spent a very long time choosing her clothes in the morning and sometimes

*just wouldn't get out of the house in time to get to her class at the university.
In therapy and after a number of role plays in which she 'courted criticism'
with her therapist, she learnt to develop an assertive defence of the self. Here
are her assertive responses:*

- *I have my own style of dress. It may not be your style, but that is okay*
- *I like wearing clashing colours. In nature I see a lot of clashing colours:
  blues with green, reds with pinks and oranges*
- *I am wise to live within my budget. This means I do not always have
  the latest fashions and that is okay*

Notice that Ayesha was not aggressive towards the person who offered
her criticism. She did not blame the other person or throw their
criticism back at them. Instead she was quietly assertive about herself.

Exercise 5.13: Courting Criticism

Practice your assertive defence of the self with a friend or a
family member. Then go into the very situations that you fear
most with your repertoire of responses. At first you may feel
like you are crumbling inside. You will have to act as if you are
confident even if you do not feel it. It is easier to act your way
into feeling than feel your way into acting. The fear will never
go away until you realize your coping abilities! Call to mind
the six responses that you have already planned in Exercise
5.12.

People may outwardly criticize you or they may not. If they
do, then use one or two of the six responses that you have
practiced. If they do not outwardly criticize you, you can still
practice assertive defence of the self by rehearsing your six
responses silently in your head. You could *look forward* to a
situation where someone will be outwardly critical of you, then
you can practice your assertive defence of the self, out loud. A
win-win situation.

Padesky encouraged a client who was worried about being unfashionable to court criticism by wearing very outlandish and mismatched clothes (Padesky, 2012). The woman was then asked to walk around a mall and go into fashionable shops. By exaggerating the situation and actively inviting criticism, the woman firstly learnt that many people were not at all interested in what she was wearing since they were too busy worrying about themselves! Secondly, she had the opportunity to practice assertively defending herself. She went into a designer clothes shop and asked the man behind the counter what he thought of the clothes she was wearing. And then she used her assertive responses to counter his critique.

CBT for Post-Traumatic Stress Disorder

Post-Traumatic Stress Disorder (PTSD) is classified as both a danger disorder and a coping disorder. If you are suffering from PTSD, I strongly advise that you seek CBT or if this is not available, any well thought of therapy from a qualified therapist. I am aware of how much pain you are probably in. Self-help is not always effective due to the extreme pain involved in exposure to very distressing traumatic events. The most effective treatment recommended for PTSD is trauma-focused CBT, led by a therapist who can build a supportive and trusting relationship with you. Despite this, if you have no means at all of access to such a therapist, there are resources in this chapter that you can use. They may be of use, especially if the PTSD is mild. However, you should try to recruit a friend or relative to act as a supporter as you do these exercises.

In PTSD, people suppress traumatic memories and try not to think about them. Imagine a cupboard full of items representing horrible memories, thoughts and emotions. In order to protect itself from these, the mind of someone who has PTSD throws all of them in and tries to close the door. However, the items keep spilling out, filling the room with chaos until the person slams the door on them again. Just like the cupboard needs to be emptied and tidied to regain order, a person with PTSD needs to open up their traumatic memories and examine them, preferably with a trusted helper.

Wild and Ehlers (2013) explain that trauma-focused CBT is based on the following principles:

- Reclaiming your life: planning activities that you used to enjoy but now avoid, for example, socializing, shopping, cooking nice meals
- Reliving or writing about the trauma: recalling the traumatic event on purpose in the context of a safe relationship in order to expose yourself to the difficult feelings you are experiencing. In other words, instead of suppressing all the thoughts and feelings you have about the trauma, you will be encouraged to lay yourself open to them, be vulnerable to them, talk about them until the memories lose their power over you
- Talking about what the trauma means to you: this should be done with a therapist, or if it is impossible, with a trusted supporter
- Updating the memory and linked meanings
- Discriminating between the past trauma and events happening now
- Dealing with avoidance
- Dealing with other unhelpful ways of managing PTSD

Ehlers and Clark, psychologists who have specialized in PTSD, write that PTSD becomes persistent when the traumatic event that happened in the past is experienced as a serious *current* threat (Ehlers and Clark, 2000). Of course, you may not be consciously aware of this.

Recently a forty-two-year-old man named David came to me for therapy presenting with PTSD. When the traumatic event happened, he was working at the cashier of a grocery store. A man came into the store completely drunk and wanting to buy more alcohol. David refused to sell him a bottle and turned back to serve the other customers waiting in queue. The man came up from behind, grabbed David by the neck and put something sharp into his back. It seemed to David that he had a gun or a knife. He was terrified, appropriately so. The other staff called the police, there was a big commotion and because of the terror that set in, David pleaded sick and absented himself from work. He began to experience flashbacks and nightmares of this event waking up in the middle of the night in a cold sweat. He left the city in which the event occurred. In subsequent years he moved every six months from city to city because he feared that the man who attacked him would trace him down. This had a very destabilizing effect on David, he could never stay long enough in any place to make friends or develop a social life. He also continued experiencing many nightmares every week.

In therapy I enabled David to tell the story again and again and again. I did this so that the retelling of it would cause habituation. In other words, he would almost be bored with the story, so bored that he could no longer feel any anxiety. This is called imaginal exposure: using the imagination to re-enter the trauma and expose oneself to it.

In the next step, together we planned that David would go to the site of the event. He had moved 500 miles away and this step required him to go all the way back up north to carry out the plan. The first time David went to the site he felt extreme anxiety and this anxiety made him drive away. He did not stay long enough at the place of the traumatic event to allow his anxiety to dissipate. If you remember the exposure graph, it takes about two to three hours of staying within the anxiety-provoking situation for it to dissipate. So we planned the second stage after some more imaginal exposure. The second time around, David was able to stay until his anxiety had diminished by 50 per cent.

As a result of his PTSD, David was able to stay until his anxiety had diminished. He was afraid to go to public places, where there were crowds and where people would be pushing up against his back because he feared being attacked. This means that he had stopped going to pubs and stopped going dancing, an activity that he truly loved. He was experiencing the traumatic event as if it was a current threat. With therapy, he was slowly able to see the difference between the past trauma and his current life. Then he started dancing again. This brought back great joy to him. And of course when he experienced joy, it was impossible to experience anxiety at the same time.

By the end of therapy, after we had done some imagery re-scripting, which I will not describe here, David reported a decrease in his nightmares. He was able to hold down a job in one place and stay in rented accommodation for a long period of time, without having to move every six months for

fear of being tracked down. He began to make friends and finally found a
person to marry. His life had opened up again. This was indeed a happy
ending for him. And as his therapist, I was delighted.

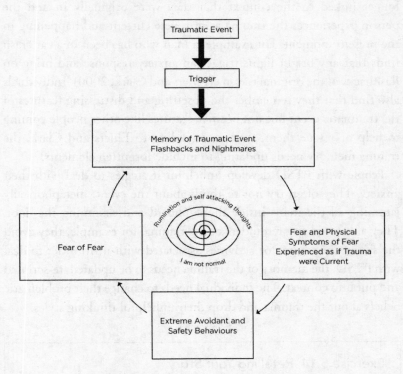

Fig. 5:9. A Maintenance Cycle for PTSD

The above model presents my simplified model of PTSD based on the
Clark and Ehlers model.

People with PTSD overestimate danger since the world seems a
much more dangerous place after the traumatic event but they also
underestimate their own coping abilities and their resources. They also
often believe that the way they felt or behaved during the traumatic
event means that they are less acceptable or able people. This leads
to avoidance of the activities that provoke fear and strong emotional
responses. The event is re-experienced mostly through sensory

memories of the event such as hearing bomb blasts or seeing car headlights coming towards you. This is because traumatic memories are not processed normally in PTSD. Sensory experiences are no longer linked to the context that they were originally in and the person experiences the trauma as if it were current and happening in the present moment. For example, a man who has been in a car crash finds that any bright lights trigger an anxiety response and bring on flashbacks of the original trauma (Ehlers and Clark, 2000). Individuals also find that they remember the upsetting and distressing features of the traumatic event but not positive features like other people coming to help or rescue them. And so according to Ehlers and Clark, the trauma memory needs updating to include forgotten elements.

People with PTSD develop unhelpful strategies to deal with their anxiety. They often try not to think about the event, metaphorically jamming all the items inside the cupboard and slamming the door. They also avoid any reminders of the trauma, for example, they avoid the site of the trauma or activities associated with it. In order to deal with PTSD, the memory of the trauma needs to be updated, re-scripted and put into context. The individual needs to change their problematic beliefs about the trauma and drop their unhelpful thinking styles.

Exercise 5.14: Retelling Your Story

Again, it would be best to do this with a qualified and experienced CBT therapist who works with people with PTSD. In the absence of someone like this, find a friend or family member whom you can trust and who is willing to spend time and effort to help you work through your memories.

In CBT, the first course of action for someone with PTSD is to re-tell their story. This can be intensely painful. Seek out a person you trust and talk to them, firstly explaining to them what happened from your point of view. Then try telling them the story from different perspectives, for example, from the perspective of a bystander or from the viewpoint of another person who was also involved in the traumatic incident. The aim of this is not to analyse or pick apart your story or for the helper to give you advice. The helper should not comment at all, except by offering sympathy and compassion. The story should be retold at least two to three times at this stage. Some therapists recommend recording yourself telling the story and replaying this recording to yourself many times. Most mobile phones have a digital recorder these days. If you do not have a recorder, then write out the story and read it to yourself and your trusted supporter over and over again. Make sure that you do not leave any detail out. Describe what you saw, heard, felt, smelt, tasted. Describe your emotions at every stage. I encourage you to tell the story as if it is happening in the present. For example, 'I am behind the wheel, the radio is on, I notice my speedometer is saying 69 m.p.h, then suddenly, out of nowhere …'

While you are retelling your story, look out for 'hot spots', which are points in the story that carry intense emotional energy for you. Note these 'hot spots'.

You are aiming for habituation. This means getting so used to the story in its proper context that you no longer feel a terrible effect when you retell it.

The purpose of this is to expose yourself to the anxiety and trauma to a small extent in a safe environment. Also, it is a means of starting to rebuild and reclaim your memories of the event. It stops you from suppressing thoughts of the trauma. At this stage, it is not recommended to revisit the site of the trauma.

GRADED EXPOSURE FOR PTSD

Like many anxiety disorders, exposure is the key to reducing distress. This means being exposed to the thing that you fear and watching your fear decrease over time. Additionally, being exposed to the thing you fear along with others who do not fear it may help reduce your fear. With PTSD, the ultimately feared stimulus is the traumatic event itself. Exposure therapy for PTSD does not expose you to the real traumatic event, of course. Instead, it is about imaginal exposure as well as exposure to the current threatening stimulus. For example, a man who had been in a car accident would not be exposed to another car accident. He might start by thinking about the accident, then acclimatizing himself to seeing sudden flashes of light (for example, by using a torch) and also practicing getting back into a car.

See Figure 5.1 in the introduction to this chapter for an explanation of how exposure works.

Anxiety drops when the person uses safety behaviours to escape the feared stimulus. However, anxiety rises again the next time the person encounters the feared stimulus. The solid line represents anxiety over time, when the person is exposed to the stimulus without escape or avoidance. Gradually anxiety will drop as the person realizes that being in the presence of the stimulus is not harming them.

The best way to overcome the fear is to gradually expose yourself to the stimulus. For that, you firstly need to develop an anxiety hierarchy. I cannot emphasize enough how much better it is to go through graded exposure under the advice of a cognitive behavioural therapist. They can help you take small steps towards conquering your fears by increasing the exposure gradually. Investing time, effort and money with someone trained in this field is worth it. However, I do include an explanation of how to do it yourself, in case you are unable to contact a cognitive behavioural therapist.

Exercise 5.15: Forming an Anxiety Hierarchy

Firstly you need to brainstorm all activities, sensory stimuli and situations that you fear, related to the traumatic event. This might include thinking about the event as well as being exposed to the stimuli. Write them down here:

1.

2.

3.

4.

5.

6.

7.

8.

Now, give each of the activities a rank in your anxiety hierarchy with 1 being the least scary and 8 being the scariest. Write the number next to the activity above.

Fill in the following table with your anxiety hierarchy, with your most feared activity at the top and your least feared at the bottom. SUD stands for subjective units of distress. Put this as a percentage. How scared are you of this activity or situation? For example, a man who had been in a car accident might write that he was 95 per cent scared of driving (it would make him highly distressed) but only 50 per cent scared of sitting in a driving simulator. You might feel that visiting the site of your trauma would make you extremely (100 per cent) distressed but reading your trauma story out loud to a close family member would only make you 70 per cent distressed.

Rank	Activity	SUD
1.		per cent
2.		per cent
3.		per cent
4.		per cent
5.		per cent
6.		per cent
7.		per cent
8.		per cent

You should never do any activities that are really dangerous and expose yourself to actual harm. You might find it difficult to judge which activities will really expose you to harm and which will expose you to imagined harm due to the trauma. That is why it is very difficult to treat PTSD without support.

Once you have filled out your anxiety hierarchy, take one of the easier ones and do it with your supporter. Then try the next one up the hierarchy, gradually exposing yourself to the feared activities, events or situations. Each time you do an activity, fill out the exposure hierarchy sheet on the previous page, predicting how many subjective units of distress (SUDs) you might feel and then recording how many you actually did feel when you did the activity.

The purpose of exposure is that ultimately habituation occurs. You no longer feel the terrible anxiety that you once did in those situations. When exposing yourself to the feared situation, you should stay in the activity until your anxiety reduces by at least 50 per cent. For example, if you started the exercise feeling like your anxiety was at 100 per cent (panic), stay in the situation until it reduces to 50 per cent (moderate anxiety).

Use this scale to measure your anxiety (SUDs) during the exercise.

0 per cent No Anxiety	25 per cent Mild Anxiety	50 per cent Moderate Anxiety	75 per cent Severe Anxiety	100 per cent Panic

Exercise 5.16: Revisiting the Scene of the Traumatic Event

Now that you have told your story and it has lost some of its emotional impact on you, it may be time to revisit the site of the trauma. Do this in a planned way and with your supporter. Expect to feel anxiety as you approach the scene of the trauma and try to stay within that scene till your anxiety has decreased by at least 50 per cent. This may take many hours or even days.

Recognize that it is not easy to do these exercises, but if you plough through them, you will come out on the other side a new person.

Note: If you have been the victim of violence or sexual abuse, it may be tempting to confront the person directly with the impact of their crime on you. Your supporter might be outraged at what has happened to you and may encourage you to do this. My advice is that you should not do this without police support and emotional support from a therapist, as you may re-traumatize yourself.

Exercise: 5.17: Updating Your Trauma Memory

You will have noticed gaps in your memory when you were retelling the trauma. If you have not noticed any gaps then retell your trauma memory to a trusted friend and ask them to ask you questions about it. In particular look at how you got from the trauma scene to now. Who was there to help? What help did you receive? In what form did it come? It is really important to fill in the gaps in your memory because these bits of information enable you to see the trauma in a new light. Instead of feeling utterly alone and abandoned, for example, you might remember a small fact like, my mother called the police or my father took me to the hospital…

_____

_____

_____

_____

_____

After you have updated your memory with these crucial bits of information, retell your trauma in writing or to your supporter adding in these pieces of lost experience.

Then ask yourself how updating the trauma memory has helped you process it and deal with it better.

_____

_____

_____

_____

_____

_____

Exercise 5.18: Reclaiming Your Life

Think about all the stuff that you used to do and be involved in but which you now avoid doing because of your trauma and the anxiety that it has produced in your life.

For example, you stopped dancing because of a fear of being attacked from behind or you stopped going to the beach because you narrowly escaped a tsunami or you no longer do any mountain climbing because you were involved in a terrible accident on a mountain in which one of your friends died.

Write down a list of these things:

_____

_____

_____

Now that the traumatic event has lost its potency and its power over you, plan how you can reclaim your life in the very areas that have been lost to you for a number of years.

Do this in a graded way, starting small and then building up.

My first step towards reclaiming my life is_____

My second step towards reclaiming my life is _____

My third step towards reclaiming my life is _____

If you approach PTSD systematically, you *will* get past the trauma and start living a healthy, productive life again. Many people find that doing mindfulness meditation can also be very useful in dealing with PTSD.

RELAPSE PREVENTION

Just as with CBT for depression, a relapse prevention plan is important so that if you feel yourself slipping back into unhelpful thought patterns, you can stop a lapse from becoming a relapse. It is very normal for people who have suffered from an anxiety disorder to experience symptoms later on, even once they have recovered. Fill out this plan so that if this happens you are prepared. If you are not sure how to fill this out, the example at the end of the chapter on CBT for depression may help.

Exercise 5:19. Relapse Prevention

1. What are the most useful ideas I have learnt from CBT for PTSD?

  1.

  2.

  3.

2. What are the most useful exercises for me?

  1.

  2.

  3.

3. What are my goals for next year?

  1.

  2.

  3.

4. What events might trigger another episode of PTSD?

  1.

  2.

  3.

---

5. What are the signs that I am succumbing to PTSD again?

1.
2.
3.

6. If I see these signs, what will I do?

1.
2.
3.

7. What will I do regularly to keep myself feeling mentally well?

1.
2.
3.

Key Points from this Chapter:

— There are two key elements of CBT for anxiety: fact-finding and exposure
— Avoidance is the opposite of exposure and keeps anxiety going
— For exposure to be effective, it must be gradual, prolonged, repeated and undistracted
— Exposure can be very challenging
— Panic disorder and agoraphobia can sometimes be resolved just by gaining a greater understanding of the bodily symptoms of anxiety and understanding how I catastrophically misinterpret these symptoms

- OCD is usually treated by monitoring compulsive behaviours and carrying out behavioural experiments. Challenging the cognitions that keep OCD going is very important
- Illness anxiety can be tackled with behavioural experiments and monitoring, checking and reassurance seeking
- GAD can be tackled by keeping a worry diary, learning to tolerate uncertainty, dropping my positive beliefs about worry and learning to problem solve effectively and immediately
- CBT for phobias is mostly about understanding beliefs and then engaging behavioural experiments that expose me to the feared stimulus
- CBT for social anxiety involves learning to recognize mind-reading and turning my eyes outward rather than keep them focused inwards upon myself. It involves building up assertive (not aggressive) defences and courting criticism and practicing my assertive defences
- PTSD is best treated with the help of a cognitive behavioural therapist since the exercises can bring up very distressing memories and emotions. CBT for PTSD involves retelling my story, updating the trauma memory, revisiting the trauma site and re-scripting the trauma memory and then reclaiming joyful aspects of my life that have fallen into disuse since the trauma. Graded exposure is also used
- Relapse prevention is very important in maintaining my resilience to anxiety over time

REFERENCES

1.   G. Butler, and T. Hope, *Manage your Mind: The Mental Fitness Guide*, Oxford: Oxford University Press, 2007.
2.   D.M. Clark, and A. Wells, 'A Cognitive Model of Social Phobia', in, R.G. Heimberg, M.R. Liebowitz, D.A. Hope and F.R. Schneier (edited by),

Social Phobia: Diagnosis, Assessment and Treatment, New York: The Guildford Press, 1995.

3. M.J Dugas, and M. Robichaud, *Cognitive Behavioural Treatment for Generalized Anxiety Disorder: From Science to Practice*, New York: Abingdon, Routledge, 2007.

4. A. Ehlers, and D.M. Clark, 'A Cognitive Model of Posttraumatic Stress Disorder', *Behaviour Research and Therapy*, 38(4):319–345, 2000,doi:http://dx.doi.org/10.1016/S0005-7967(99)00123-0.

5. D. Greenberger, and C. Padesky, *Mind Over Mood: Change the Way You Feel by Changing the Way You Think*, 2nd Edition, New York: The Guildford Press, 2015.

6. H.H. Dalai Lama, and H. Cutler, *The Art of Happiness: A Handbook for Living*, London: Hodder and Stoughton, 1999.

7. K. Meares, and M. Freeston, 'Generalized Anxiety Disorder and Worry', R. Shafran, L. Brosan, and P. Cooper (edited by), *The Complete CBT Guide to Anxiety*, 197–242, London: Constable and Robinson, 2013.

8. L. Öst, 'One-session Treatment for Specific Phobias', *Behaviour Research and Therapy*, 27(1):1–7, 1989, doi:http://dx.doi.org/10.1016/0005-7967(89)90113-7.

9. C. Padesky, 'A More Effective Treatment Focus for Social Phobia', *International Cognitive Therapy Newsletter*, 11(1):1–3, 1997.

10. C. Padesky, 'Anxiety Traps! CBT Antidotes', two-day workshop, London, 21-22 May 2013.

11. D. Richards, and M. Whyte, *Reach Out: National Programme Educator Materials to Support the Delivery of Training for Psychological Wellbeing Practitioners Delivering Low Intensity Interventions*, 2nd ed., 2009.

12. J. Wild, and A. Ehlers, 'Post-traumatic Stress Disorder', R. Shafran, L. Brosan, and P. Cooper (edited by), *The Complete CBT Guide to Anxiety*, 386–400, London: Constable and Robinson, 2013.

PART 3

Sitting Still, Bouncing Back and
Springing Forward

6

Mindfulness

'Each moment is all we need, not more.'

– Attributed to Mother Teresa

'I do not want to foresee the future. I am concerned with taking care of the present. God has given me no control over the moment following.'

– Gandhi

'Joy and happiness are born out of concentration.'

– Thich Nhat Hanh

In this chapter:

— What is mindfulness?
— Research evidence
— The key elements of mindfulness: PEACE
  ○ Presence in the moment
  ○ Engaging the senses

- ○ Accepting our thoughts
- ○ Compassion towards self and others
- ○ Equanimity
- Practicing Mindfulness

The emotional and spiritual benefits of meditation are nowadays well documented in research. More and more people are realizing that they need to learn the art of sitting still in a world that has not yet learnt to cope with the information overload produced by access to the Internet and the expectations of speed and efficiency it has brought to our work lives. TED Talks speaker Pico Iyer reminds us of the Japanese saying 'Don't just do something, *sit* there!' He also quotes Mahatma Gandhi as having said, 'Today is a busy day, I should not meditate for one hour, I should meditate for two.' (Iyer, 2014).

In January 2011, the BBC launched a Happiness Challenge, (http://www.bbc.co.uk/news/12263893) in which it encouraged its audience to do three things and then to report on whether they felt happier. These three things were:

1. Doing ten minutes of daily mindfulness meditation
2. Writing down three good things that happen to you every day and a letter expressing your gratitude
3. Doing one (or more) act of kindness each day

Being mindful, grateful and kind are indeed part of the way to being happier. In Chapter 9 we will look in greater detail at gratitude and kindness. In this chapter we will look at mindfulness meditation.

For this chapter, I interviewed a person who struggled with social anxiety and panic attacks. She had learnt to cope with this through mindfulness. Her responses are included throughout this chapter.

WHAT IS MINDFULNESS?

Mindfulness is about bringing the mind fully into the moment. When we are being mindful we are being attentive and aware of the present moment in time. We notice our thoughts, feelings and emotions without judging them. We train ourselves to focus on the present instead of dwelling on the past or rushing into the future. Although mindfulness has been shown to be effective in combating depression and anxiety, it is not a temporary solution to mental health problems but a way of living that increases resilience.

Mindfulness has a long tradition in Buddhist thought, though Christian mysticism also embodies its principles.

The term 'mindfulness' is a translation of the Pali word 'sati' or the Sanskrit word 'smriti', both of which have their roots in words meaning 'to remember'. So mindfulness is about remembering where we are and what we are doing without letting our mind wander.

Mindfulness is the seventh part of the Buddhist eightfold path to enlightenment. According to the Satipatthana Sutta, there are four kinds of mindfulness that should be practiced: mindfulness of the body, mindfulness of feelings and emotions, mindfulness of thoughts and mindfulness of reality.

As a spiritual practice, mindfulness is the call to quell over-busyness, to regularly take the time to be still. It is the call to remember our embodiment as we focus on the breath and scan our bodies to acknowledge the pain and tension that we carry. It is the call to be present in the moment rather than to dwell in the past or to rush into the future.

Meditation is an important part of mindfulness and is key to Buddhist practice but also Hindu, Jain and Sikh practice. There are also Christian, Muslim, Jewish and secular traditions of meditation.

Simran is a form of contemplative meditation that Sikhs do in order to surrender their thoughts and reveal the divine. The word 'simran' has the same etymological roots as the Buddhist words for mindfulness, meaning remembering or calling to mind.

Dhyana yoga, the yoga of meditation is described in the *Bhagavadgita* as Krishna explaining to Arjuna the importance of meditation for gaining control of the mind. 'For the being who has conquered the mind; that mind is the best of friends; but for one whose mind is uncontrolled, that very mind acts as the worst of enemies' (*Bhagavadgita*, Ch.6: Verse 6). The object of this meditation is to unite the individual consciousness with the ultimate consciousness.

Christian mindfulness is a centuries old tradition of Christian meditation initiated by the Desert Fathers and Mothers, Benedict of Nursia, Ignatius of Loyola, Meister Eckhart, St John of the Cross, Teresa of Avila, Julian of Norwich, the author of the Cloud of Unknowing, and more recently Anthony De Mello, John Main, Lawrence Freeman, Thomas Keating, Bede Griffiths, Richard Rohr and more.

The anchoring difference between mindfulness as preached by Jon Kabat-Zinn, the Dalai Lama and others of the Buddhist tradition and Christian mindfulness is that Christian mindfulness is rooted in the desire to come into the presence of a very loving God. In meditation we apprehend (though not necessarily comprehend) our Parent-God. The point of Christian mindfulness is to open ourselves and be available to our Parent-God. It is not about de-stressing, calming ourselves, relaxing and showing up to the moment. It is about presence, listening and a relationship (with God). Often from here we are led into acts of compassion and care for people (our neighbour).

Whatever your own particular spiritual persuasion, meditation is an integral element of mindfulness practice. Mindfulness meditation is different from concentration meditation. In concentration meditation, a person fixes their attention on a devotional image or item, a sentence, word or a concept. However, in mindfulness meditation the person is focused on awareness.

Today, mindfulness is becoming more and more popular as a technique, therapy and a way of life. Mindfulness meditation can be adopted as a purely secular psychological practice or a 'metacognitive' skill. So even if you don't believe in God, it is an effective practice that helps you develop a way of living healthily.

As in CBT, people who practice mindfulness say that it is not events that make them unhappy; it is their thoughts and interpretations that cause distress. Mindfulness is seen as a 'metacognitive' skill because mindfulness practitioners say that it is not our thoughts per se but our relationship with our thoughts that is important. In mindfulness practice, we do not actively try to replace unhelpful thoughts with helpful ones. Instead we cultivate an awareness that our thoughts are just thoughts and do not have power over us unless we imbue them with significance and meaning.

Practicing mindfulness is an antidote to both depressive and anxious rumination. When we are ruminating, we tend to compulsively dwell on our bad experiences from the past and to worry about the future. When we practice mindfulness we learn to centre ourselves in the present moment, disciplining ourselves not to travel into the past or to the future. In mindfulness, thoughts are not taken literally or personally, but observed and recognized for what they are, just thoughts.

WHAT ARE THOUGHTS?

But what are thoughts? In response to this question Elizabeth Dougherty in the engineering school of MIT responded that they are a series of electro-chemical impulses in the brain, that is all. How thoughts are formed and organized into perceptions that are then connected to feelings, physiological sensations and behaviour is still a mystery to all of us. But we know from previous chapters that thoughts are just that, they are not reality, even if they seem to have a ring of truth around them. We think one thought and that leads us to feel a certain emotion. We think another thought in the same or similar situation and we have a whole gamut of different feelings and behaviours. We often confuse our thoughts about reality with reality itself, and sometimes this fusion of our thoughts with reality causes us suffering.

One of my clients is a twenty-nine-year-old woman, Amanda, who is a lawyer working in a big firm in London. She hates her work but she works eleven to twelve hour days. When I asked her what would happen if she left at a reasonable time every evening, she said that it was impossible as people who do not have children are expected to stay late and she would be seen as a slacker if she left on time. I asked her what happens to people who have children. Apparently they are given leeway to leave early.

Amanda can see no way of getting a better work-life balance and she is therefore extremely stressed. I am aware of how brutal the work culture can be towards young people with no family commitments. My own daughters who are both under thirty at the time of writing this book often find it very hard to get away from the office in time for family dinners etc. But Amanda was extraordinarily stressed and overcome with feelings of despair and hopelessness. She could see no way out. And so she felt suicidal. Her thoughts were: 'People who have children can leave early. I can't, I don't have children.' She was very resistant to the fact that there are different ways of looking at reality. For example, 'Yes, Emma called me a "slacker" for leaving at 6 p.m. but my performance review indicates that I am doing well at my job.' The challenge is for her is to develop some psychological flexibility in her thoughts. The challenge for me as her therapist is to help her develop the sense that her reality is not as inflexible as she experiences it to be. One way to develop psychological flexibility is to bring ourselves into an awareness of the present moment through mindfulness.

Q: Why did you start practicing mindfulness?

A: *After I finished drama school, I just couldn't quite deal with things. I had lots of panic attacks and I was always thinking, 'I can't do it'. I felt I couldn't succeed at anything. I was very uptight and very nervous. I was very out-of-myself and nothing was a solid thing. It got to a level where it was taking over. I think that's why mindfulness works so well for me because through*

> it I get the opposite feeling to that. Now, I can say to myself,
> 'Let's just think about today, let's not worry about what's going
> to happen and what someone thinks of me.' My anxiety was
> affecting my life in a big way that it didn't need to. A lot of my
> anxiety came from comparing myself to other people. That's
> why I hate going out to parties and things because I would
> constantly be trying to read other people's minds to work out
> what they thought of me. It seems ridiculous because I went
> to drama school and I'm quite a friendly person. I was beyond
> scared of going to a party, which felt ridiculous.

Scott Bishop and his colleagues at the University of Toronto have developed a psychological definition of mindfulness as 'a mode of awareness that is evoked when attention is regulated' by adopting openness, curiosity and acceptance towards experiences in the present moment (Bishop et al., 2004). It can also be thought of as a way to reduce our vulnerability to stress and thus increase our resilience. In other words, by practicing mindfulness we can stop ourselves from becoming depressed or anxious and keep our minds healthy.

WHAT MINDFULNESS IS NOT

Mindfulness is not an attempt to try to change your mood or to stop bad thoughts. It is also not a relaxation technique or a way to calm yourself down. It is also not about making yourself feel better. These positive outcomes are likely to come about when you practice mindfulness on a regular basis but to view mindfulness as any of the above is to miss the crux of the practice.

MINDFULNESS IN TODAY'S PSYCHOLOGY AND PSYCHOTHERAPY

Jon Kabat-Zinn introduced mindfulness to modern western therapeutic practice in 1979. He was an American doctor who had been on a retreat run by Buddhist monk Thich Nhat Hanh and consequently developed a programme called 'Mindfulness-Based Stress Reduction' (MBSR). This eight-week programme still runs today and was designed for people suffering with chronic pain. It combines mindfulness meditation with yoga and is no longer just for chronic pain sufferers or people with medical complaints or stress but for anyone who feels like they could benefit from it.

In the 1990s, Zindel Segal, Mark Williams and John Teasdale took the idea of mindfulness and combined it with CBT to make a mindfulness-based cognitive therapy that they used to help people overcome depression (Williams et al.,).

Mindfulness has become increasingly popular in psychology and psychotherapy and nowadays features on mindfulness are found in many contemporary magazines, newspapers and websites. Psychologists are continuing to develop different kinds of mindfulness programmes to suit various needs and are building up clinical evidence to show that it is effective against anxiety, depression and stress.

Q: How has mindfulness helped you with your anxiety?

A: I sometimes get the beginning of that feeling of anxiety in my chest. It's a kind of ball of tension. I will sometimes get that when I am particularly stressed or very tired. In certain social situations, big groups, all that sort of stuff. I haven't had a lapse for a long time now because that feeling doesn't take over, I just accept it. When I was panicky I could induce panic whenever I wanted to. It would take me a second and I could make myself panic and cry. I can do the same thing now with calm. So when I do feel a little bit overwhelmed by something, I have that muscle memory of what calm and contentment feels like so I can go towards that instead.

> I had CBT for about four months. At the end of the sessions, mindfulness was what I held on to. For about a year after that I would have lapses. When I suddenly started feeling like rubbish again, I would get my mindfulness folder out. When I first had a lapse, it felt like if I started doing that again that I would be going backwards, that it was a 'treatment' rather than just a good thing to do. I saw it as something I was supposed to do because I was being weird.
>
> Now I know that it's taking time for myself and can help everyone, not just people who are in therapy. I think our minds can run away from us. They're so busy and I think that lots of people crash and burn. We need to look after our minds. We go to the gym, we eat well but why are we not looking after our brains? Techniques like mindfulness are like brain food. I'm like, here you are mind, have a little bath, chill out.

RESEARCH EVIDENCE

At the time of writing this there is much research being conducted into whether practicing mindfulness can help people become less anxious, depressed and stressed and if it can make them happier. A recent review looked at 209 studies of mindfulness-based therapies and found that on average it was more effective than other psychological treatments for anxiety and depression with the exception of medication and traditional CBT (Khoury et al., 2013).

Since this review was conducted, numerous other studies on mindfulness have been published, showing the effectiveness of one-to-one mindfulness meditation intervention (Wahbeh et al., 2014), online mindfulness programmes (Boettcher, 2014) and a specific mindfulness programme for young adults (Greeson et al., 2014). Most of these studies have focused on programmes derived from Kabat-Zinn's Mindfulness Based Stress Reduction or Segal, Williams and Teasdale's Mindfulness Based Cognitive Therapy.

However, there is also scientific evidence that the more traditional *Vipassana* meditation has a positive effect on people. Vipassana draws heavily on Buddhist practices of deep awareness of body and mind and the connection between them. It is taught on a ten-day residential course developed by S.N. Goenka and colleagues and is offered in different centres in India and worldwide. A study of people on a Vipassana residential course found that participants' stress significantly decreased and their well-being, kindness and mindfulness increased after the course, although the positive effects became weaker six months after the course (Szekeres and Wertheim, 2014).

Mindfulness also has an effect on the brain which can be seen using an MRI scanner. Kilpatrick et al., (2011) found that functional connectivity in the brain was improved after an eight-week mindfulness-based stress reduction course. This could explain why people who engage in mindfulness on a regular basis are able to focus their attention more easily and reflect more effectively than people who do not.

> **Q: What is mindfulness for you?**
>
> A: *It's a sense of getting back to the pace that I should be at, slowing myself down and just taking myself away from everything that can upset me, make me busy or stress me out. It's an ongoing process that I think I've learnt, built on and got better at. When I first started, I hated it, I couldn't do it. Then I went through a stage of it being my saviour. Now it's just a thing that I do to get me back to being okay with life.*

THE KEY ELEMENTS OF MINDFULNESS

In my experience, the key elements of mindfulness as I see them can be expressed using the word PEACE.

- **P** - Presence in the moment

- **E** - Engaging the senses
- **A** - Accepting our thoughts
- **C** - Compassion towards the self and others
- **E** - Equanimity

PRESENCE IN THE MOMENT

One of the most important elements of mindfulness is staying in the present moment, or what Eckhart Tolle, a writer and spiritual thinker, terms the 'Now'. Many of our worries and unhappinesses come from dwelling upon things that have happened in the past or worrying about what might happen in the future. The only thing that is really true is what is happening right now. If we bring both our body and our mind to focus on the Now, we will find that we have the ability to cope with whatever the Now presents us with (Tolle, 2005).

Nihal was on his way to a meeting with an important client. He had been advised by his office that the client had not liked the work his company had done on the marketing strategy but might be prepared to give the firm one more go. As Nihal walked down to the train station, he was imagining what he was going to say in the meeting, thinking about what negative comments the client would make and wishing he had spent more time improving the client's marketing strategy. He felt nervous and regretful. He also had a sick feeling rising from his stomach.

Nihal was not rooted in the present moment. He was busy worrying about his meeting. Eckhart Tolle makes a distinction between psychological time and clock time. Clock time is physical time – the time that you have to pick your children up from the nursery or go out to a party. It is also about learning from mistakes in the past and working towards your goals in the future. We all need to accept clock time as an intrinsic part of our human experience. On the other hand, you are living in psychological time when you allow yourself to get bogged down in ruminating about the past or obsessing with living in the future. You are also living in psychological time when you are in a state of Flow (more on this elsewhere) which is when you are so immersed in the task at hand and so absorbed in it that you do not notice the passage of time.

After reading about mindfulness, Nihal decided to try to live in the 'Now' and intensely experience what was going on around him. The next time he had a difficult meeting coming up, he found himself in the same position as before, walking down the hill towards the train station. Thoughts about how terrible the meeting was going to be started to enter his mind but Nihal focused on his present surroundings. He looked up at the sky, which was perfectly blue that day, felt the warm sun on his back and thought to himself, 'What is hurting or threatening me right now?' In that present moment, there was not a single thing to make Nihal feel unhappy, although he knew that the meeting would be difficult. He concentrated on the feeling of his footsteps on the ground, the weight of the briefcase he was carrying and the sights and sounds around him.

The thing is, when we are really in difficult situations, we deal with them and we often cope very well. When Nihal was in the challenging meeting, he was too busy with the task at hand to get worried. He used his experience of working for the marketing company to put the client at ease and prove that he could do the job well.

Similarly, we often imagine that our lives will be better in the future. It is easy to think that we will be happy when we have moved house, when we are earning a certain salary, when we get a new job, when we meet the man/woman of our dreams ... and the list goes on indefinitely. If we do this, we are not rooted in the present moment. Thus, we fail to see the birds that pepper our day with their songs, or flowers that colour our day with their vibrancy or the myriad other manifestations of the fact that 'Earth's crammed with heaven' (Elizabeth Browning).

Tanuka was unhappy with her life. She was bored of being at university and couldn't wait to get a job. She found the lessons dull and the other students uninspiring. She knew that her life would be so much better once she had graduated. When graduation time came and Tanuka got a great job, she still felt unhappy. She thought that this must be to do with being single and she decided that she would only be happy when she had a boyfriend. A few months later, Tanuka met a lovely young man and started dating him but she still felt dissatisfied. She decided that she would only be content when she was married. She began pushing too early for marriage. This was difficult for her boyfriend who decided that the relationship was not mature and developed enough for him to be able to commit to marriage.

Tanuka's main issue was not her university or her boyfriend but the fact that she was living in the future. She was so preoccupied with achieving these goals to make herself happy that she did not fully appreciate what was happening in that moment. Perhaps if she had been present in those lectures and mindfully aware of what her tutors were saying, she may have enjoyed her classes more. If she had taken time to experience the present moment, she may have been content to ride the relationship with her boyfriend a bit longer until he was ready for a commitment as serious as marriage.

Remember that you do not need to try to feel happy or calm in the present moment. You are just being aware of everything around you and within you: sights, sounds, smells, textures, your body, every minute detail.

Q: What does being in the present moment mean to you?

A: It's in knowing what's happening around me while being in a centred place. It's being able to respond right here and now and not think about what came before or what will happen after.

I know I'm in the present when I can accept thoughts and let them go. When I don't hear any noises, I know that I'm thinking about stuff too much. When I am in the present, I hear the birds singing or someone coming to the door. Sometimes I make myself listen because sounds happen in real time. If I listen to those, I know that I'm in that moment. I try to do that sometimes when I know that I'm struggling.

Engaging the Senses

Part of focusing on the present moment is making a shift from 'doing mode' to 'being mode'. So much of our time is used up concerned with schedules, calendars and to-do lists that we very rarely allow ourselves to just 'be'. While time management is important, it is equally important to spend some time just 'being'.

A good way of shifting your focus from doing to being is to engage the senses. As I am sitting here writing this, my mind is racing: what shall I write next? Is this sentence structured properly? Shall I go and have my breakfast or make a cup of tea?

I am definitely in doing mode and not in being mode! I'm going to expand my awareness to my surroundings using the five senses. You might like to do this too, after you have read this paragraph.

I am looking ahead and the garden is in front of me. I am noticing the bright colours, the blue of the sky, the green of the grass, the beauty of the trees and the sunlight illuminating patches of the grass. Next to me I can hear the fan whirring, outside the birds are singing, I can hear my daughter in the kitchen making tea. I can feel my fingers tapping the keyboard and I can feel that my neck is stiff from leaning over my computer. I can smell the *sambhar* and *idli's* I am going to have for breakfast and taste toothpaste in my mouth.

By engaging the senses, I am expanding my awareness and truly existing in the present moment. I am also turning away from thinking mode and entering into experiencing mode. As a result, I feel calm, appreciative and peaceful. However, I did not try hard to feel that way; it was merely a result of shifting to 'being mode'. It might help you to imagine that you are tuning a radio station or focusing a camera lens. Of course, we need the 'doing mode' too; otherwise we would never get anything done!

Exercise 6.1: Being Present while Mindfully Eating a Raisin

This is a traditional mindfulness exercise. It is a good exercise to start with because you have a tangible focus. You are going to eat a raisin in a mindful way. As you eat the raisin, you will need to be fully in the present moment, not thinking about future or past events. You will need to be focused on the raisin, not thinking. See if you can be aware of the raisin in the greatest possible detail. Thoughts will enter your mind as you do this: accept them. Have an attitude of loving compassion for yourself and others as you eat the raisin. If you don't have a raisin, any textured food will do. A clove, a cardamom pod, a tiny bit of sonf, anything.

Step 1: Take a raisin and hold it between two fingers
Step 2: Engage the senses

Look at the raisin – what does it look like? What colours can you see?
Touch the raisin and move it between your fingers. What is its texture like?
Smell the raisin. Can you smell anything?

Step 3: Say thank you

With a sense of compassion, say thank you to the people that brought this raisin to you: the farmers in the fields, the people who washed and packaged it in the factory, the ones who designed the packaging, the people in the supermarket that laboured to put the food on the shelves, and your wife or husband or parent or child who did the shopping.

Step 4: Put the raisin into your mouth and again engage the senses

Feel the raisin – does it feel different now that it's in your mouth? Is it soft or hard? Dry or moist? How does it feel when you bite into it?
Taste the raisin – how does it taste? Is it sweet or sour?
Listen – what kind of noise does the raisin make in your mouth?

Step 5: As you do this, be aware of your thoughts and feelings and accept them

Are you feeling hungry? Are you full? Are you feeling peaceful? Or are you feeling suspicious of this exercise? Don't try to fight your thoughts, gently accept them, no matter what they are.

This exercise is the first one recommended in both Mindfulness-Based Stress Reduction (Stahl and Goldstein, 2010), and Mindfulness-Based Cognitive Therapy (Williams et al, 2007). I like the idea of being very aware of a raisin as you eat it. When I was a young girl, my mother would give me raisins in my packed tiffin and I would pour the whole packet into my mouth and eat them in one go. Mindful eating is the opposite of this!

ACCEPTING OUR THOUGHTS

Sometimes we find it extremely difficult to shift from thinking or doing mode to being mode. The famous Indian psychoanalyst, Sudhir Kakar, likened the unconscious mind to an elephant being driven by a mahout, who is the consciousness (Kakar, 2011). The elephant is mostly good-natured although it can become moody and uncooperative. In these circumstances, the mahout cannot start up a physical fight with the elephant – he is bound to lose! He will need to be aware of what is making the elephant behave in a moody and uncooperative way and gently steer it in the right direction. The more he fights against the elephant, the more stubborn the elephant will become. Similarly, if we try to tame our thoughts, all we will do is continuously chide ourselves for not being present. Instead we need to learn how to treat the contents of our unruly minds as friends and to marshal our thoughts such that we can centre down and be still. We simply concentrate on our breathing as this is a way of pulling ourselves into the now. When thoughts come we let ourselves become aware of them, we accept them without judgement and then we let them go.

Q: How is acceptance part of mindfulness?

A: *You need to accept that thoughts are always wandering rather than pushing the thoughts out. I first tried to ignore my thoughts and tell myself, 'don't think that, don't think that' but actually that's just counterproductive.*

Exercise 6.2: Awareness of the Breath

One of the simplest ways to increase mindfulness is to practice bringing attention to your breath and breathing pattern.

- Sit or lie down in a comfortable position
- Bring your awareness to your breath. Don't try to breathe in a different way and don't count your breaths. Just be aware of your breath as it comes in and then goes out. You might like to place your hands gently on your chest to feel your breath at the same time

- When your mind wanders, observe the thought,
  acknowledge the thought and return to your breath
- If you find this difficult, it is sometimes helpful to open and
  close your hand in tandem with your breath. Breathe in, curl
  your fingers up, breathe out, and uncurl your fingers
- Continue this for about five minutes to start with but later
  on you can meditate on your breath for as long as it feels
  comfortable

You can practice cultivating awareness of your thoughts and feelings by
doing the exercises at the end of this chapter. In the previous chapter,
I wrote about negative automatic thoughts (NATs) that can be likened
to gnats buzzing round your head. By becoming aware of our NATs
and hot thoughts, we can observe them entering and leaving our minds
without engaging with them. Imagine trying to swat a wasp. The more
you hit at it, the angrier and more dangerous it gets. By being aware of
the wasp, but seeing it as a small insect that is more scared of us than
we are of it, we minimize the likelihood of getting stung. This is an
interesting comparison to our thoughts.

Sometimes we are in a bad mood without really knowing why or
even recognizing that we are in a bad mood.

*Priya arrived home from university and her mother greeted her with a
smile and asked her if she would mind setting the table for dinner. Priya
erupted with anger, shouting at her mother that she had much too much
studying to do and that her mother was always expecting her to do too much
around the house. Priya went upstairs to her room and started crying. It felt
as if her mood had come out of nowhere.*

If Priya had been cultivating a mindful awareness of her thoughts
and emotions before the outburst, she might not have snapped at her
mother. Here is an alternative way that the episode could have gone:

*Priya was coming back from university in a bus. She decided to focus on
the now. She could not find a seat and was hanging onto the top rail. People*

were pushing against her. She took a minute to pay attention to her thoughts and emotions. She noticed tension in her shoulders and a feeling of unease in her body. As she waited for the lights to change, she thought, 'This traffic is making me so late, I'll never finish my project for tomorrow! I'm doomed to fail.' Since Priya had been practicing mindfulness, she recognized this as a NAT and observed it without passing judgment. She became aware of the stress and tension in her mind and body. She did not try to think positive thoughts or push the stress away but calmly accepted it. As she reached home and her mother asked her to set the table, Priya said, 'That's fine but do you mind if I go upstairs to study afterwards? I'm feeling a little bit stressed because I have to finish my project by tomorrow.' Priya's mother smiled and said that Priya should go straight up to study and that she would take care of setting the table.

Of course, this may be an ideal situation. Being mindful will not always result in behaving better around other people. And even when you do treat other people more kindly, they may still snap at you! However, the more aware we are of our own emotions and thoughts as well as other peoples, the more chances we have of reacting in a loving and gentle way.

Being aware and accepting of thoughts, emotions and physical sensations as well as of the outside world will often result in an openness to new experiences, people and ourselves. Have you ever been bored in a meeting or a lecture? Or have you ever been in conversation with someone and found that everything they are saying is so dull that your mind begins to wander? I certainly have! However, the more aware you become of your surroundings and your own state of mind, the more open and interested you become.

In Buddhism this attitude is known as 'beginner's mind.' This means having an open, unprejudiced, curious and eager attitude to whatever we are learning or hearing about.

Two women, Charu and Tripta, were in an art class. The teacher was demonstrating how to draw a human hand. First he showed them a presentation on the anatomy of the hand, including the bone and muscle structure. Then he taught sketching techniques. Charu, a professional artist, yawned and looked away. She had seen this so many times before and felt like she had nothing to learn. What a waste of money this course was! Tripta was an experienced artist but she watched attentively, making notes and raising her hand to ask questions whenever she did not understand.

The difference between these two women's experiences was that Charu approached the class with the mind of an expert. She had heard it all before. Tripta came to the class with beginner's mind – eager, excited and curious. Even if it feels as if we are doing what we have done a million times before, there will always be new sensations to be felt and new experiences to enjoy, if we are aware of them. We do not need to be a beginner to approach things with the attitude of a 'beginner's mind'.

The Buddhist Zen teacher, Shunryu Suzuki said, 'In the beginner's mind there are many possibilities, but in the expert's mind there are few' (2011). Try to look at the world as if you are experiencing everything for the first time.

COMPASSION TOWARDS SELF AND OTHERS

In my understanding, mindfulness is a self-absorbed and selfish activity unless it leads us to feeling for and acting into a suffering world. The practice of mindfulness will naturally lead us to being empathic and compassionate towards those who suffer. Pema Chodron in her book, *The Noble Heart* outlines the *Loving Kindness* meditation where she describes how we can cultivate compassion, starting first with ourselves, then with someone we feel real gratitude for, then with a friend with whom we feel natural empathy, then with people we feel neutral towards and finally towards people we have negative feelings for, people who may have harmed us (Chodron, 2004). The loving kindness meditation is freely available on the Internet at http://marc.ucla.edu/mpeg/05_Loving_Kindness_Meditation.mp3. Loving kindness and empathy are deeply linked. Empathy is the ability to climb into another person's skin and see life through their eyes (Hutnik, 2005; Rogers, 1951). This is difficult to do because it requires us to suspend our own values and frameworks of belief and our own agendas. But when we can do this, then we develop a compassionate heart that seeks to alleviate our own suffering and the suffering of other people.

In the chapter on depression, I mentioned developing inner compassion in place of self-attacking thoughts. When practicing mindfulness, compassion needs to come from within and it starts by developing a gentle loving attitude towards ourselves (Neff, 2013). The voice of inner compassion tells us to become our own best friend, to hush the self-critical voice. Loving one's self enables us to reach out and love other people. This is empathy in action. In the next chapter on ACT, we will talk about defining our values and learning to take committed action.

My friend Dave Andrews says that love (compassion for others) is the willingness to be interrupted. It is the ability to put aside the presentation that is due next week or the cooking that will feed the family in the evening in order to listen to and meet the needs that are being expressed, in the now. On our journeys into the future we sometimes become blind to need in the now, unless we are mindfully present in the moment. With mindful presence, compassionate action becomes a possibility and we will learn to express tough-minded and tender-hearted love (King, 1963).

All major world religions have a word for what I term compassion. In Christianity it is 'agape' (Lewis, 1960), not sexual or romantic love or brotherly or familial love, but an all-encompassing compassion and self-sacrificial love for others, similar to the love Christ demonstrated as he healed and helped, taught and guided and ultimately died for others. In Buddhism it is termed 'metta' – universal love or love without clinging. According to the Quran, only those who have compassion, living in a way that benefits others, will find acceptance in God's neighbourhood (Khan 2009 cited in Andrews, 2012). Jews use the Hebrew word 'chesed', meaning God's love for his people and the main attribute of grace, benevolence, or compassion that people should possess.

EQUANIMITY

People who have practiced mindfulness meditation for a long time (such as Buddhist and Christian monks) face the world with much greater equanimity than those who do not. They are able to accept the good and the bad with calmness and composure. They are likely to be more self-possessed, level-headed and even-tempered in difficult situations and show presence of mind.

The effect of mindfulness is that we feel much greater equanimity than we did before we engaged in the practice. The practice of mindfulness enables us to develop a different platform of being. We find we are more mellow and flexible in our ability to have a balanced perspective on the things that are happening in our lives. We have learnt to still the inner buzz and have situated ourselves in the now. We find that the now is not as frightening as our thoughts about the future and not as painful as our thoughts about our past. While the now may not always be a pleasant place, it is usually a quieter, more centred place.

PRACTICING MINDFULNESS

There are many different ways to practice mindfulness meditation. Here I share the one that has been the most useful to me. I wake up naturally some time between 4 and 6 a.m. I make myself a cup of tea and then begin my meditation practice. I usually start with reading a passage of scripture or listening to a talk by someone I admire like Richard Rohr, Jim Marion, John Main, Lawrence Freeman or Timothy Radcliffe. I particularly like audiobooks for this part of my early morning meditation. I have found a comfortable chair. And I use this one regularly. My feet are flat on the ground. I make sure they're comfortable. My back is straight, preferably away from the chair and not supported by cushions; this enables me to maintain alertness. My hands rest quietly in my lap. When it is winter and cold, I tend to sit in my bed covered by my quilt. The great danger of sitting in one's bed is that you will fall asleep again.

So this is not ideal! But some meditation is better than no meditation at all. I set the timer on my cell phone for twenty minutes. If you have an iPhone you can download an app called Insight Timer that gives you a series of beautiful bells at the beginning, at five-minute intervals and at the end of your meditation. It also tells you how many people have been meditating at the same time as you around the world. It is good to feel like a part of the world community of meditators. I adjust the lighting so that I am sitting in very dim light. This is because I find bright light hitting my closed eyelids quite uncomfortable and distracting. Gradually, I bring my body into stillness. I do this first by focusing on the sounds around me. Today I heard a cock crowing and the distant rumble of thunder. Then I bring my attention to my breath. Sometimes, if I'm very distracted because of all the things that I must do in the day, I will coordinate my breathing with the opening and closing of my hand. This enables me to focus a bit better. The idea of meditation of this particular form is to slip into the gap between two thoughts. I believe the Sanskrit word for this is *Jikan*. I strive to do this because I know that this state of pure being is blissful and I almost always fail. Instead it is much easier for me to bring myself into the presence of my loving Parent-God, Ma-Baap. Some people like to say a mantra over and over again and this stills them. *Maranatha* (which means 'Come, Lord') is a common Christian mantra. *Aum* is a Hindu one. The Gayatri mantra is particularly soothing and I have used this. I have also made up a mantra for myself; 'Jesusa Christa, please take care of me.' You can do so too. I used to like to tell beads using my mantra although I no longer do this. When thoughts come in to distract me from what I am doing, I will make a note of them and let them go.

At first I could not see the usefulness of meditation. It seemed to me to be an exercise in futility. I remember that when I tried to start meditating as a teenager, my principal sensation was boredom! Feeling like a failure, I gave up. If only a wiser person had told me that feelings of boredom were to be acknowledged and accepted and that refocusing was a core part of the practice, I may have continued. Today, I meditate regularly and have done so for many years. I have persisted, sometimes with big gaps in my practice. I am now beginning to see it as my divine therapy time, a time when the unconscious part of me is being reached, healed and transformed. Since I have framed it in these terms, it has become exceedingly important that I come daily to my divine therapist. Gradually, this now happens most days and a stillness comes over me and I find myself at peace. When the timer goes off, I stop my mindfulness meditation.

If you are just beginning on the path of meditation, be kind to yourself. It is a hard discipline to acquire and it may take years to become regular and practiced at it. Know that this is true for everybody. Though I have meditated for many years, I am all too aware that on many counts I fail as a human being, as a mother, as a friend and partner. I remind myself that I am only human. This is my way of being kind to myself.

BUT I CAN'T STOP MYSELF FROM THINKING OR FEELING!!

Isha had heard about mindfulness meditation and decided to try it out. She had been feeling very stressed recently and getting upset and tearful without really understanding why. She sat down cross-legged in her room, closed her eyes and tried to think about nothing. After a few seconds, Isha heard someone shouting next door and immediately started thinking about the fight she had with her mother-in-law earlier that week. Realizing she had lost focus, Isha started to get frustrated and annoyed with herself. So she tried again but again after a few seconds realized she was thinking about what she was going to eat for dinner that night! Feeling like she was wasting her time, Isha jumped up and went out shopping. On the way out she said to her husband, 'I'm never going to be able to meditate. I cannot stop thinking, even for a few seconds!'

Mindfulness meditation is not about forcibly emptying your mind of every thought. In fact, trying to suppress your thoughts will only make them come back stronger. When thoughts come into your mind, you could use your Third Eye to observe them and then gently bring your attention back to your breath. Similarly, you are not trying to make yourself feel happy or stop yourself from feeling sad or scared.

You are not consciously trying to change your state of mind at all. You should simply recognize and acknowledge the emotion you are feeling and bring your attention back to your breath again.

Isha's experience of meditation is very typical. But meditation does not have to be like this.

While shopping, Isha bumped into a friend who convinced her to try mindfulness meditation at least once more. The next morning, she sat down in her room again and closed her eyes. This time, she did not blame herself when her mind wandered. Isha started feeling hungry so she acknowledged the feeling 'my tummy is rumbling!' and brought her attention back to the present moment. Then she remembered that she had not checked her emails, so she acknowledged the thought and then refocused on the present. Every time that a thought or feeling popped into her mind, Isha did not try to banish it but recognized it, noted it and refocused her mind. She still found it difficult to meditate but she had taken the first step towards developing mindfulness in her life.

In fact, the founders of MBCT (mindfulness-based cognitive therapy) encourage us by saying that mind wandering is not deviating from the practice of mindfulness but is the very heart of the practice itself. When judgmental thoughts enter your mind telling you that you are doing it wrong, the best thing to do is to acknowledge them for what they are and bring your attention back to your breath. As you pick up on these thoughts and sensations and refocus yourself, you are engaging in mindfulness practice. Congratulations!

EVERYDAY MINDFULNESS

> Q: What advice would you give to someone who is starting mindfulness practice for the first time?
>
> A: I'd say, make sure you do your ten or twenty minutes. Don't pretend you're done and cheat yourself! Set an alarm. You

> *don't need to think about time. Sometimes ten minutes feels like the world, sometimes it goes by in a flash. Just let that happen and keep trying. Even if you get angry, keep your eyes closed and breathe. Even if you want to get up and you want to fidget, just try to sit still and breathe through all the fidgetiness. Stick to it. Like anything, keep trying and don't give up. My boyfriend can tell if I have done it or not even if I don't necessarily feel that different. It's something that changes you. People will see the difference in you if you keep going.*

Mindfulness can become part of your day. The more you practice, the more you will be able to live each moment in a way that is truly present. Here are some ideas for when you could focus on mindfulness in your day-to-day functions:

- Waiting for public transport – focus on the senses, shift attention to your breath
- When your car is stuck in traffic – feel your hands on the wheel, pay attention to the sounds around you
- When taking a walk – feel your feet on the ground, focus on all five senses and listen to the sounds of people, animals and machines
- Going shopping – be aware of the people around you, the large number of products you have to choose from, feel and smell the food you are buying (as far as the vendor will let you!) or feel the textures of the clothes you are choosing
- When brushing your teeth – really taste the toothpaste, feel the bristles on your teeth and feel how clean your teeth are afterwards

Really, anything you do can be done in the spirit of mindfulness. However, carrying out routine actions and physical tasks might be the easiest time to practice mindfulness as a beginner. Thich Nhat Hanh, a Zen Buddhist monk, says this about everyday mindfulness:

'Joy and happiness are born of concentration. When you are having a cup of tea, the value of that experience depends on your concentration. You have to drink the tea with 100 per cent of your being. The true pleasure is experienced in the concentration. When you walk and you're 100 per cent concentrated, the joy you get from the steps you are taking is much greater than the joy you would get without concentration. You have to invest 100 per cent of your body and mind in the act of walking. Then you will experience that being alive and taking steps on this planet are miraculous things.'

When both body and mind are in the same place in the now, that is bliss.

APPLYING MINDFULNESS TO YOUR LIFE

Mindfulness is not an easy practice. Congratulate yourself that you have read the end of this chapter. You should now understand the basic principles behind what mindfulness means. However, reading and understanding is only half the battle. In order to cultivate mindfulness in your life, you will need to practice. Firstly, when you do these exercises, it is best not to aim for a specific outcome. If you do this, you are going back from a 'being' mindset into a 'doing' mindset and not being fully there in the present moment. Do not concern yourself with whether you are doing it right or wrong.

Secondly, do not expect to enjoy or gain a large amount of pleasure from the exercises. Carrying them out every day is a discipline, not a quick fix to make you feel good. Over time, you will experience greater peace and contentment. However, becoming fixated on this goal means that you are slipping into future-orientated thinking. Gently and kindly shift your attention to the present and not to what you are expecting to get out of the practice.

Exercise 6.3: The Body Scan

This is another exercise that uses a physical thing as its object as focus: your own body (Williams et al., 2007). You can lie, sit or stand for this.

Get yourself into a comfortable position and welcome yourself back to your body. Your mind may have been miles away, thinking about all the things you have to do. Try to tune in to your own feelings and switch from doing mode to being mode (existence). As you do this exercise, be aware of physical feelings as well as your internal emotions. It should help to close your eyes in order to focus your attention.

Start by focusing on your breathing. Do not try to change your breathing, breathe more deeply or in the 'right' way. Just be conscious of the air entering and leaving your body. Take some time out to give your full attention to your breath. If any other thoughts enter your mind during this time, gently acknowledge and accept them and return your attention to your breath.

Then begin your body scan by shifting your awareness to your left foot. Feel any tension or pain in it? Is it hot or cold? Strained or relaxed? Let your attention travel from your toes to the middle of your foot to the ball of your foot and then up to your ankle. Gradually allow your focus to travel up your calf and to your knee. Feel the connection between your lower leg and upper leg. Then move your attention up to your thigh. Repeat this process slowly, calmly and lovingly for your other leg.

Move up to your genitals. Tune into any physical feeling or emotions you have in this part of the body. Shift attention outwards to your hips and your bottom and then gently and slowly up to your internal organs. Feel your stomach digesting the food you have eaten and your liver and kidneys filtering out the waste. Spend a few moments focusing on this part of your body.

Then allow your focus to move up into your diaphragm. This is the muscle that controls your breathing. Experience the sensation of your diaphragm pushing up softly and your lungs inflating. Then move your attention to your heart. Can you feel it beating, pumping your blood around your body? Move up into the shoulders. Is there any tension there? Don't consciously try to relax, just feel the sensation currently in your body.

Next, move your attention to the fingers on your left hand. Feel them resting on the floor or by your side. Allow sensation to travel up the fingers into the knuckles and from there into your hand. Bring your awareness up to the wrist and from there up the arm, taking in the sensations in the elbow. Bring your focus up to your shoulder. Repeat this with your right hand and arm.

When you reach your right shoulder, continue to shift your focus up into your collarbone and into your neck. Feel the connection between your neck and your backbone where the spinal cord is located that brings messages from your body to your brain. Focus your attention onto your brain. Imagine the electrical signals it is sending from one region to another to keep your body and mind working. Move over to your eyes, nose, ears, mouth and chin. What is your tongue doing? Do you feel any sensation with your lips or teeth?

As you finish your body scan, now zoom out and feel the emotions and physical sensations in your whole body. Do not judge your feelings – just acknowledge and accept them. You might feel neutral – neither happy, sad or any other emotion or physical feeling. Acknowledge and accept this too. Congratulate yourself on completing your body scan and try to bring this attitude of awareness out into your life.

Exercise 6.4: The Three-Minute Breathing Space

This exercise comes from the Mindfulness-Based Cognitive Therapy programme (Williams et al., 2007) and is useful to learn and keep with you throughout the day. You could either schedule it in at certain times or use it as a tool for when you experience a troublesome emotion. Remember though that it is not meant to pick you up from a low mood or to help you relax but to make you aware of what is going on in your body and mind.

Step 1: Awareness

Sit or stand. Close your eyes if you can. Focus on what you are experiencing right now. Watch your thoughts pass through your mind and be aware that they are just thoughts, not facts. Bring your attention to your emotions. Are you comfortable or uncomfortable? Are you nervous or relaxed? Are you bored or interested? Focus on your physical feelings as well and note any stiffness or pain as well as hunger, thirst or fatigue.

Step 2: Breathing

Shift your attention to your breath now. Feel your breath going in and out. Focus on your stomach rising and falling and your lungs filling up with oxygen.

Step 3: Expand Your awareness

As you continue to focus on your breath, allow that focus to zoom out and extend to your whole body. If you feel any unease, sadness or pain, breathe into those feelings on every inhalation and out of those feelings on every exhalation. Tune in on the present moment. The MBCT programme suggests a mantra of 'It's okay ... whatever it is, it's already here; let me feel it.'

You may like to use a quote or personal mantra that helps you to expand your awareness or you may prefer to feel your emotions and sensations without words to distract you.

Now as you move from your practice into the outside world, try to bring the awareness you have cultivated into your everyday life.

You might find it easier to use a recording while you are doing these exercises so that you are not going backwards and forwards from the book to your practice. Here are some suggestions for good audio accompaniments to mindfulness practice.

Audio aids to help in mindfulness meditation (all available as cds from amazon or in downloadable mp3 format from audible.com)

- Pema Chodron: The Pema Chodron Collection and When Things Fall Apart
- Richard Rohr and Thomas Keating: Healing Our Violence through the Journey of Centering Prayer
- Jon Kabat-Zinn: Guided Mindfulness Meditations Series 1, 2, 3

Useful websites –
Free Mindfulness Meditation Downloads: http://marc.ucla.edu/body. cfm?id=22

Free Christian Mindfulness Meditation Downloads: http://www. mindfulworship.com/category/free-guided-meditations/

Key Points from this Chapter:

– Mindfulness has a long history in many spiritual traditions, particularly in Buddhist thought and contemplative Christianity
– Mindfulness is becoming increasingly popular in modern psychology and psychotherapy
– PEACE is a good acronym for remembering the elements of mindfulness:
- Presence in the moment
- Engaging the senses

- Accepting our thoughts
- Compassion towards the self and others
- Equanimity
- By focusing our attention on the present moment, we can prevent ourselves from falling into unhelpful thought cycles
- There is scientific evidence to support the use of mindfulness-based therapies for anxiety and depression
- One of the keys to greater well-being and resilience is to develop your own mindfulness meditation practice
- Mindfulness can be cultivated in meditation practice as well as in everyday activities

REFERENCES

1. S.R. Bishop, M. Lau, S. Shapiro, L. Carlson, N.D. Anderson, J. Carmody, Z.V. Segal, S. Abbey, M. Speca, D. Velting, and G. Devins, 'Mindfulness: A Proposed Operational Definition', *Clinical Psychology: Science and Practice*, 11(3):230–241, 2004, <http://dx.doi.org/10.1093/clipsy.bph077>.

2. J. Boettcher, V. Åström, D. Påhlsson, O. Schenström, G. Andersson, and P. Carlbring, 'Internet-Based Mindfulness Treatment for Anxiety Disorders: A Randomized Controlled Trial', *Behavior Therapy.* 45(2):241 –253, 2014. <http://www.sciencedirect.com/science/article/pii/S0005789413001044>.

3. P. Chodron, 'Noble Heart: A Self-Guided Retreat on Befriending Your Obstacles', *Sounds True*, Audio CD, 2004.

4. J. Darley, and D. Batson, 'From Jerusalem to Jericho: A Study of Situational and Dispositional Variables in Helping Behaviour', *Journal of Personality and Social Psychology*, 27(1):100–108, 1973.

5. J.M. Greeson, M.K. Juberg, M. Maytan, K. James, and H. Rogers, 'A Randomized Controlled Trial of Koru: A Mindfulness Programme for College Students and Other Emerging Adults', *Journal of American College Health*, 2014.

6. H.H. Dalai Lama, and H. Cutler, *The Art of Happiness: A Handbook For Living*, London: Hodder and Stoughton, 1998.

7. T.N. Hanh, *The Pocket Thich Nhat Hanh*, (edited by) M. McLeod, 9, Boston: Shambala, 2012.

8. N. Hutnik, 'Toward Holistic, Compassionate, Professional Care: Using a Cultural Lens to Examine the Practice of Contemporary Psychotherapy in the West', *Contemporary Family Therapy*, 27(3):383–402, 2005, doi:10.1007/s10591-005-6216-

9. P. Iyer, *The Art of Stillness: Adventures in Going Nowhere*, London: TED books, Simon and Schuster, 2014.

10. S. Kakar, *A Book of Memory: Confessions and Reflections*, New Delhi: Penguin, 2011.

11. M.W. Khan, *The Prophet of Peace*, New Delhi: Penguin, 2009, cited in D. Andrews, Bismillah ISA: Christian-Muslim Reflections, Preston Vic: Mosaic Press, 2012.

12. B. Khoury, T. Lecomte, G. Fortin, M. Masse, P. Therien, V. Bouchard, M. Chapleau, K. Paquin, and S.G. Hofmann, Mindfulness-based Therapy: A Comprehensive Meta-Analysis', *Clinical Psychology Review*, 33(6):763–771, 2013. <http://www.sciencedirect.com/science/article/pii/S0272735813000731>.

13. L.A. Kilpatrick, B.Y. Suyenobu, S.R. Smith, J.A. Bueller, T. Goodman, J.D. Creswell, K. Tillisch, E.A. Mayer, and B.D. Naliboff, 'Impact of Mindfulness-Based Stress Reduction Training on Intrinsic Brain Connectivity', *Neuroimage*, 56(1):290–298, 2011. <http://www.sciencedirect.com/science/article/pii/S105381191100190X>.

14. M.L. King Jr, *Strength to Love*, Ohio: Fortress Press, 1963.

15. C.S. Lewis, *The Four Loves*, New York: Harcourt Brace, 1960.

16. K.D. Neff and C.K. Germer, 'A Pilot Study and Randomized Controlled Trial of the Mindful Self Compassion Program', *Journal of Clinical Psychology*, 2013.

17. C. Rogers, *Client-Centred Therapy: Its Current Practice, Implications and Theory*, London: Constable, 1951.

18. B. Stahl, and E. Goldstein, *A Mindfulness-Based Stress Reduction Workbook*, Oakland: New Harbinger Publications, 2010.

19. S. Suzuki, *Zen Mind, Beginner's Mind*, Shambhala, 2011.

20. R.A. Szekeres, and E.H. Wertheim, 'Evaluation of Vipassana Meditation Course Effects on Subjective Stress, Well-being, Self-kindness and Mindfulness in a Community Sample: Post-course and Six-month Outcomes', *Stress and Health*, 2014 <http://dx.doi.org/10.1002/smi.2562>.

21.   E. Tolle, *The Power of Now*, London: Hodder and Stoughton, 2005.

22.   H. Wahbeh, J. Lane, E. Goodrich, M. Miller, and B. Oken, 'One-on-One Mindfulness Meditation Trainings in a Research Setting', *Mindfulness*, 5(1): 88–99, 2014.

23.   M. Williams, J. Teasdale, Z. Segal, and J. Kabat-Zinn, *The Mindful Way through Depression*, New York: Guilford Press, 2007.

Chapter 7

Acceptance and Commitment Therapy

'God, grant me the serenity to accept the things I cannot change, the courage to change the things I can, and the wisdom to know the difference.'

– Reinhold Niebuhr

In this chapter:

- What is ACT?
- The six core processes of ACT
- ACT and Indian thought
- ACT in Modern Western Clinical Practice
- Research evidence

WHAT IS ACT?

ACT, like CBT, is a theory of how to deal with human suffering and it spells a way of moving forward. It stands for Acceptance and Commitment

Therapy and the name explains its meaning and purpose. It is based on the serenity prayer, which encourages us to accept the things we cannot change, to have the courage to change the things we can and to be wise enough to know what can and what cannot be changed.

The litany of human suffering is endless. One of our children dies in an accident; a parent gets dementia; a friend is diagnosed with cancer in its final stages; we realize that our partner has put the family into debt which is beyond our ability to repay; a flood has ruined all our possessions; we are overlooked for promotion because of the jealousy of our bosses; war has taken our sons and grandsons. How can we live with this? What can we do to cope? Using the principles of ACT, we grapple with the fact that some suffering just cannot be avoided.

Richard Rohr, a Franciscan priest and contemporary Christian theologian says that in life there is always a certain amount of 'necessary suffering' (Rohr, 2012). Necessary suffering provides us with the occasion to become more evolved human beings. So rather than thinking that we can do away with suffering once and for all, we need to accept the fact that some suffering is inescapable. Using ACT, we can teach ourselves to live productively and constructively with the necessary suffering in our lives. Indeed, we can learn to wrestle a blessing out of it so that we become fuller, deeper, wiser and more compassionate human beings.

ACT theorists believe that human suffering is caused by **psychological inflexibility.** It is the opposite of resilience. When we are psychologically inflexible, we are rigid in our thinking, brittle in our emotions and restricted in our repertoire of behaviour. The aim of the ACT is to increase our ability to be psychologically flexible. We will suffer much less than we do if we can bend and be pliable and adapt to change easily and quickly. We can transcend our suffering if in the midst of it we keep moving in the direction of our most deeply held values.

So if psychological inflexibility is the root of our suffering, what then produces psychological inflexibility?

First and foremost, as we have noted in earlier chapters, we tend to avoid the experiences that cause us suffering. If we are socially anxious, we avoid public speaking or social occasions. If we are depressed, we withdraw from friends and family. We spend many hours protecting ourselves from contact with possible sources of germs and contamination because of our OCD. Our phobias cause us to take a wide berth around pigeons or heights or cockroaches. We avoid experiences that produce in us difficult emotions such as anxiety and depression, and our lives become increasingly limited and restricted. This **experiential avoidance** contributes significantly to us becoming psychologically inflexible.

Second, as we have learnt in the previous chapter on Mindfulness that we cause ourselves suffering by not staying in the present moment. We constantly rush into the future or dwell on the past. We ruminate about what we could have said or what we did say, what we could have done or what we did do. Why did I only point out my weaknesses to my boss in my annual appraisal? Why didn't I tell her about my strengths? Why didn't I tell my friend that I really can't afford to lend her the money she needs now? What if my husband does not find me attractive any more when we are old. Will he leave me for another woman? We then ruminate about our ruminations. Why am I so depressed, I must be neurotic! Why did this have to happen to me?

This kind of rumination causes us further suffering. Thus, our conceptions of the past and the future dominate us.

Third, we confuse reality with our thoughts about reality. ACT theorists call this **cognitive fusion**. According to ACT, thoughts are just thoughts, electrical impulses due to chemical reactions in the brain. But we give them the power to dominate our lives. We need to learn to de-link our thoughts from reality. As we have learnt in previous chapters, substituting one thought for another leads to a completely different set of emotions, physiological reactions and behaviours. If you think, 'I am not an attractive woman', you will act in a different way from the way you would if you thought, 'I am a sexy woman'. We can have control over our thoughts. We can exercise what I have termed 'choicefulness' in both our thoughts and our actions, i.e., we can choose to think thoughts that are helpful to us and to engage in behaviours that will further our well-being. A tendency to fuse our thoughts with reality is the cause of most of our suffering in life. Luoma, Hayes and Walser (2007) liken thoughts to a pair of sunglasses that you forget you are wearing. The whole external world seems to be tinted a particular colour as long as you allow your thoughts to fuse with reality. This is because in cognitive fusion, verbal and cognitive constructions are treated as the real events. By observing thoughts through mindfulness or what I have termed our Third Eye, ACT encourages cognitive de-fusion.

Fourth, we develop a narrative about ourselves, which we become very attached to, but this narrative is not necessarily useful or helpful in life. We become married to our **conceptualized selves**. For example, a person might say, 'My brother died when I was born, my parents were in mourning and were unable to give me the love that I needed as baby at the time. This is the root of my depression.' All of this may be 100 per cent true but the attachment to the story of the self does not help this person in dealing with the depression. Real solutions may not exist within the story and yet the person clings to the story, rejecting alternative ways of conceptualizing the self as being untrue or invalidating of the self. This rigidity in the stories we create to describe our lives contributes greatly to psychological inflexibility. For example, if you describe yourself as a 'worrier' you may then lose the psychological flexibility to conceive yourself as anything but a worrier and make it hard for yourself to change. Luoma, Hayes and Walser (2007) describe this way of conceptualizing the self as a 'self-created' cartoon.

Fifth, if we live our lives trying to avoid painful experiences, we may lose contact with what gives our lives meaning and direction. We are **unable to define our values**. Ordinarily, values are a compass with which we guide our lives. Or they are like a lighthouse drawing us in a particular direction while we sail upon our dark and dangerous sea. People who are psychologically inflexible and experientially avoidant often lose contact with their core values. Instead, they live by immediate goals such as avoiding upsetting others, avoiding conflict, defending ourselves and our self-narratives, and not risking loving too deeply.

Finally, our tendency to avoid important experiences, our inability to stay in the present moment, the thought-reality fusion we exhibit, our attachment to our self narratives and our inability to make contact with the things that really matter to us all lead us to a state of inaction or rigid persistence on a life course or to its opposite, **impulsivity**. People who are unable to connect with their values often come across as apathetic and lacking in vitality. They are drifting in a fairly meaningless void not knowing whether the career they are in is the right one for them, or whether the relationships they are in are the ones they want, not having hobbies or passions or indeed much engagement with life at all. This often causes them much suffering. Or they manifest impulsivity, behaving spontaneously in ways that are unconnected to a core value framework and therefore lose themselves in the process and often harm others by their impulsive actions.

To summarize, according to ACT, human suffering comes from being psychologically inflexible. We develop psychological inflexibility through:

- Experiential avoidance
- Dominance of the past and the future
- Cognitive fusion
- Attachment to our conceptualized self
- Lack of clarity with regard to our values
- Inaction, rigid persistence and impulsivity

THE SIX CORE PROCESSES OF ACT

So the antidote to psychological inflexibility and therefore to suffering is to develop psychological flexibility by developing the opposite of the six issues above. The diagram below is called the Hexaflex. It encapsulates the six major processes in ACT that contribute to psychological flexibility.

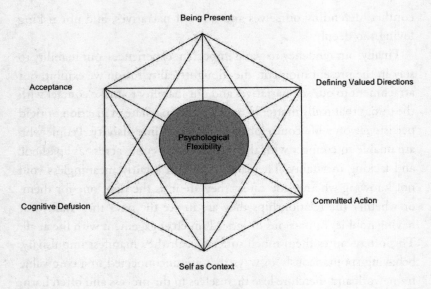

Fig. 7.1 The Hexaflex

Acceptance in Place of Experiential Avoidance

Acceptance which forms the 'A' of ACT is the process where instead of avoiding our pain, we 'lean into' it. I liken this to the process of natural childbirth. In hospital-mediated childbirth, mothers are given epidurals, nitrogen gas and other painkillers so that the pain of labour is lessened. In natural childbirth mothers in labour are told to breathe deeply and not resist the pain but to relax and allow it to wash over. Natural childbirth is not easy but some people think it is the healthier option. Similarly, with ACT psychological pain, we have the option of reducing our pain using alcohol or drugs or simply avoiding the people who cause us pain or we can 'lean into' it, accept the pain, and allow it to be. I am thinking of parents of children who have been murdered. I cannot think of anything much worse than having your child murdered. Some parents cannot get over the shock of this and they become embittered, angry, and they do things to numb themselves from the emotion of such a terrible loss. Others teach themselves to lean into the pain and if they are able to do this, they very often turn their trauma into a gift. (Parapully, 2002) This is now called post-traumatic growth. Accepting the things we cannot change is a challenging developmental task, which once mastered, lessens our suffering and causes us to evolve into wiser, more mature people. Acceptance also means embracing the thoughts and emotions that we cannot control (such as the intrusiveness of thoughts in OCD and other anxiety disorders), accepting them, letting them be without judging them or ourselves, letting them go as if floating our thoughts down an imaginary stream and moving always in the direction of our deeply held values despite the limitations that our sufferings bring.

BEING PRESENT IN THE NOW IN PLACE OF BEING DOMINATED BY THE PAST AND THE FUTURE

If we situate ourselves in this very moment of earth time, we often discover that we have what is required to cope in the moment. As we learn to breathe into our pain, accept it and bring ourselves into the now, neither thinking about the past nor the future, we find the skills we need to continue. This means being fully conscious and not lost in thought. As discussed in the previous chapter, the past exists only in memory and the future exists in our expectations (St Augustine). What we have is the present moment. This is the basis of mindfulness, a key component of ACT.

Being able to think about the past and the future means that we can learn from experience. It is the key to human intelligence and makes us able to plan and predict what is going to happen. However, it is unhelpful to constantly time travel in our minds, reliving past embarrassments and failures and indulging in future fears. The exercises on mindfulness in the previous chapter help us practice being present in the now.

COGNITIVE DEFUSION IN PLACE OF COGNITIVE FUSION

Cognitive defusion involves seeing our thoughts for what they are: just words or pictures in our minds. It is not the thought itself that causes psychological suffering or inflexibility but the way that we react to that thought. If we think, 'Nobody really loves me', and we see the thought as our reality, then we will become depressed. If however, we realize that the thought is just a thought, we can disempower the thought and disable it from doing any damage to us. ACT theorists (Harries, 2009) sometimes use the metaphor of a radio station to describe the human mind.

The mind can be compared to a radio station, let's call it 'radio doom and gloom'. It wants to grab your attention and tell you things that will make you listen, even if they are horrible and nasty. It is constantly broadcasting and since you have it switched on all the time you often forget that you are listening to the radio at all. It broadcasts stories of past failures and future disasters. Some of the stories it broadcasts are based on reality or contain elements of truth but they also include opinions, judgements, beliefs and evaluations. Sometimes it is useful for us to listen to the stories and sometimes it is very unhelpful. The most important thing is to recognize that what it is broadcasting is not the complete truth. Don't try to switch it off or drown it out with other noise. Just close your eyes and listen to what your 'radio doom and gloom' is telling you.

This is a useful exercise to start the process of cognitive defusion. More exercises can be found in this chapter.

Cognitive fusion leads us to get caught up in our thoughts but cognitive defusion allows us to disentangle ourselves. The first step towards cognitive defusion is to use our Third Eye to notice our own thoughts. Some of the most common types of thoughts that become indistinguishable from reality in our minds are the rules we have for ourselves, the reasons we give ourselves and the judgements we make about ourselves. Here are some examples of common thoughts that people fuse with reality:

- Rules: I shouldn't feel like this; I can't go out when I am feeling so anxious
- Reasons: I can't change because ... I feel too depressed; it's genetic; I can't handle it
- Judgements: I'm ugly; I'm stupid; I am a bad mother; I'm pathetic at my job

These are just thoughts, but thoughts lead to feelings and then physiological sensations and behaviours. If we think that 'these are just thoughts', the quality of our emotions, physiological sensations and behaviours will be entirely different.

Cognitive defusion is a basic mindfulness skill that can be developed by practicing many of the exercises in the previous chapter. There are also some specifically developed ACT exercises to work on cognitive defusion.

Exercise 7.1: Leaves on a Stream

This is a cognitive defusion exercise that will help you mentally separate thought from action.

- Find a quiet and peaceful place where you will not be disturbed. Set your alarm for five or ten minutes to start with. The more you practice this exercise, the easier it will be to sit for longer durations of time. Close your eyes
- Picture a calm stream flowing beside you. There are leaves gently floating down the stream. Take a few moments to imagine this as vividly as you can
- As thoughts come into your head, place each one gently on a leaf and allow it to flow down the stream. The thought might be upsetting, exciting, happy, sad or intrusive

- If you have any thoughts about the exercise itself, like 'this is silly' or 'am I doing it right?' put them on a leaf too and allow it to flow down the stream
- Do not try to make the stream flow faster to wash away the thoughts. If any leaf gets stuck, allow it to remain. The aim is not to push your thoughts out or destroy them but to gently allow them to float past you
- Every now and then, a thought will grab you and you will drift away from the exercise into that thought. When a thought grabs you, start from the beginning of this exercise and imagine the stream again

Continue the exercise until your timer goes off. How did you find it? Were there any thoughts that really grabbed you and brought you out of the meditation? What were those thoughts?

Remember that the purpose of this exercise is not to control your thoughts. It is also not to make you feel better or to get rid of the thoughts that you do not like. It is to defuse your thoughts from reality and become present to the moment.

Self as context in place of Attachment to the Conceptualised Self

In order to cope with and manage our suffering, we need to develop psychological flexibility around our self-narratives. Using our Third Eye, we develop a more distanced awareness of the struggles that we face and the battles that we fight. We develop the skill of looking in upon our lives as if it were happening to someone else. This once-removed vantage point enables us to see our suffering in perspective rather than to focus on the immediacy of the issues. When we begin to be able to see the self as context, our self-narratives loosen their grip on our minds and emotions and we are able to flex our psychological muscles.

One of the common examples given by ACT theorists to explain self as context is as follows:

Think of a chessboard. The white pieces represent your positive thoughts such as 'I am an intelligent person', 'I am kind' and feelings of hope, joy and love. The black pieces represent negative thoughts such as 'I am worthless', 'I am ugly' and feelings such as depression, anxiety, hopelessness and pain. We try to knock the black pieces off the board by waging war against them. Sometimes it looks like the white pieces are winning and other times it looks like the black pieces are winning. The problem with this is that we are waging war against ourselves. Both white and black pieces are a part of the conceptualized self playing upon that part of our self that is the chessboard. The chessboard is not affected or damaged in any way by what the white and black pieces on it are doing. It is separate from the battle and holds both white and black pieces without changing in itself. The chessboard represents the observing self that carries and watches the pieces. It is the self as context.

In Chapter 3 we did a number of exercises on developing our Third Eye, which exists alongside the thinking self. In the resilient person, the Third Eye or the observing self is stable, friendly and choiceful. It can view the content of our lives as if standing apart from it. It can be imagined as a large, interconnected context that holds all of our experiences, thoughts, feelings and actions. You might like to think of it as the soul. This transcendent 'I' (eye) is a place that is unchanging and not threatened by internal thoughts and emotions, just like the chessboard is not affected by the battle of white against black. In a non-resilient person, the observing self turns against itself, becoming critical and vicious. This happens in anxious rumination or depressive rumination. 'Look at me, so depressed and useless. I am a waste of space.' When this happens, we need to learn techniques to halt these sorts of unfriendly observations. This is more on this in a later chapter. More often than not, our Third Eye is an invaluable asset enabling us to stand back from our lives and mindfully watch ourselves being who we are.

DEFINING VALUED DIRECTIONS IN PLACE OF LACK OF CLARITY WITH REGARD TO VALUES

Values are central to ACT. Why? Because when we are in touch with our most deeply held values, we can commit ourselves to moving in those directions while carrying with us our own particular limp, our psychological baggage or our necessary suffering. When we have a clear framework of the values we hold dear, we will more easily know what to do and when. Our values act as guiding lights, enabling us to make decisions we are proud of. For example, Linda has a high functioning Asperger's twenty-eight-year-old son. Even though he is highly intelligent, he will not get himself a job and stays in front of his computer all day, not even getting out of his pyjamas. She feels trapped in her motherhood of this child who should have flown the nest by now. But one thing Linda knows for sure: she will never forsake her commitment to her son despite the suffering it causes her. Her most deeply held value is to be a loyal and reliable mother. Thus, Linda takes on more and more work in order to support herself and the family.

Acceptance and defusion are a means of managing difficult thoughts and emotions in order to focus on our most deeply held values. Values are what we stand for, statements of how we want to behave in our daily lives and the person we want to be.

Just like a compass that shows us the direction we need to travel in, values keep us on the track to where we want to go in life. We choose the direction of our journey and continue to travel towards that point. Values are not goals. Goals are achieved and finished with. They could be compared to the cities we visit on holiday. Values endure for the whole length of the journey. Acting on a value is like heading east; there will always be further to go. When acting upon goals, we may reach our destination, a city in the east, but when our value is to 'travel east' there is always more travelling to do. This image from the ACT literature explains a few key concepts related to values.

Firstly, values guide our present moment decisions. Whereas a goal can only be achieved in the future, our values define how we act in the now. Secondly, they are qualities that can be applied to a wide range of different circumstances. An example of a value could be 'treating other people fairly and justly'. This can be worked towards immediately and in different spheres of our life: at home, out shopping, at work or at a social occasion. Living according to our values results in repeated patterns of behaviour.

Values do not need to be explained or justified. When trying to work out what our own values are, we need to think beyond the rules dictated by society or tradition or even religion unless these are what is truly most important. Values are expressed verbs. I asked one of my friends, Imogen, to tell me about her values. Here is what she said:

- To treat people kindly
- To make an effective and useful contribution to society
- To take care of my family lovingly
- To experience life deeply and fully
- To build loving and respectful relationships
- To keep my body and mind healthy

Values will sometimes need to be prioritized. For example, Imogen tries to make an effective and useful contribution to society in her work. If she worked overtime every night helping other people solve problems in the workplace, she probably would contribute more to society. But then she would be neglecting her value to take care of her family and to keep her body and mind healthy.

The other important point to remember is that values are not rigid rules. ACT's purpose is to encourage psychological flexibility, not slavish obedience. They are to guide you, not to be followed rigidly under every circumstance.

If you are not sure of what your values are, try asking yourself these questions (Johnstone and Akhtan, 2008):

- What are some of the things that I really care about?
- What are some of the things I see in society that make me sad or angry?
- If I were marooned on a desert island, what five things would I take with me?

When I ask myself these questions, these are some of the ideas I come up with. I share them with you to stimulate your thinking about what you value.

- I care about beauty; what is a feast for the eyes is food for the soul
- I care about friendships; they are the only things that I can carry into the next life
- I care about my children; I want them to remember me as a loving mother
- I care about producing good quality work
- I want enough money to be comfortable and mobile in old age
- I want to keep my body and mind as healthy and as flexible as possible throughout the rest of my life
- I want to learn to sit still at the beginning of my busy day
- I want to use my therapeutic skills to alleviate suffering

Things in I see in society that make me sad or angry:

- I am saddened by how lonely and vulnerable many older people are
- I am angered when I see people being sexist or racist

Desert island question:

- At least one person I love, to keep me company
- Matches and a toolbox to keep me warm, fed and sheltered
- A spiritual text to remind me that there is more than the material world around me

- The Internet and my computer to keep me connected and to message for help
- Ponds cold cream to keep my skin from drying out

I also have a more generic set of morals that tend to guide my behaviour. Morals are principles of right and wrong. Values are different from morals. They are about what we hold important in life. You might like to think about what your fundamental morals are in relation to God, other people and possessions. My morals are informed by the 10 Commandments in the Old Testament of the Bible, the great new commandment in the New Testament, 'Love your neighbor as you love yourself' and some of the stories found in written accounts of Christ's life. You might like to think of the source of your morals. Where do they come from? What or who informs them?

But for now let us try to determine what our most deeply held values are.

Exercise 7.2: Exploring values

- What are some of the things you care about?

  _____

  _____

  _____

  _____

- What are some of the things you see in society that make you sad or angry?

  _____

  _____

  _____

  _____

- If you were marooned on a desert island, what five things would you take with you?

_____

_____

_____

_____

_____

Exercise 7.3: Shopping at the Values Mall (adapted from LeJeune, 2007)

ACT is focused on values. We aim for clarity in relation to what is important to us. Here is a simple questionnaire to help you think further about your values. Imagine you have Rs 10,000 to spend on anything you want, as long as it is sold in the values mall. The values mall has a number of stores: the career mart, the leisure and learning lane, the family and friends store, the community corner, the spirituality shop, the love boutique and the mind-body connection store. Anything you buy, you can have in your life. Anything you do not choose will be absent from your life. The prices have been allocated randomly to reflect the reality that the costs to individuals will differ depending on a large number of factors. You can buy anything from any store as long as it is within your budget. You do not have to distribute your money equally between stores; you can spend it all in two stores if you want.

Afterwards look back at the choices you made. Was it easy or difficult to make those choices? How do they reflect your values? At the moment, are you living your life in accordance with your values?

Career-Mart	Leisure and Learning Lane
Making a lot of money Rs 800	Travelling Rs 600
Doing work that is challenging or creative Rs 700	Learning new things Rs 800
Helping others Rs 800	Relaxation and meditation Rs 700
Flexibility and autonomy Rs 500	Enjoying a hobby or sport Rs 500
Doing something easy and low-stress Rs 900	Enjoying art, music or literature Rs 600

The Family and Friends Store	Community Corner
Helping loved ones in need Rs 900	Being politically aware and involved Rs 800
Hanging out and laughing with loved ones Rs 800	Volunteering to help others Rs 600
Emotional intimacy and personal sharing Rs 600	Protecting the environment Rs 500
Meeting new people Rs 700	Patriotism Rs 700
Belonging to a club or group Rs 500	Being ethical and fair Rs 600

The Spirituality Shop	The Love Boutique
Prayer and meditation Rs 700	Long-term commitment and fidelity Rs 900
Knowledge/understanding of spiritual writings Rs 700	Companionship and shared interests Rs 500
Believing and practicing a specific religion Rs 900	Physical intimacy and sex Rs 700
Belonging to a spiritual community Rs 500	Romance and excitement Rs 800
Feeling connected to a higher power Rs 600	Emotional connection with partner Rs 900

The Mind-Body Connection	Grand Total
	Now add up your totals. Your grand total should not exceed Rs 10,000
Eating healthy foods Rs 700	
Exercising regularly Rs 900	Career Mart _____ Leisure and Learning Lane
Psychological awareness/mental health Rs 600	_____ The Friends and Family Store
Managing stress well Rs 700	_____ Community Corner _____ The spirituality Shop _____ The Love Boutique _____
Living as long as possible Rs 600	The Mind-Body Connection _____ Grand Total _____

Exercise 7.3: The Bullseye

This is an exercise that will help you determine how close you are to the centre of your soul. Think about your values in the four main areas of valued living: work/education, leisure, personal growth/health, relationships. At this present moment, how close or far are you from living by those values? On the dartboard diagram below, mark an x to show where you are today. Mark an x for each area of valued living. If you are close to the bullseye, you are living fully by your values and are close to the centre of your soul. If you are far from the bullseye, you are not living by your values enough. The question you will then need to ask yourself is, 'How do I re-align my life so that I am living close to the centre of my soul?'

This was downloaded from the free resources that are available at http://www.thehappinesstrap.com/upimages/ACT_Made_Simple_-_Client_Handouts_and_Worksheets.pdf

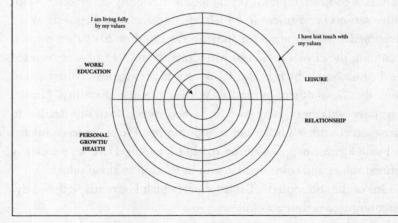

I am living fully by my values

I have lost touch with my values

WORK/EDUCATION

LEISURE

RELATIONSHIP

PERSONAL GROWTH/HEALTH

COMMITTED ACTION IN PLACE OF INACTION, RIGID PERSISTENCE AND IMPULSIVITY

When you have learnt to accept your thoughts and feelings non-judgementally and to accept the necessary suffering in your life without resisting it, when you are able to live in the now, when you are able to see your thoughts as thoughts and not as reality itself, when you are able to take your stories about yourself less seriously and can see your suffering in the context of the larger picture of your life, when you are able to determine your life direction and where you want to go, then you are ready to take the first few action steps towards travelling towards your most deeply held values.

This is the whole purpose of ACT: to enable people to take action from a place of empathy towards the self and others in order to travel in the direction of their most deeply held values even while carrying their particular burden of suffering.

A great example of the philosophy of ACT in real life is the Paralympics. Paralympians are people with physical disabilities who achieve sporting excellence while carrying the knowledge, awareness and reality of that disability with them. Paralympians do not allow their physical limitations to stop them from moving in the direction of their values, but take committed action towards their own deeply held values. Here is a good example of psychological flexibility in practice. Born with a serious impairment in his left leg, Girisha Nagarajegowda won a silver medal in high jump for India in the London 2012 Paralympics, becoming the eighth Indian to win a medal. In 2013 he was awarded the Padma Shri which is the fourth most prestigious civilian award from the Government of India. With a lifetime disability, Girisha Nagarajegowda must have had to be very psychologically flexible to have even considered becoming a high-jumper. He has even competed and won against people with no disabilities at all. Here we see clearly defined values and committed action in relation to these values.

One of the common ACT metaphors (which I have adapted slightly) for committed action is as follows:

Imagine that you are a bus driver. Your bus is headed towards the Central Secretariat in New Delhi. You pick up and drop off passengers. Some passengers are cheerful and pleasant. They compliment you on your driving. Others are rowdy and rude. They try to cause trouble and try to get you to take a different route to avoid a traffic jam. You know beyond a shadow of a doubt that you cannot do this and so you continue on your route while accepting and dealing with both types of passengers. If we use the bus as an analogy of our life and the final destiny of the bus as the values that guide us, then the passengers on the bus are our thoughts and feelings, some of which are pleasant and others unpleasant. Committed action means being sure of the route that you are taking (having already defined your values) and not stopping to argue with the unruly passengers on the bus. Committed action also means continuing to travel in the direction of your values whilst carrying the painful experiences as well as the joyful experiences along with you.

Committed action depends on defining what you value and working out how to go about living out those most deeply held values while carrying along whatever happens to hinder you.

GOAL SETTING

In order to take committed action, it is helpful to set some goals for ourselves. Our goals need to be based on our values but in order to be achievable they are more specific than our values.

SMART goals are goals that are specific, measurable, achievable, realistic and time-framed. Therapy in CBT usually starts with the client defining SMART goals. The ACT adaptation of SMART goals is as follows: (Harris, 2009)

Specific – Our goals need to be precise and exact. For example, 'I will be nicer to my mother-in-law' is not a specific goal because 'niceness' cannot be measured. However, 'I will buy my mother-in-law flowers this Sunday to show her how much I appreciate her' is specific.

Meaningful – Rather than being driven by should's and must's our goals need to be a meaningful outworking of our values.

Adaptive – Our goals need to demonstrate our ability to be flexible and adaptive and should take us in a direction that will improve our life.

Realistic – We need to be able to actually achieve our goals. Can I turn into a loving, kind, caring and compassionate daughter-in-law overnight?

Time-framed – We need to define a time frame for the achievement of our goal. 'Within six months, I would have expressed so much appreciation for my mother-in-law that our relationship would have significantly improved.'

ACT AND INDIAN THOUGHT

ACT originated from cognitive behavioural therapy and was not based on any spiritual belief system. It is a scientifically based therapy and can be used independently of any religious or spiritual belief. However, Hayes (2001) explores similarities between concepts in Buddhism and ACT, drawing interesting parallels between them. Many ACT ideas also relate to Hindu thought.

Buddhism's emphasis on mindfulness, as discussed in the previous chapter, is very relevant to ACT. Cognitive defusion, one of the key ACT processes, is rooted in mindfulness. 'Let no man ever cling to what is pleasant, or to what is unpleasant.' (Dhammapada, 2939) Whilst ACT does not require renunciation of emotion, the idea that we should stop 'clinging' to or fussing over thoughts, sensations and emotions is central to it. Similarly, in the *Bhagavadgita*, Krishna tells Arjuna that, 'When the senses contact sense objects, a person experiences cold or heat, pleasure or pain. These experiences are fleeting; they come and go. Bear them patiently, Arjuna.' (*Bhagavadgita*, p90) This cognitive defusion allows you to travel in the direction of your values through committed action. This is also reminiscent of ideas in the *Bhagavadgita*: 'The senses have been conditioned by attraction to the pleasant and aversion to the unpleasant. Do not be ruled by them; they are obstacles in your path.' (*Bhagavadgita*, p107) This can be compared to the ACT 'passengers-on-the-bus' metaphor. Thus we learn to carry our pleasant and unpleasant emotions together as we travel in the direction of our values.

Another parallel between ACT and Indian thought is the idea of self as context. Krishna continues to state that, 'The Self cannot be pierced or burned, made wet or dry. It is everlasting and infinite, standing on the motionless foundations of eternity. The Self is unmanifested, beyond all thought, beyond all change. Knowing this, you should not grieve.' (*Bhagavadgita*, p90) This idea can be likened to the ACT metaphor of the self-as-context being like a chessboard, containing all the thoughts, feelings and sensations but being independent and unaffected by them.

Both Buddhism and ACT (and Christianity for that matter) share the belief that suffering is an intrinsic part of life (Hayes, 2001). Additionally, the Buddhist idea of craving as the source of human suffering and the need to let go of attachment is similar to the ACT concept of acceptance.

We can also draw parallels between ACT and Hindu thought in the way that the concept of pain is dealt with. Whitman (2007) discusses how pain and suffering are viewed by the Hindu religion. If God encompasses everything, including pain and suffering, we should not see it as something bad, to be defeated and vanquished.

ACT IN MODERN WESTERN CLINICAL PRACTICE

ACT was developed in the 1980s by Steven Hayes, Kelly Wilson and Kirk Strosahl but has only become popular very recently. Many practicing clinical and counselling psychologists now offer ACT as one of the treatments they provide, or integrate ACT-based ideas into their practice in general. ACT involves getting people to 'lean into' the suffering in their lives by accepting it rather than resisting it. Encouraging people to develop a mindfulness practice so that they are living in the present is an important step. Helping people to treat their thoughts as just thoughts is a further therapeutic intervention.

This might involve all sorts of weird exercises like speaking one's thoughts in a Donald Duck voice in order to recognize the non-reality of thoughts. Facilitating people to clearly define their values and life direction is another step. Enabling people to step in the direction of their most deeply held values while carrying their own particular brand of suffering is the final step. Essentially the way I see ACT is:

A = Accepting the fact that there is suffering in life and that each of us carry our own particular limitations that perhaps we cannot change

C = Choosing a valued direction

T = Taking action to move our lives in the direction of our most deeply held values despite our limitations and our pain

Now let us see how ACT works in therapy.

Sally, fifty-nine, came into the therapy room in a state of distress. She was a mother of two and had been married once before but was now in another relationship. Her current partner was a good man, extroverted, friendly and approachable when in public. But in private he turned into something of a monster. He was dominating and controlling and perfectionistic. When things were not 'just so', he became critical of her and in later years took to shouting. He raised the volume of his voice and bore down upon her in an intimidating fashion. He even did this in public sometimes, not concerned about what other people thought of him or of them as a couple. This public diminishment was unbearable to Sally. Even though she did not believe he would be violent towards her, she hated living in a state of hyper-arousal. She began to tiptoe around him, becoming exceedingly careful about how things were done around the house so that they were in line with his expectations. She was a shadow of her original self. She began to indulge in her hobbies furiously, thus avoiding her pain and avoiding thinking about her situation. In her mind she was always thinking about what had to be done tomorrow and the day after so that she could avoid a conflict with her partner or what she had done to produce the violent temper yesterday. She told herself that she was rubbish at relationships.

The sex in their relationship became a thing of the past and there was little positive intimacy. Her children retreated into their bedrooms and stayed there because of the high conflict levels in the house. In spite of efforts to contact them, she had very little knowledge of what they were going through and what was happening in their lives. She therefore began to tell herself that she was a useless mother. She felt like she had no control over her life and that her life was drifting in no particular direction. It seemed as if she had lost sight of its meaning and purpose. Even though in the past she had been a woman of good, sound values, now it seemed as if she was unable to connect with them.

But the choices she faced were difficult. With two salaries coming into the house, hers and her partner's, she was physically very comfortable and she knew that her old age would be taken care of. Her children were experiencing a high standard of living. They had their own cars, computers, TVs in their room and they were able to take expensive courses and travel abroad. Since her partner was friendly and sociable at a superficial level with others, they were able to have large parties in their house. Besides, her partner gave her ample space to indulge in her hobbies, which she was passionate about. Also, there were weeks at a time in which they bumbled along quite happily together, not in any intimate fashion, but in parallel lives. So if she left the relationship she would be giving up the security and safety of all of this.

She entered therapy ambivalent and torn, not knowing what her values were or what her life direction was. The first step for her was to accept the suffering in her life, being mindful of it moment by moment, non-reactive and calm. This meant that she had to learn to put her hobbies aside at least for a time in order to carve out time to be still and look at her pain. Instead of distracting herself from her pain she learnt to lean into it. She developed a daily mindfulness practice. She began to do the body scan, which helped her to identify the location of the difficult emotions as they expressed themselves in her body. Using the exercise of thoughts on a leaf, she learnt to defuse thoughts such as 'I am a failure at all my relationships' and 'I am a rubbish mother', seeing them for what they were, just thoughts and then allowing them to float down an imaginary stream. This enabled her to see her life in the bigger picture, to refuse critical self-attacking thoughts, to develop a more compassionate way of looking at herself and to develop a new self-narrative that incorporated both the good and the bad, the beautiful and the ugly and the whole context in which her life was being played out. The next step was a difficult one: it was to enable her to define her values and her life direction. Some of her values conflicted with each other. For example, she wanted to provide a secure stable family home for her children. But she also wanted a deep, meaningful intimate relationship. In her current relationship the first was possible but not the second. I then asked her what proved to be a critical question, 'Who would you like to have around your deathbed?' This led to the important insight that she definitely did not want her current partner to be at her deathbed. This knowledge went a long way towards resolving her ambivalence. In the remainder of our therapy sessions together, Sally gradually came to the realization that she did not need to have a partner in order to provide a stable family home for the children. After some research and financial advice, she realized she had the financial wherewithal to move into a three-bedroom house. Her nest would not be feathered to the same degree and she would have to work a lot harder. Was this worth it? Sally decided it was. The next step was to go beyond inaction and onto the pathway of committed action. She would have to tell her partner that the relationship was no longer viable for her. In therapy, she recognized that she would have to deal with his tantrums in response to her news and she would need courage for this. She would also have to face the pain of telling her children that she was breaking up the family home for a second time. She used the skills she had learnt in mindfulness and acceptance to lean towards these unpleasant tasks so that she could move herself in the direction of her most deeply held values. Recently, Sally wrote to me telling me that the move was complete, that she felt her own woman again, that she was happy, that the children had adjusted to the new situation quite easily and that she was living an empowered life. To me this was indeed a happy ending to therapy.

RESEARCH EVIDENCE

Both mindfulness and ACT are further developments of classic CBT. They are post-modern outgrowths of the fact that some people find that the left brain, science-based, logical techniques of thought challenging and behavioural experimentation, hallmarks of classic CBT, are less useful in dealing with depression and anxiety than using more right-brained methods described in mindfulness and ACT. Thus, in mindfulness meditation, our brain activity is very different to when we are, for example, running up and down the stairs to convince ourselves that we are not going to die due to breathlessness as we might do in classic CBT treatments for panic disorder. In mindfulness and ACT the focus of our attention is not on the content of our thoughts as it is in classic CBT, but in our relationship to our thoughts. This is the essential difference between classic CBT and mindfulness and ACT and both are important and both are useful and effective.

An evidence-base evaluation (Ost, 2014) showed that ACT is not yet well-established for any disorder. This study concluded that it is probably efficacious for chronic pain and tinnitus, possibly efficacious for depression, psychotic symptoms, OCD, mixed anxiety, drug abuse and stress at work. However, evidence for ACT's effectiveness is growing and it is increasingly considered to be a useful therapy for many problems such as depression, anxiety and chronic pain, addiction etc (A-Tjak et al., 2015). The A-Tjak study found that ACT was more effective than treatment as usual and placebo conditions and that there was no significant difference between ACT and classic CBT.

I would say that the studies that have been done on ACT so far do testify to its effectiveness. Swain and colleagues (2013) reviewed papers written on ACT as a treatment for anxiety disorders and found that it was effective for combating social anxiety, OCD and Generalized Anxiety Disorder and there is some initial evidence that it can help against PTSD and panic disorder. Churchill and her team of researchers (2013) also found positive results for a range of 'third wave' therapies, including ACT, for the treatment of depression. However, again there is still considerable research to be done before ACT can be considered a truly empirically backed treatment. Since ACT has only recently become a popular therapy of choice, it has not been studied in the same depth as traditional cognitive behavioural therapy and therefore it does not enjoy the same high level of empirical support from the scientific community.

What we do know is that people who do not find traditional CBT useful can often benefit from ACT. Additionally, ACT can be used to enhance and extend CBT for everyone.

Key Points from this Chapter:

— Everyone experiences psychological suffering, not just those with mental health problems
— There are six problematic processes that lead to psychological inflexibility: experiential avoidance, cognitive fusion, dominance of the conceptualized past and future, attachment to the conceptualized self, lack of values, clarity and inaction, rigid persistence and/or impulsivity.
— ACT posits six core processes that people should work on to replace the problematic processes. These are: acceptance, cognitive defusion, being present, self as context, defining valued directions and committed action
— ACT is about increasing psychological flexibility
— To do this, it combines acceptance and mindfulness with commitment and behaviour change techniques
— ACT can be summarized with this acronym:
  A = Accepting the fact that there is suffering in life and that each of us carry our own particular limitations that perhaps we cannot change
  C = Choosing a valued direction
  T = Taking action to move our lives in the direction of our most deeply held values despite our limitations and our pain

- There are many similarities between ACT concepts and ideas in Buddhist and Hindu thought
- Research evidence for the effectiveness of ACT against anxiety and depression is growing and it is becoming part of the mainstream practice of many psychologists and psychotherapists today

REFERENCES

1. J.G. A-Tjak, M.L. Davis, N. Morina., M.B. Powers, J.A. Smits, and P.M. Emmelkamp, 'A Meta-analysis of the Efficacy of Acceptance and Commitment Therapy for Clinically Relevant Mental and Physical Health Problems', *Psychotherapy and Psychosomatics, 84*(30), 30-36, 2015 DOI: 10.1159/000365764.

2. R. Churchill, T. Moore, T. Furukawa, D. Caldwell, P. Davies, H. Jones, K. Shinohara, H. Imai, G. Lewis, and V. Hunot, 'Third Wave Cognitive and Behavioural Therapies Versus Treatment as Usual for Depression', *Cochrane Database of Systematic Reviews*, 2013.

3. K. Hancock, C. Hainsworth, and J. Bowman, 'Acceptance and Commitment Therapy in the Treatment of Anxiety: A Systematic Review', *Clinical Psychology Review*, 33(8):965–978, 2013. <http://www.sciencedirect.com/science/article/pii/S0272735813000901>

4. R. Harris, *ACT Made Simple*, Oakland, USA: New Harbinger Publications, 2009.

5. S.C. Hayes, 'Buddhism and Acceptance and Commitment Therapy', *Cognitive and Behavioral Practice*, 9(1): 58–66, 2002. <http://www.sciencedirect.com/science/article/pii/S1077722902800414>

6. S.C. Hayes, M.E. Levin, J. Plumb-Vilardaga, J.L. Villatte, and J. Pistorello, 'Acceptance and Commitment Therapy and Contextual Behavioral Science: Examining the Progress of a Distinctive Model of Behavioral and Cognitive Therapy', *Behavior Therapy*, 44(2): 180–198, 2013. <http://www.sciencedirect.com/science/article/pii/S0005789411000669>

7. S. Hayes, K. Strosahl, and K. Wilson, *Acceptance and Commitment Therapy: An Experiential Approach to Behavior Change*, New York: Guilford, 1999.

8.   S.G. Hofmann, A.T. Sawyer, and A. Fang, 'The Empirical Status of the "New Wave"', Fang, A. of Cognitive Behavioral Therapy', *Psychiatric Clinics of North America*, 33(3): 701–710, 2010. <http://www.sciencedirect.com/science/article/pii/S0193953X10000481>

9.   C. Johnstone and M. Akhtar, *The Happiness Training Plan: Practical Strategies for a Happier Life from the New Science of Positive Psychology*. Audio CD. www.happinesstrainingplan.com

10.   C. LeJeune, *The Worry Trap: How to Free Yourself from Worry and Anxiety Using Acceptance and Commitment Therapy*, Oakland, USA: New Harbinger Publications, 2007.

11.   F.M. Mèuller, *The Dhammapada: A Collection of Verses*, Champaign, Illinois: Project Gutenberg.

12.   L.G. Ost, 'The Efficacy of Acceptance and Commitment Therapy: An Updated Systematic Review and Meta-analysis', *Behaviour Research and Therapy*, 61, 105-121, 2014. DOI: 10.1016/j.brat.2014.07.018

13.   J. Parapully, R. Rosenbaum, V. Daele, and E. Nzewi, 'Thriving After Trauma: The Experience of Parents of Murdered Children', *Journal of Humanistic Psychology*, 42(l):33–70, 2002.

14.   R. Rohr, *Falling Upward: A Spirituality for the Two Halves of Life*, London: SPCK Publishing, 2012.

15.   R. Tagore, *Stray Birds*, New York: Macmillan, 1916.

16.   S.M. Whitman, *Pain and Suffering as Viewed by the Hindu Religion*, London: Churchill Livingstone, 2007.

8

Bouncing Back – Resilience

'The greatest glory in living lies not in never falling, but in rising every time we fall.'

– Nelson Mandela

'When we tackle obstacles, we find hidden reserves of courage and resilience we did not know we had. And it is only when we are faced with failure do we realize that these resources were always there within us. We only need to find them and move on with our lives.'

– APJ Abdul Kalam, former president of India

'If I can't make it through one door, I'll go through another door or I'll make a door. Something terrific will come no matter how dark the present.'

– Rabindranath Tagore

In this chapter:

— What is resilience?
— Why are some people more resilient than others?

- The road to resilience
- Resilience and spirituality
- The centenarian study
- Padesky and Mooney's Model of Resilience Training
- Hutnik's Resilience Awareness Instrument

In this chapter you will learn the skills to become resilient. You will learn to bounce back quickly to a place of fullness and vibrancy and nurture a zest for living after you have been knocked down by the trials of life. But by bouncing back, I do not mean you are blithely able to shed the pain and struggles of everyday life without a second thought. Indeed, part of being truly resilient is the ability to experience and process difficult emotions as they arise in the face of difficult life events. The term 'bouncing back' signifies robustness, but that does not mean you will go back to the same place before the stressful life event happened. To become truly resilient we need to use our stressful life events and experiences of failure to learn new patterns of behaviour that are adaptive and engineered so that they produce a greater sense of well-being within us.

The fact that you will experience being knocked down is a given. But there are many types of 'knocking down'. There are the big 'knocking downs': losing a family member, being the victim of rape, receiving a diagnosis of terminal illness, losing your house and possessions. Then there are the small 'knocking downs': your printer isn't working just when you need a printout, your client called to cancel at the last minute after you rescheduled a holiday to be available to him, the new puppy made a huge mess just before guests are due to arrive, you have overbooked your day and are seriously pressed for time. Some people collapse under the strain of these knocking downs. Others take even the big ones in their stride. If you are someone who tends to collapse, then there is good news for you. You can teach yourself to overcome your fragility and become robust. Since the psychological processes underlying resilience are the same for both the big knockings and the small knockings, I will no longer make the distinction between the two.

WHAT IS RESILIENCE?

The English word 'resilience' comes from the Latin '*resiliens*', meaning the property of a material to return to its original form after being bent, stretched or squashed. The Japanese proverb, 'The bamboo that bends is stronger than the oak that resists' conjures up a powerful image of a resilient plant in the wind. Resilience is not the strength to resist every storm or stay stiff and upright without showing any signs of weakness. But it is the ability to undergo difficulties and struggles without being crushed by them. The concept of resilience invokes words like pliability, flexibility, springiness, buoyancy and robustness. An example of a material that is not resilient is glass. It is brittle and fragile and breaks as soon as you drop it. Rubber, on the other hand, is resilient. You drop it and it bounces back (Robertson, 2012).

Swami Vivekananda (2014) also presents an interesting image that can inspire resilience: 'The world is the great gymnasium where we come to make ourselves strong.'

As we undergo difficulties in our lives, we build up our 'resilience muscles'. By learning and practicing the tools and techniques described in this book, you can strengthen your psychological muscles so that you have the resources to bounce back despite whatever life may throw at you.

SIGNIFICANT ADVERSITY: STRESSFUL LIFE EVENTS

Masten et al., (2009) see resilience as 'patterns of positive adaptation during or following significant adversity'. For these authors, resilience is manifested in the ability to make changes which move us in the direction of our greater well-being and happiness following a life event that may have been significantly damaging to us.

See the following example of a non-resilient response to significant adversity.

Meera had a child who died unexpectedly after a very brief illness. Meera became depressed, she lay in bed the whole day and she stopped doing things that she normally used to, like cooking, going to work and helping her two other kids with their homework. She felt terribly guilty about her child's death and blamed herself for not being careful and responsive enough to her child's needs. She could not function well. She went into therapy, but found no meaning in it. After two years, the grief for her child was as strong as when her child had died. She kept his room exactly as it was on the day he died. She put up photos of him all over the house and visited his grave regularly. Meera became dysfunctional and was unable to put the pieces of her life back together. Her husband, Sunil, was stretched to his limits in coping with her depression and sense of bereavement. He functioned for her and for the whole family, trying to keep it together for the older two kids. But this was taking an immense toll on him and began to harm their marriage. Finally, they entered therapy together and Meera recounted the story of the child's death in minute detail. Even though she felt comforted by the therapist who understood the pain she was going through, Meera did not want to let go of her grief. Thus, she did not benefit as much from therapy as she could have. Three years down the road she was still mourning the little boy, visiting his grave daily, having given up her job because she could not cope with it all.

Of course, in this example the death of Meera's child was a tragedy. There is a natural grieving period when you lose someone very close. As a therapist, I will wait till people have grieved for at least a year before I see them in therapy. My mother died two years ago and I still feel occasional bursts of intense sorrow and longing for her presence. But I contain my grief and function as normally as I can. When life becomes dysfunctional and depression takes over the person like a demon, we are talking about a non-resilient response to bereavement. Although we can all imagine how the sudden death of a child can whack the breath out of us, we can also envisage the possibility of learning to live again after a terrible event such as this.

WHY ARE SOME PEOPLE MORE RESILIENT THAN OTHERS?

Many people develop depression, anxiety and other mental health issues as a result of significant adversity. This has led resilience researchers to believe that only a minority of people are resilient. However, more recently, researchers have realized that large numbers of people manage to endure the temporary upheaval of loss or potentially traumatic events with no significant disruption in their ability to function at work or in their close relationships and they seem to move on to new challenges with ease (Bonanno, 2004). This indicates that resilience is more common in the general population than once believed, leading Ann Masten to refer to the quality as an 'ordinary magic' (Masten, 2001).

Some people do appear to have a natural propensity towards resilience. Waaktar and Torgersen (2012) conducted a study on identical twins which led them to conclude that resilience is largely genetically determined. Other studies have also found that our environment is equally important in making us resilient (Amstadter, Myers and Kendler, 2014). Irrespective of whether we have a natural tendency to be resilient or not, it is possible for everyone to increase resilience in their own lives. Doctors Steven Southwick and Dennis Charney found ten qualities that highly resilient people showed (Southwick and Charney, 2012):

- Realistic optimism
- Facing fears
- A moral compass
- Religion and spirituality
- Social support
- Resilient role models
- Physical fitness
- Brain fitness
- Cognitive and emotional flexibility
- Meaning and purpose

Famous people who showed remarkable resilience to adversities include Mahatma Gandhi, Nelson Mandela, Aung Sung Suu Kyi, Winston Churchill, Abraham Lincoln and Mother Teresa. Winston Churchill and Abraham Lincoln became great world leaders despite struggling with depression throughout their lives. Churchill dealt with his 'black dog' of depression by painting. Aung Sung Suu Kyi was under house arrest for over fifteen years, meaning she missed saying goodbye to her husband before he died and lived for a period of time without a roof or any electricity due to cyclone damage. A recent example of resilience is Malala Yousafzai, the young Pakistani girl who wrote a diary of her life under the Taliban when she was eleven years old. Fifteen-year-old Malala was shot in 2012 and was seriously injured but continued to be an activist for women's right to education. She is the youngest person ever to win a Nobel Prize.

My own role model of resilience is my mother. She immigrated from India to the United States when she was seventy, learnt to drive on the 'other' side of the road, developed a whole network of friends and was totally fulfilled and content having made such a great change so late in life. Can you think of people that you know who embody resilience to you?

A recent review of a number of studies (Domhardt, Münzer, Fegert and Goldbeck, 2014) investigated resilience in people who had been sexually abused as children. They found that between 10 and 53 per cent of the survivors of child sexual abuse participating in psychological studies in the past had been able to function normally despite these traumatic early experiences. The most important factor that promoted normal functioning was having support from their family and their wider social circle. There were also other key factors which promoted resilience: education, emotional and interpersonal competence, the belief that they could be in control of their lives, active coping, optimism, social attachment and being able to blame bad experiences on external factors rather than blaming themselves.

THE ROAD TO RESILIENCE

The American Psychological Association (APA, 2002) has brought out a blueprint for resilience, the main points of which are:

• Maintain good relationships with family, friends and others

- Avoid seeing situations as insurmountable problems and look for ways forward
- Accept certain circumstances as being outside of your control where necessary
- Set realistic goals, in small steps if necessary and plan to work regularly on things that are achievable
- Take decisive action to improve your situation rather than simply avoiding problems
- Look for opportunities for personal growth by trying to find positive or constructive meaning in events
- Nurture a positive view of yourself and develop confidence in your ability to solve external problems
- Keep things in perspective by looking at them in a balanced way and focusing on the big picture
- Maintain a hopeful and optimistic outlook, focusing on concrete goals, rather than worrying about possible future catastrophes
- Take care of yourself, paying attention to your own needs and feelings and looking after your body by exercising regularly and engaging in enjoyable, relaxing and healthy activities, perhaps including practices such as mediation.

RESILIENCE AND SPIRITUALITY

The 'ordinary magic' of resilience is an important concept in all of our major world religions. Steven Wolin spent a career researching resilience and as part of this, he asked representatives of the major world religions to describe how their faith presents or encourages resilience (Wolin, 2009).

A Buddhist he spoke to said that Buddhism recognizes that pain is an inevitable part of the human condition but that ongoing suffering comes from how we relate to our pain. Within each of us, Buddhists believe, exists a 'Buddha-nature', which is an innate illuminating divine perfection. Although pain and sorrow exist in our lives, they cannot damage the enlightened being within us. If we can discover our Buddha-nature, we can persist despite any pain. According to a Hindu speaker, Hindus perform karma yoga, undertaking activity in a dedicated manner without becoming too attached to the fruits of that action. By surrendering the fruits of the action to the higher power, Hindus can practice resilience in facing difficulties in their lives. A Muslim contributor said that Muslims look to the example of the Prophet Mohammed for inspiration on resilience. Mohammed was born into poverty and both his parents died when he was young. He taught tolerance, forgiveness and how to reconcile with others. A Jewish woman who took part in the discussion spoke about the Jewish Exodus from slavery in Egypt and the Passover tradition of the Seder. At the Seder, stories are told about the Jews' suffering as slaves in Egypt and their escape to freedom through the desert. A Christian participant added that in Christianity, the ultimate image of resilience is of Jesus Christ who underwent human suffering and death but continued to be faithful, ultimately conquering death and being resurrected, thereby finding renewal and regeneration, and quite literally bouncing back to life.

THE CENTENARIAN STUDY

Recently, my colleagues and I carried out two qualitative studies in which we interviewed British people who had lived beyond the age of a hundred. These centenarians had a great deal to tell us about resilience. Like no other generation before or after, they had each experienced a century of change: they were born at a time when there were no inside toilets or central heating and women did not have the right to vote. They lived through both World Wars in which many lost husbands, brothers and sons. They saw the rise of capitalism, the dismantling of communism, the sexual, the music and the technological revolution. At the time of their birth, cars and airplanes were rare, radio, television, washing machines, dishwashers, countless other kitchen appliances and the World Wide Web had not been invented. They probably never expected to live to see the twenty-first century.

In the first study we were interested in investigating the socio-emotional texture of the lives of these centenarians (Hutnik, Smith and Koch, 2012). We were amazed at how engaged these centenarians were in their lives. One was the president of his bowling club, another learned Tai Chi at the age of 101, a third had been given an honour by the Queen for her skill at glass engraving and a fourth had marched against the Iraq War at the age of 102. What shone through their interviews was their stoicism in the face of loss and change, and that each of them reported being happy and they had had a good life. Yes, there were sources of frustration, their eyes and ears were no longer working as well as they used to and some of them were wheel-chair bound, but they had enough social support and expressed gratitude for the amount of care they received from people. Not many of them talked about death, but those who did seemed to have made a friend of it.

In the second study (Hutnik, Smith and Koch, 2016) we used a CBT lens to look at resilience in their stories. We found that most of them had developed some key psychological skills.

1. They had developed the ability to use positive language to frame the very difficult events that they had lived through
2. With that stiff upper lip stoicism that we had discovered in the first study, they were determined to cope with whatever life threw at them
3. Part of the first two skills was the art of pushing worry away. They just would not entertain it
4. They learnt to adapt to change quickly, demonstrating the psychological flexibility that we talked about in the chapter on ACT
5. They continued to see and to take opportunities for personal growth and development, demonstrating engagement and interest in life

Here are some interesting quotes from the interviews:

Olive: 'Herb (Olive's husband) had a stroke very soon after he retired, when he was sixty-five. I've always thought that was through stress. He had four strokes. Luckily for me, he never lost his speech. Some people can't speak anymore, but he managed. But I had to wheel him around in a wheelchair if we went out. I don't know how I managed the wheelchair up the hill. Despite the fact that he had a stroke, he had a good sense of humour and he never stopped giggling. He would start telling a joke and was laughing so much about it, he couldn't finish it.' This showed Olive's ability to frame difficult 'knocking-down' events in positive language.

Phyllis: 'Well you just have to cope with it, don't you? I'm afraid I'm one of those resilient people, I don't just sit down and cry when it comes, I've just got to get on with it. You know fully well it's probably the end and you think your life is going to change but you've just got to go on. And I think it's just living sensibly quite honestly.] Yes, you've just got to get on with it; you've just got to get on with it.' This showed Phyllis's determination to cope with whatever life threw at her with stoicism.

Nita: 'If you can manage and you've not got pain, you've got to try and push worry away and not be miserable. Try to be happy and try and join in every day with what's going on. Accept what comes. Think about being thankful to be alive.' Nita was determined to push worry away and to be happy.

Albert: 'If you can't change it and alter it, don't worry about it.' Here again we see the habit of pushing worry away.

Bob: 'At twenty-one, I went to Newcastle to work in a marine engineering works as an apprentice. It was a big change from being a middle class student to being an apprentice who could be teased and made fun of and generally made to carry tools around for other people. But I didn't suffer at all, I loved it. I accepted it.' Bob adapted to change and accepted it, showing psychological flexibility.

Marion: 'Never give up. I don't think of death. I think of living and what I am going to do and what I am going to enjoy.' Marion at over a hundred years of age, showed a level of engagement and interest in life that is significant. She does not actively think of death even though just mentioning it suggests that she knows it is not far away.

It seems to me that the core of resilience is a positive attitude towards life, taking any blows that life deals us squarely on the chin, refusing to enter into cycles of rumination and regret, adapting to change quickly and having a growth mindset. According to Neenan, a cognitive behaviour therapist, resilience is all about attitude, forward movement and learning from experience (Neenan, 2009). We never return to the same place as before we were knocked down, we revisit it from the vantage point of having learnt the lessons that life has taught us.

Even though these centenarians did indeed experience significant adversity in their lives, when they talk about resilience it is in the context of the normal vicissitudes of life, the everyday ups and downs, and the little things. For the remainder of this chapter we will be looking at how to develop resilience in the face of the small knocking-downs. In this context, it might be useful for you to have a baseline measure of your own resilience before you begin to develop it further. Do take the questionnaire below.

Exercise 8.1: How Resilient Are You?

The Brief Resilience Scale (Smith et al., 2008) can help you to assess how resilient you are already. Don't panic if you end up with a low score. Resilience can be learnt and developed. There are a number of statements and below each statement you can tell us how much you agree or disagree with the statement. Circle the one that most closely reflects the way you are.

SA = Strongly Agree
A = Agree
N = Neither Agree nor disagree
D = Disagree
SD= Strongly Disagree

Please use the key above to indicate your agreement or disagreement with the items below.

1. I tend to bounce back quickly after hard times

SA(5)   A(4)   N(3)   D(2)   SD(1)

2. I have a hard time making it through stressful events

SA(1)　　A(2)　　N(3)　　D(4)　　SD(5)

3. It does not take me long to recover from a stressful event

SA(5)　　A(4)　　N(3)　　D(2)　　SD(1)

4. It is hard for me to snap back when something bad happens

SA(1)　　A(2)　　N(3)　　D(4)　　SD(5)

5. I usually come through difficult times with little trouble

SA(5)　　A(4)　　N(3)　　D(2)　　SD(1)

6. I tend to take a long time to get over set backs in my life

SA(1)　　A(2)　　N(3)　　D(4)　　SD(5)

Scoring: Next to each of your responses is a number. Add up these numbers for all six items. Then divide the total sum by 6.

If your score is above 3 you are moderately resilient. If it is nearing 5 you are very resilient and are able to bounce back easily after stress. If it is 1 or 2 it means that you will really benefit from reading this book and learn how to increase your ability to bounce back.

PADESKY AND MOONEY'S MODEL OF RESILIENCE TRAINING

Christine Padesky and Kathleen Mooney, who are leading lights in the field of CBT, have developed a systematized CBT model that facilitates the development of personal resilience in the face of everyday stress and difficulty (Padesky and Mooney, 2012). The theory underlying the model is that people already have some areas in which they exhibit resilience. It may be that come what may, hell or high water, they always take the dog out for a walk or they always read the newspaper before the end of the day even if the day has been impossibly busy. If they can uncover these 'never-miss' activities, they will develop an awareness of their hidden strengths. Once aware of their strengths, it is important to know what makes them continue in these activities even in the face of obstacles. What strategies have they developed that enable them to be persistent in these activities even when they are difficult to carry out? What values keep them going? What images do they have of themselves in coping mode? Once people are aware of their own personal model of resilience (PMR), they can learn to transfer the awareness of these already existing strengths and strategies into the areas of life that have knocked them down and caused them to develop depression and/or anxiety or other mental disturbances. The idea behind all of this is not necessarily to achieve a positive outcome, but to stay resilient irrespective of the outcome. This model represents a real development in CBT since we have moved from treating negative states to bringing positive states into being.

DEVELOPING YOUR OWN PERSONAL MODEL OF RESILIENCE

According to the Padesky and Mooney model (2012) there are four steps to building your personal model of resilience (PMR):

Search:	Where are your hidden strengths?
Construct:	Build your personal model of resilience.
Apply:	Transfer this to your area of difficulty.
Practice:	Keep practicing staying resilient in different difficult areas in your life, using the PMR.

I will now use an example to show you how to search, construct, apply and practice.

Tanya was a thirty-five-year-old mother of three. She was also an executive in an important IT company. She was married to Tilesh who was forty years old and who seemed to be going through a mid-life crisis. Tilesh was very successful in his work and stayed very late at the office. He travelled a lot and was often away during the weekends. He hardly saw his children because they were always asleep by the time he got home at night. Tanya was feeling depressed and lonely and insecure about whether Tilesh really loved her at all. She was also resentful that Tilesh spent such little time with the family, leaving her to deal with both the physical and the psychological needs of the children, as well as doing a demanding job. But she found herself unable to express any of these feelings to Tilesh. She thus suffered in silence but her feelings were growing in intensity within her, leaving her acting sulky and prickly when she was with Tilesh. This caused him to withdraw more into his work and spend even less time at home. Tanya learnt about resilience training and decided to build her own personal model of resilience to help her face these stresses.

SEARCH: UNCOVERING HIDDEN STRENGTHS

Tanya asked herself, 'What do I do every day which is so important to me that no matter what happened, I would do it?'

Tanya decided that her never-miss activity was that no matter how ill or bad she was feeling she would always see that there was food on the table for her children. From this, and in discussion with a therapist, she became aware of the strengths underlying her dogged determination to ensure that her children don't go hungry no matter how rotten she was feeling. She identified her strengths as:

- I am committed to my family
- I am a good mother. I want my children to remember me with great love when I am gone
- I know how to nurture well
- I am a great cook. I have skills and aptitudes that are valued

- *I am well organized*
- *I have a great deal of determination when it comes to things that are important to me*
- *I am good at communicating what I want done*

CONSTRUCT: THINK ABOUT STRATEGIES THAT ARE USED TO OVERCOME OBSTACLES AND IMAGES THAT CAN BE CALLED UP AS EASY WAYS TO REMEMBER THESE STRATEGIES

Tanya's cooking was her never-miss activity. She loved cooking and she valued being a good parent so the two together enabled her to develop strategies to overcome difficulties that came her way. Sometimes Tanya's job was very pressurizing, her company was meeting tough deadlines and she had to stay late at work which meant that her cooking time in the evening was severely cut down. To overcome this, she planned and organized the whole week's meals in advance, having everything ready in the fridge. She enlisted extra domestic help to get the basics done while she was at work and when she came home, she always put the finishing touches on herself. If the domestic help called in sick, she was ready with hand-prepared food frozen in advance. She also made it a priority to never leave from work so late that she was absent at the children's meal times. Tanya wrote down strategies of what she did when completing her never-miss activity was threatened:

- *To be a good mother I have to schedule my work to be present for my children when they are home from school*
- *To nurture well, I am able to walk the tight rope between love and discipline*
- *I have learnt how to be both tender-hearted and tough-minded appropriately*
- *I have applied my intelligence and talent to learning to cook well*
- *When things go wrong such as the domestic help has misunderstood my instructions, I use this as an opportunity to learn how to communicate better and more clearly*

Tanya's Personal Resilience Model		
Never-miss activity: Cooking for my Children		
Strengths	**Strategies**	**Image**
• I am committed to my family • I am a good mother. I want my children to remember me with great love when I am gone. I know how to nurture well • I am a great cook. I have skills and aptitudes that are valued • I am well organized • I have a great deal of determination when it comes to things that are important to me • I am good at communicating what I want done	• To be a good mother I have to schedule my work to be present for my children when they are home from school • To nurture well, I have to be able to walk the tight rope between love and discipline • I have learnt how to be both tender-hearted and tough-minded appropriately • I have applied my intelligence and talent to learning to cook well • When things go wrong such as the domestic help has misunderstood my instructions, I use this as an opportunity to learn how to communicate better and more clearly	Intelligent and nurturing vibrantly coloured kingfisher

APPLY

Tanya recognized her inability to be resilient with Tilesh. She was caught in a cycle of sulks and pouts. She was avoiding the task of addressing some difficult issues with Tilesh. She was not confident about her ability to do so without getting into a huge fight. She also realized that it would be advantageous to develop some ability to be resilient with her husband. If she could do this, she would re-open the lines of communication between them and this would give her a better chance of being satisfied in the relationship.

Tanya, therefore, looked at the strengths, strategies, images and metaphors that she had identified as being part of her PMR.

There were two strengths that Tanya identified as important and significant for developing more resilience in talking to Tilesh: being committed to her family and being good at communicating what she wanted done. The fact that she already had these two strengths in a different area of life told her that she was not starting from scratch and this boosted her confidence. She decided she would try to have a conversation with Tilesh at some point over the next few days. She tried to anticipate the obstacles she would face: Tilesh would say he was tired and not really willing to talk and she would feel fearful of an argument and retreat rather than stand her ground.

Tanya then asked herself if she had any strategies, images or metaphors in her tool bag that would enable her to overcome these obstacles. In order to be committed to the well-being of her family she knew she had to be both tender-hearted and tough-minded with Tilesh. She had already developed this skill with her children. She knew it would not be easy to exercise but she had done it effectively with her children. She drew upon her considerable time-scheduling capacities to make sure that the children were elsewhere, occupied, when she planned to have this conversation with Tilesh. She knew she could communicate clearly and effectively with her domestic helper. With her husband, she decided she would use the age-old couples' communication strategy: when you do this (X), I feel (Y) and I would like you to do (Z).

Tanya planned this statement carefully. She decided she would say, 'When you stay late at the office so many times a week, I feel lonely, depressed, insecure and unattractive to you. I also feel a little angry and resentful that I am running the household single-handedly and that you do not spend any time with me and the kids. I would prefer you to come home in time for the children's dinner at least three times a week and for us to be together as a family on weekends, without you checking your mobile phone and your work emails at least on Saturdays.'

Tilesh was silent and unresponsive when he heard Tanya's statement. Tanya remembered that the goal of the exercise was to stay resilient rather than anything else and so she refused to let his non-responsiveness get to her. She called to mind the image of herself as a beautiful kingfisher. To her very great surprise, even though he had not said anything, Tilesh came home on Monday, Wednesday and Friday and spent the weekend with his family.

Practice

Emboldened by her success in staying resilient rather than cave in to her emotions of fear and anxiety, Tanya decided she would practice this in other areas of her relationship with Tilesh too. Over time she was able to go out one evening in the week to join a gym, while Tilesh looked after the kids and gave them dinner. Paradoxically, Tilesh discovered he enjoyed being with his kids and he found that his colleagues at work admired him for prioritizing his family. Eventually, Tanya was able to initiate sex instead of waiting for Tilesh to do so. This required her to risk rejection and to stay resilient even when Tilesh was not interested. She constantly brought to mind the image of herself as a kingfisher. Thanks to her increasing resilience, both of them arrived at a much better place in their relationship and Tanya felt enriched and empowered.

Now why don't you try it? Go through the exercises below one by one and see if you can build your resilience.

Exercise 8.2: This exercise consists of 4 parts: Search, Construct, Apply, Practice

8.2.1: Searching for your own hidden strengths

The first step towards making your own personal model of resilience is to search for your hidden strengths. Think of areas in which you are already resilient. It is really important to look at your daily never-miss activities or things that you are passionate about that you would do even when there are obstacles in the way. Under each section I will give you two examples, one from my life, the other from Karim who loves dogs. Look at these examples and think about your life and write down your particular items. For example, the thing that I am most passionate about is painting. It is my 'never-miss' activity. Karim's never-miss activity is taking his dog out for a walk.

Think about what this 'never-miss' activity is for you. Some ideas might be looking after a pet, child or other relative, playing a musical instrument, going to work, art, writing, reading, etc. It could be something very simple. Try to think of something that you currently do. Write down what the activity is here:

My never miss activity is painting.

Karim's never miss activity is taking the dog out for a walk.

What is yours?

_____

_____

_____

_____

_____

What is special about this activity for you? Why do you enjoy or value it?

I love creating things that are pleasing to look at in colour and form. When I am painting I lose myself and the hours fly past without me noticing the time. I am often in 'flow'. Karim loves animals and in particular dogs. He thinks they are wonderful companions and need to be treated with care and respect

_____

_____

_____

_____

_____

Exercise 8.2.: Searching for your own hidden strengths

What strengths did you demonstrate when you did the previous activity? Here are some tips for looking for your hidden strengths:

- Have you used your intelligence to solve a particular problem?
- Have you shown any particular insights into a situation that were not immediately obvious?
- Have you been creative in resolving an issue?
- Have you shown tenacity and persistence in certain areas of your life?

Strengths: My strengths in painting are: I have a good eye for aesthetics, I am able to solve knotty problems related to composition and colour, and I am keen on experimenting with new materials and texture. Karim's strengths are persistence and commitment to his dog, being able to organize his time in a way that he always has time after work to take his dog out, being highly empathic with the dog being cooped up in the house the entire day)

Exercise 8.2.2: Constructing Your own Personal Model of Resilience (PMR)

Keeping your passion in mind, what are some of the obstacles that you face when pursing this activity? What difficulties do you run into while doing your never-miss activity? My obstacles are: a lack of formal art education, lack of talent and skill, lack of practice.

The obstacles Karim regularly faces are bad weather, a dog that is sometimes difficult to manage when he is with other dogs, work and family commitments, wanting to stay in bed another hour.

Now think of what obstacles you encounter when pursuing your passion or your never-miss activity

_____

_____

_____

_____

_____

Which values enable you to persist despite frustrations and difficulties? If you have difficulties with this stage, you could try asking a friend to help. Look back to what you wrote in 8.2.1.

_____

_____

_____

_____

_____

The next step in constructing your PMR is to think of the strategies you use that enable you to overcome the obstacles you encounter. For example, to overcome a lack of formal art education, I take many series of short courses at reputed art colleges. I know that a lack of talent and skill can be somewhat overcome by practice and hard work. Therefore, I carve out some time from my busy schedule to do at least some art every week.

Karim's strategies include being properly equipped with water bottles, sun hats, comfortable open sandals, dog leads, and being efficient and time-conscious at work so that he always finishes on time and takes on no more or no less than he is able to do within work hours. To make your strengths and strategies more memorable, you might find a particular image or metaphor of your own resilience useful to take with you into your week. For example, Tanya saw herself as a beautiful kingfisher who built its nest by water and cared for its chicks by inviting them to cuddle beneath its wings. Another image could be that of a lorry driver delivering an important package and continuing down the highway despite heavy rain and wind pelting down on the vehicle. Try to make the image personal to you. Link it to your own values if you can.

_____

_____

_____

_____

_____

Rather than or as well as writing this as a paragraph, you might prefer to draw a picture or create a diagram. Some people like to make a poster that they can put on their wall to remind themselves of their strengths and strategies. You might already have an image or a metaphor that you use to help you stay resilient. If you do, write it down here. Otherwise, you might need to start practicing your resilient strategies in real life before you can think of an image:

_____

_____

_____

_____

_____

In the next exercise, there is a blank personal resilience model for you to fill in. When completing your own personal resilience model, think about the difference between strengths and strategies. The strengths are qualities that you show in your never-miss activity whereas the strategies are how you cope with obstacles and frustrations in your never-miss activity.

Exercise 8.2.2 My Personal Resilience Model

My passion/Never-miss activity: _____

Strengths	Obstacles Encountered	Values I hold about my passion/never miss activity
	Strategies I use to overcome these obstacles	Image of myself as resilient in the face of obstacles

Exercise 8.2.3: Applying Your PMR

Just like Tanya, me or Karim, you can learn to apply your PMR to transfer your strengths and strategies from your area of confidence to your area of difficulty. Firstly, think about your area of difficulty where you want to be more resilient. For Tanya, this was her relationship with her husband. For others it might be dealing with a difficult boss or colleague, meeting deadlines with school or university work, bringing up children or ill health. Think of only one area.

Write your area of difficulty in the space below:

_____

_____

_____

_____

_____

Using your strengths and strategies, and holding the image of your resilient self in front of you, write down how you might apply your PMR to your difficult situation. You might benefit from discussing this with a dear friend first.

_____

_____

_____

_____

_____

_____

8.2.4: Practicing Your PMR

The final step in building resilience is to practice using your PMR in everyday life. In doing this, you will develop new neural pathways to resilience in place of pathways to fear, anxiety and collapse. In order to do this, try out your PMR in smaller, less threatening situations first and then practice it in larger, more difficult situations. For example, in Tanya's case, she started with clear communication about how she was feeling about the kids and his absence from their lives and what Tilesh could do to help. It is only when something had shifted and changed, and she found herself still standing despite her fears and anxieties, that she tried the next step which was to initiate sex and not be upset or feel rejected but still stay resilient even when Tilesh was too tired or not in the mood.

Make sure that you challenge yourself in the coming days and weeks to put yourself into situations that you find difficult. See difficulties and obstacles as fantastic opportunities to practice your resilience. The test of how resilient you are is if you can stay resilient and robust regardless of the outcome.

_____

_____

Being resilient might not make you feel better immediately. It's not about suddenly feeling great about your life. According to Christine Padesky:

> 'Being resilient doesn't mean you'll be happy about what you are facing. It just means you are still standing at the end of the day.'
> (Padesky and Mooney, 2012)

HUTNIK'S MODEL OF RESILIENCE

Padesky and Mooney's model (2012) is designed to be used in conjunction with CBT with people who are moderately depressed. They state clearly that it is not an intervention in itself.

I have developed a model which is influenced by the Padesky and Mooney model, but which can be used independent of classic CBT, with people like you and me who sometimes experience low mood and may be stressed and anxious about life and its vicissitudes. My own assumption about resilience is that most of us show a great deal of it, that indeed it is an 'ordinary magic' (Masten, 2001). We are often resilient in the difficult times in our lives and also in the times when we are meeting and overcoming obstacles in areas of positive achievement. But we are often not aware of how resilient we actually already are. And so, part of building resilience is to become aware of it. Thus, I have developed a resilience awareness instrument to help us out. Rather than use a never-miss activity or an area of passion, I look at resilience in broader terms in the context of our lives as a whole.

I use a timeline to help people discover how they have been resilient in difficult life events and also in achieving positive things. A timeline is a kind of graph of your life, which is divided into chunks of, say ten years. I will take you through an example and then guide you as to how you can go about doing the timeline for your own life.

Tanuja was a fifty-nine-year-old woman who had had many difficulties in life but who had also been able to achieve a lot of positive things. At the age of three she became very ill and had to be hospitalized. She lost a dearly loved maid at the age of five. Her studies were really important to her but at sixteen her father got posted to another state and she found in her new school that she did not have all the subjects she needed to do her O levels. At thirty she experienced three deaths in the family, her sister and her brother-in-law died in a crash and her best friend died of cancer. At this time she was also facing pressure at work, needing to meet strict deadlines. At thirty-six her husband had an affair and her marriage broke down. At forty her company was facing bankruptcy and she found herself at risk of losing her job. At forty-five her mother died.

After Tanuja plotted some of the difficult events in her life, I asked her to plot some of the positive things she had achieved during her lifetime. She had finished her degree, gotten married, brought up her children and written a book. Several years after her divorce, she had found a new husband and was now engaged in nurturing him and the new melded family.

Difficult Life Events

- 3 yrs. Almost died of appendicitis
- 5 yrs. Lost my nanny
- 16 yrs. Shifted schools in my final year of school and found that the new school did not have some vital subjects that I needed for my career
- 30 yrs. 3 deaths in the family in 1 year while meeting deadlines for book publication
- 36 yrs. Marriage breakdown: fear of being alone and anxiety about how to manage practical things like plumbing, computers, paying bills etc.
- 40 yrs. Restructuring at work : job being made redundant
- 45 yrs. Mother died

_____

20 yrs.   21 yrs.   23-28 yrs.   30 yrs.   36 yrs.   38 yrs.   39 yrs.   50 yrs.

Positive Achievements

- Finished my degree
- Got married
- Had children
- Wrote a book
- Started painting
- Separated
- Found a new job
- Remarried

RESILIENCE IN THE DIFFICULT TIMES

Taking each difficult life event into consideration, I asked Tanuja some questions to uncover her hidden strengths and coping strategies. What did she do to cope with her knocking-down situation? Who helped her? What resources did she use to overcome the situation? What hidden strengths can she see in herself?

After she had uncovered her coping strategies, I asked her if she could come up with a resilience rule that she has lived by as a result of the difficult life event in question.

It is quite a skill to uncover your hidden strengths and resilience principles. In the next chapter there are more instructions on how to find these hidden strengths. It is enough to give you the names of a few hidden strengths: courage, grit, persistence, compassion, caring, kindness, leadership, planning and organization.

Here is how Tanuja responded to my probing.

Difficult Life Events	How I Responded	My Hidden Strengths	My Resilience Principles
Hospitalized and almost died	I let time heal me. I relied on my mum and dad to support me	Drawing on people for support when I need it	I learnt that given time and general good health I can heal from most things, even the most invasive of procedures
Lost my beloved maid	I just lived with this pain, not denying it	Acceptance of things that cannot be changed	I can still survive even though I have lost some very important people
Shifted schools in my final year – not the right subjects	Collected the data to show that I could not do my O levels in the new school and therefore convinces my parents to go back to the old school	Ability to be rational and to problem-solve	I can solve problems well by collecting data and using it to convince people of what I need to do

Three deaths in the family while meeting my deadlines at work	I paid from my pocket for extra help to support me at work	Ability to manage difficult emotions and to keep functioning	I can solve problems well
Risk of losing my job	Employed an organizational coach. My job was reinstated because of a letter I wrote to the authorities	Courage to tell it like it is	I can recruit people to help and advise me when necessary. I can also speak up about things that are important to me
Mother died	I cried for many months and then decided I must put my mourning behind me and rejoice in her presence in my history	Accepting and integrating death as part of the natural cycle of life	People we love may die but they are just as alive in memory as if they were physically here

RESILIENCE IN POSITIVE ACHIEVEMENTS

Next I turned her to look at the positive things she had achieved in her lifetime. There were many and we listed a few of them. I then asked her what obstacles she had faced in achieving these positive things, and she listed them. The next question I asked was, 'What resilience rule could you come up with to encapsulate your ability to deal with obstacles in achieving these positive things?'

Positive Achievements	Obstacles I Faced and How I Overcame them	My Hidden Strengths	My Resilience Principles
Finished my degree	Severe time pressure. I asked family members to help me meet my deadlines	Able to manage time well. Able to plan and to organize my work. Able to recruit help from family	I can work well under pressure
Got married to someone from outside my caste	Faced opposition from parents and society but did it anyway	Courage and grit	I can stand my ground and still remain connected to those I love
Had children	Problems in pregnancy: had Caesarian sections	Ability to realistically appraise risk and take decisions	I can sometimes take risky decisions for my own well-being
Wrote a book	Juggling many time commitments. Wrote lists and made timetables	Good problem-solving abilities	I am good at time management and problem solving
Separated	Disapproval from parents. Kept in contact with both ex-husband and parents despite arguments	Perseverance but then being able to know when enough is enough	I can keep connected to the people who were important to me while having major disagreements with them

Found a new job	My age was an obstacle. I created a new career for myself	Creativity	I am flexible enough to start again
Remarried	Disapproval from parents but I kept talking to them rather than avoid them	Persistence	I have learnt that my parents will stay connected with me and I with them whatever I do

SUMMARIZING RESILIENCE PRINCIPLES

We then took the resilience rules from the difficult life events and the resilience rules from the positive life events and put them together in a summary. Here is Tanuja's summary:

When life is difficult:

I am surprisingly resilient. I heal well. I recover well from relationship losses. I have a great source of strength in my meditation practice. I am a good problem solver and in certain cases I can adopt a 'who cares' attitude that really helps me cope with stress.

The positive things I have achieved reveal my innate resilience:

I work well under pressure and can carve out the time for things that are really important to me despite many competing commitments. I can take important and sometimes risky decisions. Even in the face of opposition I have the courage to stand my ground. I can seek advice and help when I need and am good at forward planning and organizing.

LOOKING FOR IMAGES OR SONGS TO SYMBOLIZE RESILIENCE

We then looked for images and songs that would help Tanuja remember her ability to be resilient. She came up with several images. The first was that of a bop bag, one of those inflatable punching bags that always return to standing position. The second was an image of the Hindu goddess Durga, who has many arms and sits upon a tiger, embodying the very essence of a powerful woman. When I asked her about songs, she came up with two, the refrains of which were very important to her.

'I *get knocked* down' by Chumbawamba and *'I will survive'*, by Gloria Gaynor. A slogan that she used for herself was: freedom is just another word for nothing left to lose.

PRACTICING RESILIENCE IN CURRENT KNOCKING-DOWN SITUATIONS

Next, we looked at the areas of Tanuja's life, which were currently proving difficult for her. She told me that her dog, who had been her companion for over twelve years, was dying. She also told me she was having difficulty at work with a colleague who was bad-mouthing her.

We then looked at her resilience summary to see if there was anything there that she could draw upon to deal with these situations. Her challenge was to use her resilience rules in the situations she was finding difficult, with the goal being merely to stay resilient at the end of the encounter rather than to produce a desired outcome. Staying resilient sometimes means accepting the things we cannot change. In relation to her dying dog, Tanuja looked at the way she had faced death in her life, when she had lost her help and family and friends. She realized she can still survive even though she has lost some very important people in her life. By focusing on the fact of her past, resilience seemed to help her cope with her current difficult life situation, leaning into it, accepting it and knowing that time will heal her and that she will be able to live happily again after a period of grief and mourning. She was determined to actively focus on her meditation practice as she grappled yet again with the reality of death. With regard to her colleague, Tanuja realized she had good problem-solving skills and that she was able to seek advice from someone who knew how to deal with such situations. She could plan forward and take risky decisions. So, remembering her bop bag image and the Chumbawamba song, she planned to ask her colleague if there was something she had said or done to upset her. Tanuja was also determined to employ the skills of an organizational coach who would help her deal with the bad-mouthing.

There are many advantages to building resilience in our repertoire of coping strategies. The first advantage is that in being determined to be resilient, we forsake the victim position in life and become the author of our own happiness. The second advantage is that we can begin to see difficulties as the practice ground for building resilience. Thus, we change our relationship with our 'knocking-down' events and instead see them as opportunities for growth and positive development.

It is your turn now to become aware of your own resilience.

First plot both difficult life events and positive achievements on your lifeline. Then use the template below to do this.

Exercise 8:3 Hutnik's Resilience Awareness Instrument

Here are some steps that you can follow to arrive at an understanding of your existing resilience and how to use it to build even more resilience in your current 'knocking-down' situation.

1) Use the timeline to plot difficult events in your life on the upper half of the line. Then plot your positive achievements in the lower half of the line
2) Enter two to three of the most significant difficult life events into the table on the next page
3) In the next column titled 'How I Responded', look at the objective facts of what you did in the situation
   a. Can you outline how you bounced back and are here today?
   b. What did you do to cope? Did you recruit people to help you cope?
   c. What was the outcome?

4) We learn things through failure and when things don't go right for us. Go through each significant life event that you have chosen and try to get to the moral of the story and make this into your resilience rules

   a. What did you learn from this experience?

   b. What values or resilience principles helped you bounce back?

5) What are some of the positive things you have achieved in your life? We are not looking for things like 'I had a happy childhood', or 'My parents are the best'. Instead, look for facts like I won a gold medal or I was chosen to be captain of the football team

   We want actual events. These may be large events or very small ones in which we find real joy.

6) For the next column, when we look at the things we have achieved, we have usually had to overcome a number of obstacles. Detail these obstacles in the column titled, 'Obstacles I Faced and How I Overcame Them', and in the following column, try to arrive at your resilience principles

7) Now make a summary of your resilience principles

8) What images, slogans or songs remind you of your resilience principles

9) The final step is to practice applying your resilience principles in the current 'knocking-down' situation. What will you do to strengthen your ability to bounce back? Outline actual steps. For example, if you are avoiding your boss because of her tendency to be over-critical, how will you apply your resilience principles in this situation? Be specific and remember that the goal is to be resilient whatever be the outcome

My Timeline

Difficult Life Events

0–10	11–20	21–30	31–40	41–50	51–65

Positve Acheivements

Difficult Life Events	How I Responded	My Hidden Strengths	My Resilience Principles
For example: marriage breakdown	I developed a meditation practice I found a good therapist	Grit Can-do attitude Courage Problem solving	Even in the midst of the most horrendous turmoil I have learnt to sit still mindfully and am able to help myself in times of emotional difficulty

Positive Life Events	Obstacles I Faced and	For example: marriage breakdown	For example: marriage breakdown
For example: finished my degree	Severe time pressures Recruited family members to help	Good time management Very high quality standards	I can work well under pressure

Summary of my Resilience Principles

Images, slogans or songs that remind me of my resilience principles

Steps I will take to apply my resilience principles in the current 'knocking-down' situation.

1.
2.
3.
4.

Key Points from this Chapter:

— Resilience means being flexible and springy in the face of stress, adversity and change

— Everyone experiences difficult, unpleasant and even traumatic events in their lives

— Humans on the whole are very resilient. Some people are more resilient than others, either due to their nature or nurture, but everyone can learn resilience

— Factors leading to resilience include: optimism, social support from friends and family, physical fitness, psychological flexibility, meaning and purpose and continuing to develop and grow

— By speaking to people who have lived to the age of a hundred, we have discovered that resilience may be key to living long lives

— Our centenarians showed determination to cope with whatever life throws at them and to push worry away, psychological flexibility in the face of change, the art of positively framing what could be construed in negative terms and the ability to see and take opportunities for continuing growth and development

— If you are moderately depressed and have taken yourself through behavioural activation, then you can use Padesky and Mooney's technique of building up a personal resilience model. Padesky and Mooney's personal resilience model has four stages: search, construct, apply and practice

— Otherwise, you can use Hutnik's Resilience Awareness Instrument to increase your resilience. This involves plotting difficult life events and positive achievements, then looking for how you coped and/or how you overcame obstacles on your course and then arriving at your resilience principles derived from your own life. The final step is to apply your resilience principles to the current 'knocking-down' situation

- The goal of resilience training is not to achieve a desired outcome so much as practicing habits that enable us to keep standing in the face of potentially 'knocking-down' events

REFERENCES

1. American Psychological Association, *The Road to Resilience*, 2002. http://www.apa.org/helpcenter/road-resilience.aspx.

2. A.B. Amstadter, *J. Myers,* and K.S. Kendler, 'Psychiatric Resilience: Longitudinal Twin Study', *British Journal of Psychiatry*, 2014.

3. A.T. Beck, A.J. Rush, B.F. Shaw, and G. Emery, *Cognitive Therapy of Depression*, New York: Guildford Press, 1979.

4. G.A. Bonanno, 'Loss, Trauma and Human Resilience: Have We Underestimated the Human Capacity to Thrive After Extremely Aversive Events?', *American Psychologist*, 59(1):20–28, 2004.

5. K.M. Connor, and J.R.T. Davidson, 'Development of a New Resilience Scale: The Connor-Davidson Resilience Scale (CD-RISC)', *Depression and Anxiety*, 18:76–82, 2003.

6. M. Domhardt, A. Münzer, J. Fegert, and L. Goldbeck, Resilience in 'Survivors of Child Sexual Abuse: A Review of the Literature', *Trauma, Violence & Abuse*, Published online before print, doi:10.1177/1524838014557288 10 November 2014.

7. S.C. Hayes, J.B. Luoma, F.W. Bond, A. Masuda, and J. Lillis, 'Acceptance and Commitment Therapy: Model, Processes and Outcomes', Behaviour Research and Therapy, 44(1):1–25, 2006.

8. N. Hutnik, P. Smith, and T. Koch, 'What Does It Feel Like to Be 100? Socio-Emotional Aspects of Well-Being in the Stories of 16 Centenarians Living in the United Kingdom', Aging Mental Health, 16(7):811–818, 2012.

9. N. Hutnik, P. Smith, and T. Koch 'Using a Cognitive Behavioural Lens to Look at Resilience in the Stories of Centenarians in the UK', *Nursing Open*, doi: 10.1002/nop2.44.

10. U. Lau, and A. van Niekerk, 'Restorying the Self: An Exploration of Young Burn Survivors' Narratives of Resilience', *Qualitative Health Research*,

21(9):1165–1181, 2011, doi: 10.1177/1049732311405686, Epub 13 April 2011.

11. A.S. Masten, 'Ordinary Magic: Resilience Processes in Development', *American Psychologist*, 56:227–238, 2001.

12. A.S. Masten, J.J. Cutuli, J.E. Herbers, and M.G. Reed, 'Resilience in Development', C.R. Snyder and S.J. Lopez (edited by), *Oxford Handbook of Positive Psychology*, 2nd ed., 117–131, New York: Oxford University Press, 2009.

13. M. Neenan, *Developing Resilience: A Cognitive-Behavioural Approach*, London: Routledge, 2009.

14. F.H. Norris, and L.B. Sloane, 'The Epidemiology of Trauma and PTSD', M.J. Friedman, T.M. Keane, and P.A. Resick (edited by), *Handbook of PTSD*, 78–98, New York: Guilford Press, 2007.

15. R. Owen, *Facing the Storm: Using CBT, Mindfulness and Acceptance to Build Resilience When Your World Is Falling Apart*, Hove: Routledge, 2011.

16. C.A. Padesky, and K.A. Mooney, 'Strengths-Based Cognitive-Behavioural Therapy: A Four-Step Model to Build Resilience', *Clinical Psychology & Psychotherapy*, 19(4):283–90, 2012. http://padesky.com/clinical-corner/publications.

17. D. Robertson, *Build Your Resilience: How to Survive and Thrive in Any Situation*, London: Hodder Education, 2012.

18. B.W. Smith, J. Dalen, K. Wiggins, E. Tooley, P. Christopher, and J. Bernard, 'The Brief Resilience Scale: Assessing the Ability to Bounce Back', *International Journal of Behavioral Medicine*, 15(3):194–200, 2008.

19. S. Southwick, and D. Charney, *Resilience: The Science of Mastering Life's Greatest Challenges*, New York: Cambridge University Press, 2012.

20. T. Waaktaar, and T. Svenn, 'Genetic and Environmental Causes of Variation in Trait Resilience in Young People', *Behavior Genetics*, 42(3):366–377, 2012.

21. S. Wollin, 'Resilience in Young People', In F. Walsh (edited by), *Spiritual Resources in Family Therapy*, 2nd ed., New York: The Guilford Press, 2009.

9

Springing Forward – Flourishing

'Flourishing is everyone's birthright.'

– Steve Jurvetson

'Reaching beyond where you are is really important.'

– Martin Seligman

In this chapter:

- What is flourishing?
- Learned helplessness and learned optimism
- Strengths
- What makes us flourish?
  - P- Positive emotion
  - E- Engagement
  - R- Relationships
  - M- Meaning
  - A- Accomplishment

- Flourishing in old age
- Integrating death: The ultimate letting go
- Hutnik's model of resilience and flourishing

WHAT IS FLOURISHING?

When I look outside my bedroom window I see a riot of pink, purple, red and yellow flowers. My neighbour's plants flourish under her hard work and tender loving care. Each bloom is lush, fecund and stunningly beautiful. But this hasn't happened by accident or chance. After having cleared the soil of sticks and stones and the remnants of builder's rubble, Fredrika has conditioned the soil to make it fertile, putting alkaline compost here and acidic compost there. Then she has chosen the plants carefully to grow where they are best suited to the patterns of sun and shade.

I am using Fredrika's garden as a metaphor for human flourishing. This metaphor is not original to me. Martin Seligman, the author of the book *Flourish,* first used it to broaden the task of psychotherapy. Once we have cleared away the rubble of depression and anxiety and restored the soil to good health and resilience, how then are we to bring ourselves to the place where we are flourishing, like Fredrika's flowers?

When I looked up the word 'flourish' in an online thesaurus, this is what I found: 'to flourish is to abound.'

It is a verb and means to exist in abundance

- Be alive with
- Be all over the place
- Be knee deep in
- Be plentiful
- Flow
- Overflow
- Proliferate

- Swell
- Teem
- Thrive

So this chapter is all about how you can bring your life into a state of fullness and abundance.

To date, psychology has focused almost exclusively on removing the disabling conditions of life, on clearing away the sticks and stones of depression and anxiety. The assumption was that happiness was the absence of these difficult moods. But this is far from the truth. Yes, in order to flourish we need to clear away the sticks and stones, but we need to do more, so much more. We need to create the conditions that enable us to spring forward and grasp life in all its goodness, to flourish. This has been the reasoning behind the growth of a new science called positive psychology (Seligman, 2011).

LEARNED HELPLESSNESS AND LEARNED OPTIMISM

Martin Seligman, the founder of positive psychology, began his work as an experimental psychologist looking at the responses of dogs to electric shock. Long ago and before animal rights came into existence, he trained dogs to avoid receiving an electric shock by jumping over a barrier when they saw a light come on. This was the sequence of learning.

Phase 1:

Red light ———→ Dog Jumps ———→ Avoids shock

Since the shock was so painful, the dogs in the experiment all learnt to avoid the shock when they saw the red light come on.

In the second part of the experiment, the dogs jumped when they saw the red light in the hope of escaping the shock on the first side and jumping to safety on the second side. But then they were given shock on the second side as well, so they jumped back to the first side, where they received yet another shock, then to the second side where they still received a shock and so it went on, until they gave up trying to escape, curled up in a ball and looked depressed.

Phase 2:

Red light ———→ Dog jumps ———→ Receives shock on the second side as well ———→ Jumps back to the first side ———→ Receives shock there too ———→ Repeats the same sequence hoping to escape shock ———→ Discovers that there is no escape ———→ Curls up in a ball looking depressed

Seligman termed this curling up behaviour 'learned helplessness' and it became the big explanation for depression in human beings.

Some of us suffer life events similar to that of the dogs who could not avoid the shock. Learned helplessness is very typical of depression because people believe that there is nothing they can do to escape shock, trauma and a negative experience. The tsunami in Sri Lanka and southern India in 2004 meant that many people lost their homes and families. Some of us live in extended families in which the mother-in-law is cruel to the daughter-in-law. People suffer rape and other acts of violence across India, as recent cases in the news have highlighted. Prejudice and selfishness perpetuate class-based injustices such as when I see families walk into a restaurant to have a lavish feast and the domestic help comes in holding the baby and is not given any dinner. Religious violence leads to great suffering all across the world. For example, anti-Muslim, anti-Hindu, anti-Christian and anti-Sikh violence has resulted in many people being killed, maimed and displaced. Muslims in particular have been targets of violence, for example, the events in Gujarat in 2002. They have equally perpetuated violence in the world. At the time of writing this, violence in Kashmir on the border between India and Pakistan has been in the news again.

All of the above represents the big knocking downs that I talked of earlier. But there are small ones that also leave us damaged. You may be living in a family where your father is dominant, controlling, critical and contemptuous of you. Or your partner is so jealous that she gives you no freedom to form friendships with other women. Or you have an autistic child and the burden of care that you carry for that child seems heavy and endless. Or your partner has got you into so much debt that you know neither of you can earn enough in a lifetime to pay it off. You may argue (and with justification) that what I have termed 'small' is not so small after all!

In such cases, it is likely that many people will become depressed and will exhibit the human equivalent of learned helplessness. People with depression share a common attitude: 'There is nothing I can do to get out of this situation, so what is the point?'

Seligman became very famous for the learned helplessness experiments on dogs. But gradually something new dawned on him. This was the fact that about one third of the dogs in the second phase of the experiment never gave up, they kept jumping back and forth, they never curled up into a ball and looked depressed, they never gave up the hope of escaping the shock. Soon Seligman began to study the reasons for why some dogs were 'optimistic' despite the odds.

Seligman's work on learned optimism is now well known. The main thrust of this work is that optimism can be taught. This is good news for all of us.

Learning to be optimistic has well known effects on our health. We are at less risk of developing cardiovascular disease or cancer if we have an optimistic thinking style (Seligman, 2011). This is documented in study after study. Pessimists are more likely to die earlier than optimists and have a greater risk of cardiovascular disease. This trend is found to be true for infectious diseases as well. People with high positive emotions are less likely to get the common cold. While pessimists believe they are helpless to change, optimists take action to have healthier lifestyles. Also having good social support systems in place prevents early death.

Learned optimism is one of the key strengths that people can develop in order to flourish in life.

STRENGTHS

In order to flourish we need to be aware of and build upon our strengths. When we are operating from within one of our strengths, there will be changes in our body posture, facial expressions, eye movements, hand gestures and tone of voice. All of these will point to the fact that we are feeling confident about whatever it is that we are engaged in. A person who knows she is good at communicating, for example, will naturally be relaxed and engaging when she is talking to a group of people. With just eye contact she will be able to draw people into the group and hold their attention. She will not be self-conscious about the way she is standing or sitting and her words will flow smoothly and easily and will have the impact that they were intended to have.

Some psychological research has shown that being aware of our strengths is associated with higher levels of happiness and lower rates of depression and if you use your strengths consciously you become happier (Seligman et al., 2005). Higher levels of strengths such as optimism, forgiveness and gratitude are associated with lower levels of social anxiety among people in combat situations (Kashdan et al., 2006). This can even have an impact on your physical health. Strengths such as bravery, kindness and humour are associated with recovery from illness (Peterson, Park and Seligman, 2006). Additionally, psychotherapy that uses a strengths-based focus was found to be better than Treatment As Usual or Treatment with Anti-Depressant Medication (Seligman, Rashid and Parks, 2006).

It is really important that we discover our strengths. In Seligman's own words, 'The belief that we can rely on shortcuts to happiness, joy, rapture, comfort, and ecstasy, rather than be entitled to these feelings by the exercise of personal strengths and virtues, leads to legions of people who, in the middle of great wealth, are starving spiritually.' In the previous chapter on resilience we looked at two ways of uncovering our strengths.

But we are not trained to look for them. We may be even embarrassed to own them. Since we do not often talk about our strengths, they are hidden to our eyes. When asked about what our strengths are, we often come up with a list of abstractions: 'I am kind, I am warm, I am gentle, I am intelligent.' For the purposes of becoming more robust in life, we need to become much more specific about our strengths.

According to Biswas-Diener (2010) there are three simple questions we can ask ourselves to help us identify our strengths:

1. From your past, what are you most proud of?
   Your educational achievement? Your long marriage? Your ability to stay slim when all your friends have put on loads of weight?
   Your strengths: ability to absorb information, perseverance and self-discipline

2. What energizes you in the present?
   The book you are writing? The course you are completing? The marathon that you are training for?
   Your strengths: your academic skills, your physical abilities

3. What are you looking forward to in the near future, i.e., the coming weekend or the coming month?
   Watching a movie with a friend? Joining a meditation group? Beginning singing lessons? Trying out the clothes that you were given for Diwali?
   Your strengths: a passion for a creative outlet and companionship

The third question is particularly potent in identifying your strengths.

Let us look at Riya's strengths in the following example:

Riya had planned to go on holiday with her dear friend Ishita, who suffers from a type of OCD where she constantly avoids the number 3 or multiples of 3. Ishita is a creative artist who plays the piano and teaches music to young children, and is not terribly well off because of her chosen vocation. She has been looking for a job in a school but has not been able to land one in several years because she will not travel on buses with the number 3 on them. Riya offered to organize everything related to finding accommodation for the two of them and asked Ishita to take care of the flights. Riya found and booked the accommodation, Ishita found the cheapest flights on the Internet. Riya took out her passport and was about to give Ishita her passport number but Ishita refused to do anything further, telling Riya that her OCD was the issue. Riya, who at that point was very tired from meeting deadlines at work, felt impatient and upset. She asked Ishita whether she could get her brother to book the flights. Ishita refused. Since it was nearing midnight Riya told Ishita that they would revisit the issue the next day. Next evening, Ishita told Riya that she had suddenly been offered a job and therefore could not go on holiday with her. Riya knew how important getting a job was for Ishita and told her how glad she was that something had finally come her way. Ishita apologized for not being able to go on holiday with Riya and thanked her for understanding. Riya then rang up all of her friends, none of whom were available at such short notice to come on holiday with her. She contacted her two nieces and both agreed without any coercion or pressure to go on holiday with their mum. The three of them had a wonderful time and came back energized, relaxed and happy.

Can you identify the strengths that Riya showed? Before you read on, try to think of at least three strengths.

1. _____

2. _____

3. _____

Here are some of Riya's strengths:

- Ability to plan: Riya showed great planning throughout. She organized the accommodation and then when things went wrong, she sensibly altered her plans to go with her daughters
- Ability to delegate tasks: Riya did not obsess over keeping control and doing all the planning herself, even though it was one of her strengths. Riya asked her friend Ishita to book the flights, easing her own workload and giving Ishita a part in the planning

- Ability to be inclusive of friends who have mental health issues: not everyone finds it easy to stay friends with people who have conditions such as OCD. Riya had clearly taken the time to understand Ishita's OCD and make allowances for it while still enjoying Ishita's company enough to want to go on holiday with her
- Ability to be gracious when her friend told her about her job offer: many people would feel bitter and resentful. Riya might have felt a little annoyed but she was able to join in with Ishita's happiness at getting the job rather than snap at her
- Ability to problem-solve and be resilient: in the face of the fact that she had already booked the accommodation, Riya was able to quickly think about what to do and make the situation a success rather than moping around and complaining that she had been let down
- Ability to let go of the original plan of spending time with her friend and enjoy the time with her daughters: Riya was flexible in her thoughts and actions in order to alter the plan. Then she was able to actively enjoy the changed situation

Being able to ferret out and identify our hidden strengths is the key to flourishing.

Seligman and his colleagues have developed a questionnaire that will help you identify your own particular strengths in certain domains. This is available at www.authentichappiness.org. Below is a list of signature strengths. How many of them are characteristic of you? I encourage you to do the online questionnaire so that you are aware of where your strengths lie and what your under-developed strengths might be. However, for now read through the list and think of which might apply to you.

- Curiosity/interest in the world
- Love of learning
- Judgement/critical thinking/open-mindedness
- Ingenuity/originality/practical intelligence/street smarts

- Social intelligence/personal intelligence/emotional intelligence
- Perspective
- Valour and bravery
- Perseverance/industry/diligence
- Integrity/genuineness/honesty
- Kindness and generosity
- Loving others and allowing yourself to be loved
- Citizenship/duty/teamwork/loyalty
- Fairness and equity
- Leadership
- Self-control
- Prudence/discretion/caution
- Humility and modesty
- Appreciation of beauty and excellence
- Gratitude
- Hope/optimism/future-mindedness
- Spirituality/sense of purpose/faith/religiousness
- Forgiveness and mercy
- Playfulness and humour
- Grit
- Zest/passion/enthusiasm

Some people like Biswas-Diener (2010) believe that strengths are a given and that it is best to concentrate on the strengths one already has rather than develop the ones that are not so well developed. However, Seligman and his colleagues believe it is possible to teach people to acquire signature strengths. For example, we can learn to become optimistic about ourselves, the world and our future.

TRAINING OURSELVES TO BECOME OPTIMISTIC

People who have developed a pessimistic way of looking at the world can be trained to start seeing it in more optimistic terms. We have already looked at how to do this in Chapter 3 but I will give a brief summary here. We can train ourselves to dispute or battle with our NATs and come up with alternate, more helpful and balanced ways of thinking and this often leads to us feeling more energized and empowered to deal with situations. The thought record is a powerful tool enabling this process to happen quickly and systematically. If you have skipped Chapter 4, I encourage you to go back and acquire the skills of cognitive restructuring. You will find yourself much happier as a result of battling with your catastrophic thinking, fortune telling or mind reading. You will learn about the ABCDE of resilience and flourishing. (A=antecedents or Triggers, B=your beliefs about A, C=the consequences of your beliefs about A in terms of feelings and/ or behaviours, D=disputation, E=energizing). Thus, slowly but surely you can teach yourself to become optimistic, to regularly see the glass as half full rather than half empty.

Other character strengths can be taught too. For example, children can be taught to develop grit by being rewarded by their teachers and parents every time they show grit in difficult situations. Grit is the ability to be passionate about and to persevere towards very long term goals (Duckworth, 2014). When they fail, people who show grit see failure as an opportunity to learn to do something differently. They do not interpret it pessimistically or take it personally, seeing themselves as worthless or inadequate. They have a 'growth' mindset and are able to exert the self-control required to delay immediate gratification for a long-term reward.

WHAT MAKES US FLOURISH?

Martin Seligman has done considerable work on what makes us flourish. He uses the acronym PERMA to help us remember the five key elements of flourishing.

P: Positive emotion
E: Engagement
R: Relationships

M: Meaning
A: Accomplishment

Research conducted in India has found Seligman's PERMA theory to apply here as well. For example, Srivastava (2008) found that Indian school children cited being in the company of family and friends (relationships) and the successful completion of tasks and studies (accomplishments) as their main sources of happiness.

P – POSITIVE EMOTION

People who are flourishing experience joy, happiness and laughter. We can produce positive emotion in our lives by thinking of a few things we can do in a day to induce positive emotion and this can make a big difference to our overall mood. We might choose to watch a comedy programme rather than a tense drama or plan to spend time expressing our love to our children or our partner. Positive emotion increases productivity and enhances our ability to problem-solve. Positive emotion has also been found to increase longevity. Deborah Danner and her colleagues (Danner et al., 2001) studied Catholic nuns in the US. They read letters that the nuns had written when they entered the order in their early twenties and then looked at data on how long the nuns had lived. They found a very strong link between the degree of positive emotion expressed in the letters the nuns had written at an early age and their longevity. The happier nuns lived longer. This is a particularly interesting study because the nuns lived similar lifestyles: none had married, none smoked or drank alcohol to excess and all worked in similar professions.

Just the simple act of laughing while in a group with other people creates positive emotion. Dr Madan Kataria has become famous for his laughter yoga groups, which started in a local park in Mumbai and have now spread all over the world. Voluntary laughter, i.e., when you make yourself laugh on purpose, gives your body and mind the same benefits as spontaneous laughter and can also become genuine laughter.

Researchers from Oxford University found that laughter, both genuine and forced, elevates pain thresholds so that the subjective feeling of pain is reduced (Dunbar et al., 2012).

Positive psychology has developed many exercises that increase levels of positive emotion. One is the Three Blessings exercise (Seligman, 2011).

Exercise 9.1: Three Blessings

Before you go to bed tonight, take ten minutes to write down three good things that happened today. They can be small things like, 'I had a delicious dinner' or big things like 'I got my results today and I got a first division.'

Next to each of those blessings, write why they happened. For the dinner, you might write 'Because my wife is a fantastic cook.' For the results example, you might write 'Because I worked hard and also I am blessed with intelligence.'

Repeat the exercise two to three times in a week and you will feel happier.

_____

_____

_____

_____

_____

_____

_____

_____

_____

I tried a similar exercise at a time in my life when I was feeling miserable. I actually found it hard to single out only three blessings, so I decided to up the challenge for myself and write down five to ten things. The impact on my mood while I was doing this was incredible and when I was having a difficult time during the day, I thought back to my blessings and it made me smile.

Seligman has another exercise to enhance your mood. This is called the Gratitude Visit (Seligman, 2011). It requires a bit of courage!

Exercise 9.2: The Gratitude Visit

Bring to mind somebody still alive who did something important for you. It could be a relative, a teacher, a former or current work colleague, a friend or anybody else who has changed your life for the better. This person has to be somebody who you could meet face-to-face next week. Think of that person and write them a letter to thank them for what they did for you. Make sure that letter specifies exactly what the person did and explains the precise effect that had on your life. Tell the person you are writing to about how your life is different because of their impact in it.

After you have written the letter, call the person and tell them you want to visit them. Be vague about the purpose of the visit. When you see them, read out the whole letter to them. If they interrupt you, tell them that you really want to finish reading it out. Afterwards talk to them about the contents of the letter, explaining to them how you really feel about them.

These exercises will increase the amount of positive emotion that you experience. You will need to keep practicing the exercises and finding opportunities to laugh and be joyful to keep feeling positive. Moods naturally fluctuate over time and psychologists have found that each of us has a 'set-point' for happiness. This means that although good and bad things happen to us, in time each person will drift back to their default level of happiness. For the optimists amongst us, this is a high level of happiness. For others, this is a low level of happiness. While this set-point was once thought to be genetically determined, we now know that we can learn to change our set-point. We need to keep generating positive emotion in order to bring our natural 'set-points' up.

If positive emotion was the only important element of flourishing, this would be bad news for those of us who are easily discouraged or depressed. However, philosophers, theologians and psychologists have, for many years, argued that there is more to life than just positive emotion. In fact, we cannot always feel positive emotion. This links strongly back to ACT (see Chapter 7). Our determination to work towards our most deeply held values can give our lives meaning even when we experience difficult emotions.

E – Engagement

The second component of PERMA is engagement. It refers to our level of interest and involvement in the world. It points to our openness to new experiences and our eagerness to learn new things. People who show engagement seem to be engaged in a pathway of lifelong learning and are energized by the new things that come their way. They have strong ties with other people and to the environment in which they live. It seems they really throw themselves into whatever they do and enjoy what they do to the utmost, even if the tasks are tedious or challenging. They seldom find life boring and seem to be in control of their lives and are confident in their ability to take what comes their way because they have developed a confidence in their ability to solve problems and to cope. Thus, they are able to manage anxiety well because they do not overestimate danger and have a keenly developed sense of their own abilities to live life well.

One way of upping the level of engagement in your life is to find a 'flow' activity that you are passionate about (Csikzentmihalyi, 1990). You experience a state of flow when you are so completely engaged in what you are doing that you lose your sense of time. Your concentration is intense as you bring all your skills to bear upon a particular task. As Seligman points out, 'You go into flow when your highest strengths are deployed to meet the highest challenges that come your way.' (Seligman, 2011) When you are in a state of flow, you feel elated as if you are on a high.

For different people, this state is reached during different activities. People could achieve flow while painting, dancing, doing research, having good conversations, jogging, skiing, playing bridge, scrabble or making music or any number of different activities. When people are in a state of flow, they lose the awareness of the hours passing by and what 'flows' out of them is their best performance. Thus, a surgeon within a state of flow may not recognize that eight hours have passed while she/he was performing a complicated operation. Time seems to pass by much faster; hours pass as if they were minutes. But occasionally the opposite happens. Time seems to stand still and is expanded and extended such that performance reaches its peak like when doing a complicated dance move. It is suffice to say that when in a state of flow, the experience of time seems to have little to do with the progression of the clocks.

Csikzentmihalyi (1990) describes a number of characteristics of flow. The characteristics that seem most important to me are:

- Intense concentration in the flow activity
- A loss of awareness of the self
- A complete disregard for the passage of time

Csikzentmihalyi (1990) has also pointed out that to be in flow we need to undertake activities that are just challenging enough to keep us on our toes. If we choose activities that are too challenging in relation to our current level of skill, we will become nervous and anxious and might even give up on the activity. On the other hand, activities that are not challenging at all because we are very skilled at them will just bore us.

In order to be in a state of flow when undertaking these activities, we need to make sure we are in the flow channel.

Figure 9.1 (adapted from Csikzentmihalyi, 1990) demonstrates how matching our skills to the level of challenge in a task will allow us to achieve flow.

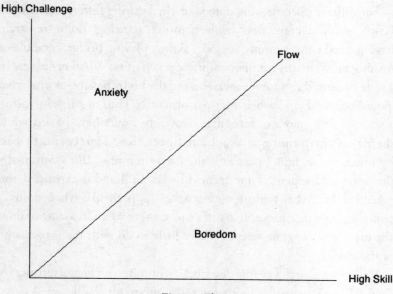

Fig 9.1: Flow

Learning to drive a car is tense and difficult at first. There is so much noise, so many cars doing unpredictable things and so many signs to read all at once. The level of challenge is high and your skills are low. This means you will experience anxiety. But once you have acquired and practiced the skill many times and become adept at it, you are then likely to enter the boredom quadrant. You find yourself in a state of flow when your skills are in proportion to the challenges that you face. If you have been driving confidently on Delhi roads for many years but are then offered the opportunity to enter a race through the foothills of the Himalayas, it may be that your skills are not commensurate with the challenges presented and you may suffer extreme anxiety. Keeping yourself in flow then becomes the challenge in itself because you must know when to accept new opportunities that are offered and when to refuse them.

Exercise 9.3:

1. What are the activities I would engage in that used to bring me into a state of flow?

_____

_____

_____

2. What are some new flow activities that I can develop for myself?

_____

_____

_____

3. What action can I take to increase the level of flow in my life?

_____

_____

_____

R – RELATIONSHIPS

We flourish when we have a set of positive relationships and are usually at our most joyful when we are with other people. Think of the last time you had a guffaw, or what I call a belly laugh. Almost always these situations occur in the context of other people. According to Cacioppo (2008), loneliness is such a disabling condition that we now believe 'that the pursuit of relationships is a rock bottom fundamental to human well-being'. In order to flourish we need to value our relationships and nourish them. One way of doing that is to do little acts of kindness for those we love.

My dear friend Dave Andrews has a song, '*Kindness is my religion...*' (http://www.daveandrews.com.au/songs/01_kindness.mp3). It is a good one to learn and to sing to yourself. The exercise below is one that Martin Seligman suggests is a real mood lifter (Seligman, 2011).

Exercise 9.4:

Find one act of kindness that you can do for a loved one and just do it. Notice what happens to your relationship and to your mood.

The language we use in our relationships is a very important indicator of the level of flourishing. Fredrickson and Losada (2005) found that the ratio of positive to negative statements made in relationships and organizations determined whether they flourished or languished. In relationships that flourished, a ratio of three positive statements for every negative statement was found. John Gottman, the Western expert on marriage and divorce, found that this ratio needs to be even higher in marriages (Buehlman, Gottman and Katz, 1992). They transcribed couples' conversations and rated them for the frequency of positive and negative statements: their ratio was 5:1. In a marriage a 3:1 ratio of positive to negative means that you are headed for divorce! Although the exact mathematics of this was later questioned, the principle behind it still holds: positive affirmation of others leads to positive relationships. However, excessive positivity is perceived as insincerity, so we can't use these ratios as precise measures. We need to trust our Third Eye here.

Padesky (2012, personal communication) likens couple relationships to a bank account. When couples are in trouble it is likely that they have spent too much without replacing it and without replenishing the bank account. The caring days procedure (adapted from Stuart, 2004) is a technique to help couples replenish their couple emotional bank account. An example follows.

Jaswinder asked his wife Jasmeet what she would like him to do as a means of showing he cared for her. Together, they came up with the following list:

- *Ask how I spent the day*
- *Offer to take care of the kids for a whole day*
- *Look at our bank account together to see how we can economize*
- *Buy me a present*
- *Offer to read rough drafts of the reports that I have to present, make comments and give suggestions for improvement*
- *Call the parents-in-law just to say hi*

Then Jasmeet asked Jaswinder what she could do to show him she cared. Again, they made a list:

- *Every now and then, call me up at work just to see how I am*
- *Cook me my favourite dessert*
- *Come out to dinner with me and get a babysitter to look after the kids for a night*
- *Spend a whole day once a month with me and the kids and leave the emails and your mobile phone at home*
- *Make me tea*
- *Tell me how you are really feeling*

Jaswinder and Jasmeet looked at the criteria for their lists and made charts as shown. The original caring-days procedure asks both to come up with a total list of at least eighteen items. They tried to do each of them once a day and if this was not possible, then at least once a week. When they noticed their partner had done one of the items on the list, they wrote the date underneath that entry on the list. They put the chart on the fridge so they could see what they perceived they were receiving in the form of care from their partner.

Jaswinder's Chart (Items generated by Jasmeet: how I want to be cared for)	Jaswinder's Dates	Jasmeet's Chart (Items generated by Jaswinder: how I want to be cared for)	Jasmeet's Dates
Ask how Jasmeet spent the day	21/6, 22/6, 26/6, 30/6, 2/7, 4/7	Every now and then, call me up (Jaswinder) at work just to see how I am	21/6, 30/6, 5/7
Offer, without Jasmeet asking, to take care of the kids for a whole day	25/6, 1/7	Cook me (Jaswinder) my favourite dessert	4/7
Buy Jasmeet a present	5/7, 15/7, 22/7	Spend a whole day once a month with me (Jaswinder) and the kids and leave the emails and the mobile phone at home	22/6, 23/7
Offer to read rough drafts of the reports that Jasmeet has to present and make comments and give suggestions for improvement	21/6, 30/6, 6/7, 13/7, 20/7	Make me (Jaswinder) tea	2/7, 3/7, 4/7, 12/7, 20/7
Call Jasmeet's parents and say hi	23/6, 30/6, 7/7, 13/7, 22/7	Tell me (Jaswinder) how you are really feeling	21/6, 30/6, 6/7, 13/7, 20/7

At the end of a month of doing the things they had asked for as symbols of care, both were feeling much better about their relationship.

Exercise 9.5: The Caring Days Exercise (Adapted)

Get your partner/spouse to do the following exercise with you. Each one ask the other, 'How would you like me to express my care for you?' Make a list of five things.

For this exercise to work, the lists have to fulfil the following criteria:

- Items must be positive (for example, 'stop shouting' does not qualify because it is not a positive action)
- Items must be specific ('be good to me' does not qualify because it does not tell the other person how being good would look)
- Ideally, items must be small behaviours that can be done at least once a week
- Finally, items must not have been the subject of recent sharp conflict. (In the example below, if Jaswinder and Jasmeet regularly quarrel about finances, then the item referring to looking at their bank account together would not qualify as a valid caring-days item)

Keep a note of the dates on which you received the care you asked for.

Partner 1	Partner 1 Dates	Partner 2	Partner 2 Dates

Sometimes couples become so conflicted in their relationship that it is best while doing the caring-days technique to 'act as if' you care about the other person. This technique often jump-starts a floundering relationship and gets it back on track so that deeper couples work can be done thereafter.

Positive psychology is interested in turning good relationships into excellent ones (Seligman, 2011). And this is true not just of couple relationships but parent-child relationships, boss-employee relationships and the relationships between friends. The manner in which we respond to good news that the significant people in our lives tell us about is crucial in whether our relationships will flourish or flounder. We can look at how we respond on two axes placed at right angles to each other. The first dimension refers to how active or passive we are in our response. The second dimension refers to how constructive or destructive we are in our response. Thus, there are four ways in which people typically respond to others' reports of success.

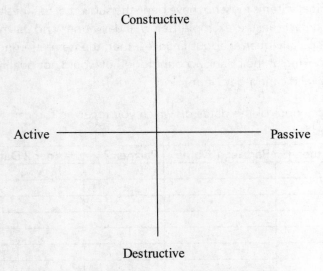

Fig. 9.2 Ways of Responding to a Report of Success

Jasmeet comes home from work one day and tells Jaswinder that her boss really liked the report she wrote. Jaswinder now has a choice. He can respond in one of four ways, only one of which will enable their relationship to flourish.

Response 1 Jaswinder: Oh that's nice.

And he continues to read his newspaper. This is a passive constructive response.

Response 2 Jaswinder: Mmm … I've had a bad day today.

This is a passive destructive response. It does not offer any feedback to Jasmeet and it turns the attention away from her to himself.

Response 3 Jaswinder: Well, I would think so! After all the feedback that I have given you on it!

This is an active destructive response. It diminishes Jasmeet's role in creating the report and is actively hostile and contemptuous.

Response 4 Wow! That's great! I know you worked really hard on it and it was so important to you. What did she say?

This is an active constructive response, affirming the other person and encouraging more communication and dialogue.

In order for our relationships to flourish we need to teach ourselves to respond in an active constructive way to our partner's success and good news. This takes practice and requires us to be mindfully present for our partner, forsaking the activities we might be involved in at the time.

The following exercise will help you get familiar with each of the four styles of response. Put yourself in the situation described in the first column, then think of the language you would use if you were responding in each of the four styles. Write this down in the third column.

Exercise 9.6: Practicing Active Constructive Responding

Situation	Response Type	Response (In this column think of all four response types and write them down so that you know the difference)
Your four-year-old child has come home with a picture she/he has drawn that does not make much sense to you	Passive constructive: Passive destructive: Active destructive: Active constructive:	Oh how nice! Come on now, it is time for your dinner That is not how a tree should look and you have used the wrong colour for the sky. Wow! It looks like you have put a lot of thought into this. Come and tell me more about this and what it is
Your partner is wearing a new outfit	Passive constructive: Passive destructive: Active destructive: Active constructive:	

Your boss is excited about a new development that she has initiated	Passive constructive: Passive destructive: Active destructive: Active constructive:
Your colleague tells you of a compliment that her new boyfriend gave her	Passive constructive: Passive destructive: Active destructive: Active constructive:
Your best friend is really pleased at the success of an event that she had organized for her company	Passive constructive: Passive destructive: Active destructive: Active constructive:

You may find that one of the other three categories is your most characteristic style of responding. It takes some real hard work to think of active constructive ways to respond to those who are near and dear to you.

In order to flourish, we need to learn to let go of the pain and resentment that we have suffered at the hands of other people who are significant to us. Increasingly, psychologists are looking at how forgiveness increases our well-being. Yes, people have done bad things to us but instead of adopting the 'victim' position, we enhance flourishing in our lives by adopting a position of forgiveness.

> 'What you are doing with forgiveness is changing your egoist involvement in your own painful story – which too often becomes your ticket to sympathy and sometimes your very identity.'
>
> (Rohr, 2013, Pg. 31)

We only hurt ourselves when we hold on to resentment, blame and anger. Forgiveness is not easy. Below is an exercise for you to develop the habit of forgiveness.

Exercise 9.7: Giving Forgiveness

Think of a situation in which you were really wronged by someone. Allow yourself to feel the pain of that situation in your body. Let this memory become visceral, otherwise your forgiveness will only be cerebral. Enter into a state of mindful meditation, holding this person in mind. As you focus on your in-breath, breathe in peace and loving kindness as you focus on your out-breath, breathe out forgiveness towards this person. Tell them during your mindfulness meditation that you forgive them for hurting you. Allow yourself to cry if you need to. Forgiveness is so painful that tears often accompany it. Now let the situation go, let the pain go. Put it behind you.

In addition to us forgiving those who have hurt us, it is important to become aware of how we have hurt other people. This is much more difficult because we are often blind to how we have impacted others. These are our blind spots. Here is an exercise that might help you uncover some of your blind spots.

Exercise 9.8: Asking for Forgiveness

Think of your most difficult relationship.
Name the person _____

What do you contribute to damaging the relationship? What have you heard them tell you about how you hurt them?
    Are you over-controlling, under-responsive, lazy, unapologetic, moody, worried, Machiavellian, indecisive, unfaithful, over-critical, contemptuous, bullying, bad-tempered?
    Own your part in why the relationship is difficult. Perhaps it is time to speak about this to the other person.
Can you bring yourself to approach them and ask for forgiveness?

_____

_____

_____

_____

_____

_____

_____

_____

Alcoholics Anonymous uses the principle of giving and asking for forgiveness as one of the fundamentals to be achieved in enabling de-addiction from substance misuse. In my opinion, the giving and receiving of forgiveness creates the soil in which we can flourish.

M – Meaning

When we are involved in something larger than ourselves, our lives have meaning. This may be politics, God, writing, philanthropy, social issues or myriad other reasons that people find to imbue their lives with meaning. It is no coincidence that the people who find a cause greater than themselves to live for are often the most resilient. This brings to mind Gandhi's commitment to civil rights and freedom, Mother Teresa's dedication to bringing God to people who are suffering, Malala Yousafzai who continues to fight for women's right to education, Muhammed Younus who developed the idea of microfinance and microcredit to enable poor entrepreneurs to start businesses and Kailash Satyarthi who continues to fight for children's rights to end child labour. The incredible thing about human diversity is that we all have different interests and talents which we can use to create meaning in our lives.

You might be wondering what the meaning of your life is. I came across an interesting exercise on a CD called the Happiness Training Plan (Johnstone and Akhtar, 2008), which is intended to get us in touch with what may be the larger meaning of our lives. I have mentioned this exercise in a previous chapter, but here it is again. As I take you through this exercise, I will use myself as an example.

First of all, ask yourself what your particular strengths are. In my case, I think one of my particular strengths is communication. I lecture, I write and other people tell me that I am good at both of these things. Next ask yourself what activity gets you into flow. What are you passionate about? For me, the activity that most enables me to lose my sense of time and get into a state that is near ecstasy is painting. Finally, what are the things you see in society that make you angry? Is it poverty? Domestic violence? The rape of the planet? Sexual abuse? Drugs? Difficult man-woman relationships? Gender inequality? Homophobia? The loneliness and isolation of older people? In my case, I feel particular empathy for the loneliness of older people among other things. Putting these three together I am led to the conclusion that perhaps I should paint about the loneliness and isolation of older people.

Exercise 9.9: Finding Meaning

Answer the following questions:

1. What are your strengths? It is a good idea to ask others what your strengths are since sometimes it can be hard to identify them yourself.
2. What is your flow activity?
3. What makes you angry?

Now put these together to come up with an activity that will bring meaning to your life.

_____

_____

_____

_____

_____

One of Parminder's most deeply held values was to feel connected with another person. She was not a party animal, she was often awkward, could never tell jokes and felt insecure in a group like she didn't belong. However, she had learnt that party going is worth it if she had at least one deep and meaningful conversation with someone at the party. She spent her time looking for this person and often came away unsatisfied. If for whatever reason she could not find such a person, she considered the evening to have been a waste. Thus, she looked for something that was meaningful to her in the moment.

One night Parminder was at a celebration dinner and ended up sitting next to a gay man. She embarked on an extremely absorbing conversation with him. He told her that he had been in a relationship with another man for over twenty-five years and that his partner was twenty-five years older than him. He was in his late forties and his partner was in his seventies. He told her about the prejudice he had experienced as a little boy, discovering his sexuality. Parminder found all of this extremely absorbing and came away feeling like she had made a deep connection with another human being and that this was intensely meaningful to her.

Meaning can thus be achieved in the moment as well as in the long term vision of our lives.

A – ACCOMPLISHMENT

Seligman has added accomplishment as a separate category in the process of flourishing. We have people who achieve a lot in their lives and contribute significantly to the development of human society; Van Gogh, Freud and others. In their time, their accomplishments did not produce much in the way of positive emotion, meaning or relationships. Indeed they were ostracized from the circles of accomplishment by what they wrote or painted. But because they allowed their creativity free rein, living about the need for social approval, their works have lasted and stood the test of time.

Accomplishment can be defined as the simple joy of exerting mastery over one's environment. It is found in activities that are pursued for their own sake even when it brings no positive emotion, no meaning or positive relationships. The closest antecedent to this concept is Allport's (1968) concept of functional autonomy. Our current motives are independent of our past. I may have taken up playing Scrabble in order to prove to my husband that I am every bit as intelligent as he is, but now I play just for the sake of it. It gives me a sense that I can master my environment. I continue to play, even if I lose many games in succession. This is because the act of striving to achieve mastery is in itself enough to drive activity. Thus, we may not be Van Gogh or Freud but we can fulfil our need for accomplishment in momentary things.

Even though I love painting, I have to admit to myself that I will never be a great painter. Nonetheless, I enrol in art and drawing classes just because I want more mastery in this area. My hand-eye co-ordination is poor. I cannot understand why my hand cannot execute what my eye sees, but I love the challenge of trying to teach it new tricks. Occasionally, enough to keep me going at it, it all works into a beautiful painting.

Exercise 9.10: My Accomplishments

What are my accomplishments? How have I demonstrated resilience in achieving these things? How do they increase the level of flourishing in my life? How can I further fulfil my need for accomplishment?

_____

_____

_____

_____

_____

_____

_____

In the previous chapter, we looked at identifying positive achievements in our lives. Buried within these positive achievements or accomplishments is the root of our resilience. We are determined to accomplish this particular task and are able to exhibit huge reserves of persistence and perseverance in overcoming the obstacles that come our way in doing so. Thus, we are resilient.

FLOURISHING IN OLD AGE

I am writing this section because I do not believe that we have thought through the issues of later life well enough. So many older people die lonely, depressed and anxious, unable to cope and all too ready to give up. The question that we as individuals and as communities need to ask is, 'How can we structure society and condition ourselves so that the final stage of life is the best one, the one when our garden is a riot of flourishing flowers?' Despite our failing bodies and minds (which we have mindfully accepted), I think it is possible to be at our peaks when we die, not in the very doldrums of life. Structures of society should be created to support old people to reach these pinnacles of life.

Exercise 9.11: Imagining the Future

In your imagination add forty years on to your age (if you are over seventy you might have to add fewer years). Imagine what will be happening in your life – how you will look, where you will live, how you will spend your day, what will happen to your relationships, etc. Identify three changes you could make both now or in the near future that will improve your quality of life in forty years.

_____

_____

_____

_____

_____

_____

_____

It is hard, in today's society, to imagine how Seligman's PERMA can apply to older people. Older people face inevitable physical and often mental decline. Physical bodies change with age, hearts, lungs and muscles grow older and less functional. Sexuality takes on different meaning. One cannot rely upon trusted responses such as orgasm or memory. Work is no longer a source of identity or satisfaction (Accomplishment). Friends and spouses die (Positive Relationships that one has relied on are no longer a source of sustenance) leaving us facing our own deaths and therefore, facing the ultimate meaning of our lives (Meaning). Play, getting into flow (Positive Emotion) and being active becomes difficult with pain, arthritis, increasing immobility and dependence upon others for transport etc., (Engagement). So it seems that we would be forgiven for thinking it is difficult to flourish in later life.

But the facts show us something different! Studies have found that life satisfaction rises, falls and then rises again across the lifespan, in a U-shaped curve. For example, the *English Longitudinal Study of Ageing* found that more than half of over 10,000 people over fifty years of age tracked since 2002, experienced increase in well-being with age. In America, the *US National Academy of Sciences Study* discovered that the overall enjoyment of life declined through early adulthood, beginning to rise again around age fifty and peaking in people's seventies and eighties. This is wonderful news! It means that some people have learnt to flourish in later life. So what have they done? How have they accomplished flourishing despite physical and mental decline, despite loss of role, relationships and accomplishment? Two factors remain: while life may rob us of all that we have accrued to ourselves in terms of accomplishment, relationships and engagement, it cannot steal from us our ability to experience positive emotion and our skill at imbuing our lives with meaning.

Throughout this book we have discovered the potency of thought in the creation of positive emotion. As we grow older, perhaps we learn to become more balanced, to be more 'even-thoughted', as one of my clients said to me. This is bound to produce contentment, well-being and joy. Also, we can continue to travel in the direction of our most cherished values, regardless of whether we can actually move or not. Thus, we do not lose meaning. Our most dear relationships may have vanished into eternity, physical ill health may mean it is difficult or impossible to engage in those activities that used to bring us flow, most people will have forgotten our accomplishments and achievements but what remains is the possibility of experiencing positive emotion and meaning. Even for people who suffer from dementia, positive emotion and meaning can remain if the surrounding structures and people are trained to support it (James, 2009). This, in my opinion, is the essence of flourishing in old age.

My colleagues and I are engaged in CBT research for resilience and flourishing in the oldest old. In our study of centenarians mentioned earlier, we found that many had intuitively developed key skills that had caused them to become wise, abounding in grace and wisdom (Hutnik, Smith and Koch, 2016). This is discussed in more detail in the previous chapter on resilience.

We have discovered how powerful CBT is in facilitating people to change their unhelpful thinking styles into helpful ones. In the centenarians we studied, we discovered tremendous stoicism, which enabled them to be resilient and to flourish in the midst of very difficult situations.

Change is aversive to the best of us. We would much prefer to trundle along with things remaining the same as they have always been. Yet change is inevitable in life and a quick adaptation to it is at the heart of resilience. In Chapter 8, we learnt that while there are things that just cannot be changed (for example, a diagnosis of a terminal illness or increasing frailty) we can use the strengths we already have to adapt to new things in our life.

CBT is especially powerful in helping us develop the same kind of stoic attitudes that our centenarians showed in just getting along with life. ACT enables us to be stoic, encouraging us to counter difficult life events by reminding ourselves to de-link our thoughts about reality from the reality itself. There will be some things we cannot change; accept them. For example, I can now no longer see as well as I used to even when I wear my glasses. I accept this and just get on with it (Robertson, 2012).

However, there are some things that we may be too passive about, things that we can change and which will indeed improve the quality of our lives, like high cholesterol or excessive weight. We may too quickly accept that we can do nothing about these things.

Exercise 9.12: Accepting the Things We Cannot Change and Changing the Things We Can

Part of being stoical is to accept the things we cannot change. What are the things in my life that I cannot change? Let me 'lean into' these irreversible choices that I have made.

For example: my body? Some career choices? Decisions I made about where to live?

_____

_____

_____

Are there some things I have passively accepted that I can now change?

_____

_____

_____

_____

On the following page we look at how we can use the thought record to alter unhelpful thinking styles when we are old. As we regularly use the thought record we can teach ourselves to overthrow habits of unhelpful thinking and teach ourselves to be more optimistic about life. Kailash challenged his unhelpful thought that he is inadequate and in doing so his low mood came down from 90 per cent to 40 per cent. This is a significant decrease in low mood.

Kailash, seventy-nine, began thinking negative automatic thoughts about how 'no one needs me anymore' because after his heart attack he is unable to do the little practical things he used to for his grown-up son and daughter-in-law and their two children. Using the thought record, he changed this unhelpful thinking style to 'I cannot do some of the things I used to for them, but I can do other things. For example, I can baby sit my grandchildren so that Krishna and Kavita can go out for dinner together.'

Kailash's Thought Record

Think of a recent situation that made you mildly upset.

- Situation: (Describe what you were doing, who you were with, the time and place the situation occurred.)

My daughter-in-law came over with her children. She said she needed some shelves put up in the children's bedrooms. I used to always help out but now I am too weak and unsteady on my feet to climb ladders.

- Mood: (Describe the mood or moods you were feeling at the time and rate their intensity on a scale of 0–100 per cent.)

Low 90 per cent

- Automatic thoughts: what was going through your mind, who were you thinking about, how do you feel about yourself, what made you feel that way, what does this mean, what memories went through your mind, and anything else you may have been thinking about at the time. Circle one hot thought. This is the one that has the most emotional energy and is responsible for driving the mood that you have mentioned above.

No one needs me anymore.

I am inadequate. This is the hot thought
I am worthless.

- Evidence for the hot thought: (Write down any factual evidence that supports your hot thought.)

I can no longer fix things for other people by myself.
My body does not allow me to be as active as I used to be.
I'm not earning any money for the family anymore.

- Evidence against the hot thought: (Write down any evidence that does not support your hot thought.)

I provide emotional support for my family, especially since my wife died.
I can babysit when my son and daughter-in-law want to go out for dinner.
I have so much life experience that I can often suggest a practical solution to problems that other people struggle to solve.

- Alternative/balanced thought: (Write an alternative or balanced thought and rate your belief in it.)

I cannot do some of the things I used to for them, but I can impart practical wisdom. I can also do other things, for example, I can babysit my grandchildren so that Krishna and Kavita can go out for dinner together.

90 per cent.

- Re-rate your mood: (Copy your feelings from 2 and re-rate the intensity of each feeling.)

Low 40 per cent

Letting Go

The developmental tasks of young and middle adulthood are very different to those of late adulthood. In old age the very things that one has striven for need to be gracefully relinquished and with wisdom. In Hindu tradition, the attainment of *moksha* is the ultimate aim of all existence. Moksha (freedom or self-realization and the achievement of oneness with the infinite) in the last years is associated with the relinquishing of the *grahasthya* stage (the stage of the householder with all its joys, cares and burdens) and the taking on of the stage of *vanprastha* (a retreat into the forest, symbolic of withdrawal) and the stage of *sannyas* (or renunciation) (Kakar, 1978).

Similar processes of letting go of attachments are described in the contemplative tradition in Buddhism and Christianity. In Rohr's understanding, the task of the first half of life is the forging of an identity in love, work and play (Rohr, 2012). Eckhart Tolle (2006) calls this self 'the little me'. In the second half of life, the task is to let go of this very identity. The art of letting go becomes a vital skill to develop.

Joan Erikson, the wife of the famous developmental psychologist Erik Erikson has added a ninth stage to her husband's Eight Ages of Man (Erikson, 1998). She says that, in this ninth stage, the despair of stage eight is magnified by the experience of one's deteriorating body and mind, which results in the lowering of self-esteem and confidence. She talks about how important it is to come to terms with these dystonic parts of the life cycle:

- We can no longer trust our bodies to do the things they used to be able to do. Thus we need to integrate Mistrust
- In the last stage of old age, we often have to relinquish our autonomy to adult sons and daughters who make decisions for us rather than with us. This may cause rebellion or resignation and certainly questions our Autonomy
- Work is no longer compelling, our competence is often questioned by the younger generation who are able, quick and know it all better than we do. Thus, we can develop a sense of Inferiority

- We have retired and people no longer remember nor seen interested in how we spent our work lives, what roles we have had or how we contributed to society. Thus, we risk Identity Diffusion
- Our partners and best friends have died or are no longer geographically present around us. Isolation is a very real issue
- The younger generation do not seem to need us to nurture them anymore. We will therefore be tempted to become Stagnant and Self-absorbed
- Thus, Despair in our inevitable physical frailties and growing dependence on others can overwhelm us. We may become Disgusted and Frustrated with ourselves and others

'To face down despair with faith and appropriate humility is perhaps the wisest course,' writes Joan Erikson (J. Erikson, 1998, p. 106). This is another way of saying that it is important to gracefully let go.

The inevitability of death becomes ever more prominent. The way in which an older person faces the reality of it will determine not only their own inner serenity, grace and wisdom but will profoundly affect children, grandchildren and others who may be watching and learning. As Erik Erikson says, 'Healthy children will not fear life if their elders have the integrity enough not to fear death.'

Rohr (2012) talks about the art of 'falling upward'. People who flourish in the second half of life are people who are able to look death in the face and embrace it. Like a ripe apple that ultimately must detach itself from the branch and the tree and fall to the ground to become part of the soil, we too need to 'lean in' to growing older, rather than resist it. Unlike the east, contemporary western culture is focused on resisting ageing or defying age. If we are to flourish in our later years, this is a futile endeavour. Falling upward is all about recognizing that the next stage is a fall into death and it is the ability to trust that fall, to trust our heaviness. Part of the process of 'positive ageing', as opposed to 'successful ageing', is the ability to integrate death as part of the cycle of life.

In Erik Erikson's terms, positive aging is the ability to look back upon one's life with integrity, to re-evaluate and reconsider the choices and decisions one has made through life and find them to have been good. We certainly found this to be evident in our study of resilience in centenarians.

Older people, who are unable to look back upon life with a sense of integrity, often experience despair, which manifests itself in depression and anxiety. They also often experience disgust, which shows itself in the form of anger, over-critical attitudes and resentment.

Those of us who can embrace the dystonic aspects of old, old age are in Joan Erikson's terms 'gerotranscendent'. As we learn to do the dance of old, old age, we enter the stage of 'gerotranscen*dance*.'

'To reach for gerotranscen*dance* is to rise above, exceed, out do, go beyond, independent of the universe and time … Transcen*dance* may be a regaining of lost skills, including play, activity, joy, and song, above all, a major leap above and beyond the fear of death. It provides an opening forward into the unknown with the trusting leap.' (J. Erikson, 1998, pg. 127)

INTEGRATING DEATH: THE ULTIMATE LETTING GO

As we have seen, part of the process of flourishing is to come to terms with death, whatever age you may be.

I have thought a lot about how to accept and integrate death into our lives. I realize that many OCD fears related to contamination and germs and most of illness anxiety (see Chapter 2) come from an avoidance of the reality of death. So below I have formed two exercises that you can use to come to terms with the fact that one day you will die. Take these exercises slowly. The first is a meditation on letting go and the second is a meditation on death itself. Do these over a number of days or weeks. Write out the answers to each of the questions or do the exercise. If your cell phone has a recording device, you can speak these sentences out loud into your cell phone and then do the exercise as a guided meditation. Alternatively, you can download an Mp3 of this meditation for a small fee from www.cbtintheuk.com. The exercises below are not just for older people. All of us need to 'lean in' to the reality of death in order to lose our fear of life.

Exercise 9.13: Meditation on Letting Go

Close your eyes and imagine that you have been told you have just six months to live. What is your reaction to this news? Who is the first person you will tell? How will you tell them?

What are some of the things you would really like to do before you die? Do you realistically have enough time to do them? Who would you like alongside you as you do these things? Are there some things that you will necessarily have to leave unfinished?

Think of your work life and your career. Use your art of positive framing to construct this narrative. Let go of the victim position if you have one. Forgive the people who have hurt you.

What about your family and your intimate relationships? What needs to be done here to let go and say goodbye? Who are the people you would like to say goodbye to? How will you do this? Are there people you need to forgive? And people you need to ask forgiveness from?

Think of the activities that have brought you into flow and a sense of accomplishment. Let them go...

Have you fulfilled the meaning of your life? Is there anything in this area that remains to be done?

Now think of the things that have brought you great joy like sights, smells, sounds and tastes. Become mindfully aware of each of your senses as you do this. Say goodbye to them.

Now allow yourself to come mindfully into the present again.

Exercise 9.14: Meditation on Death

Imagine you have just died and it is your funeral. Who is there? What are they saying about you? Who is delivering the eulogy? What are they saying in it? What strengths did you show and what were your accomplishments? Visualize the scene as vividly as you can. What colours can you see? What can you smell? Are there flowers? Which ones? There is music playing. What song or piece are they playing and how does it make you feel?

What are your beliefs about life after death? Is there God or a higher power in your belief system? Is there a welcome for you after you have lived your life on earth?

Now it is a year later. Your body has been buried or cremated and your possessions are with your family, although some have been sold or given away. Some people who knew you gather on the anniversary of your death to remember you. What have they written on your gravestone? What are they saying? Again, engage the five senses. What can you see, hear, smell, taste and feel?

Ten years on, the anniversary of your death is no longer important. You live on through some memories in the minds of people whose lives you touched. Who are those people? What do they remember of you?

Fifty years later, little remains of you, your memory or your achievements. What might still remain?

One hundred years on, no one is left alive who ever directly knew you. Try to imagine this. Access the feelings. What are your thoughts? Are you able to integrate the fact of your death into your life? If you are able to do this, what impact does this integration have on your anxieties and fears in the now? If you are unable to do this, what do you need in order to face the reality of your own death?

On the planet new life goes on. Babies are being born, new fashion trends rise and fall, musical tastes change, technology advances, humour and love remain.

When I did this exercise with one of my clients who suffered from both OCD and illness anxiety, she reached a turning point. After we had done a number of exposure and response-prevention exercises and also looked at how unhealthy self-focus causes bodily symptoms to manifest themselves, she still had some residual OCD and illness anxiety. I decided to take her through a guided meditation on death that I created. She closed her eyes and listened attentively to the words of this meditation. She turned it over and over in her head that death was inevitable and she would die one day. This dawning realization and its accompanying attitude of acceptance brought her liberation from her OCD and her illness anxiety. I have described her story in Chapter 5.

In summary, I have extended flourishing to include the ability to appropriately let go of roles, status and people and to accept the process of ageing. When we are resilient we bounce back reasonably well without collapsing under the strain of life and then we spring forward to embrace life and flourish. When we flourish we experience positive emotion and meaning despite our losses. We are able to look back at life forsaking resentment, and with integrity and are able to see that it has been good. We are able to be resilient in the face of change and stoical with the things we cannot change. We are able to accept death without fear, trusting the fall.

HUTNIK'S MODEL OF RESILIENCE AND FLOURISHING

So, now that we have all the elements in place, let us look at the difference between a non-resilient response to a 'knocking-down' situation and a resilient one. In the diagram that follows (Fig. 9.3), the non-resilient response is to respond to our current trigger situation with a negative appraisal of the situation. (Oh no! This is a catastrophe!) This negative appraisal of the situation causes us to experience difficult emotions such as grief, rage or fear with all the accompanying bodily symptoms. Thus, our heart rate increases, we may cry, our faces become flushed, we sweat, we tremble, etc. In other words, our negative appraisals are associated with difficult emotions that set our autonomic nervous system into action. All of this causes us to engage in unproductive behaviour. We develop rigid, inflexible coping styles of experiential avoidance and create a gamut of safety behaviours to protect ourselves. We enter malicious, non-resilient cycles of depression and/or anxiety. When we look at ourselves in these cycles of depression and anxiety, we ruminate about why we are so depressed and anxious. Our metacognitive processes, i.e., our Third Eye is self-attacking and unhelpful. Whichever way we look at ourselves we cannot see a way out. We turn things this way and that, lurching from the past to the future, unable to stay grounded in the present. We find ourselves caught in a vicious cycle of maladaptive thoughts, emotions, behaviours and physical sensations. Our thoughts about our thoughts, feelings and behaviours are unkind, leading to despair and exhaustion. This is a fragile, non-resilient and floundering response to a situation that threatens to knock us down.

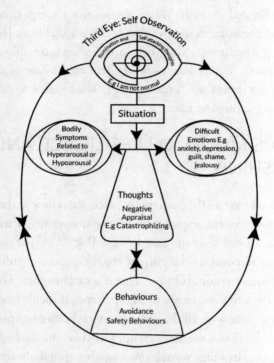

Fig. 9.3: Fragility: The Non-Resilient Face

Let us now look at the resilient response to a knocking-down situation. In the diagram on page 418 (Fig. 9.4) we respond to our current trigger situation with 'even-thoughtedness' and realistic optimism. We have taught ourselves to challenge our negative automatic thoughts and to positively frame even difficult situations. This produces a realistically optimistic appraisal of danger and loss. We are also in touch with our coping skills and the resources we have at hand to cope. Because we have worked to uncover them, we know our character strengths and how they can bear upon the current situation to make it work for our well-being. We have developed a set of resilience principles that engage previously used, tried and tested strategies that have worked in the past for overcoming obstacles. We now call upon our resilience principles to help us resolve the issues in the current situation and regardless of outcome, to still stay standing and strong.

Since we have learnt to manage our minds, the thoughts that we have about our 'knocking-down' situations will be balanced ones and balanced thoughts produce appropriate emotion and physical sensations. We may, for example, feel deep grief at the death of a loved one, but because we have done some seminal work on integrating death into our lives we are able to process our grief so that it does not overwhelm us. Or we may mourn the loss of a cherished relationship but we know this mourning will cease and we opt to cope with whatever life throws at us. We learn to pick up the pieces and try again. We open ourselves up to the experience of ecstasy and joy and even love as we immerse ourselves in our flow activities in order to deal with 'knocking-down' situations. We therefore experience appropriate and proportional emotion. Our bodies respond accordingly.

We have taught ourselves to drop our avoidance and safety behaviours and to 'lean into' the things that alarm us most, exposing ourselves to our fears and to the fears of our fears. When we find ourselves becoming inactive and passive because we are feeling low, we have learnt to schedule pleasurable activities into our daily lives so that we overcome depression with activity. We have also realized that inactivity and passivity are often products of a lack of clarity about our values. So we spend time asking ourselves what our valued life directions are. What steps can we take to orient ourselves towards travelling towards our most deeply cherished values? We have also learnt that relentless activity is not the answer to a low mood. It is important that we sit still and be mindful, developing a meditation practice that enables us to learn the important skill of staying in the present moment rather than swinging from the past into the future and back again in an uncontrollable fashion. There is a quality of 'choicefulness' about our behaviour. Quietly and courageously because we have worked on what really matters to us, we pick up with acceptance the unrelenting burdens that life has given us to carry and move ourselves, with our particular burdens in the direction of our values. Thus, we learn to flourish, to not only bounce back with resilience from situations that threaten to knock us down but to spring forward and embrace life with all its fullness. We look upon our life with our Third Eye and find that it is good and that we have learnt to be resilient.

So in dealing with our cognitions and our behaviours we have learnt to heal and manage our difficult moods ourselves. This is what CBT is all about.

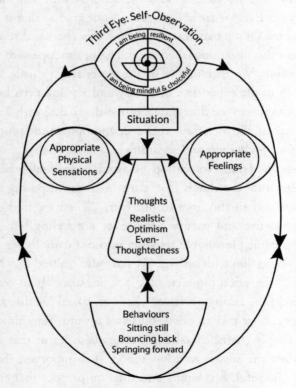

Fig. 9.4. Flourishing: The Resilient Face

In the table below I have compared and contrasted the non-resilient response style with the resilient one in the first two columns. In the third column I have outlined some of the things you can do to increase your resilient responses to 'knocking-down' situations.

Non-resilient responses to 'knocking-down' situations	Resilient responses to 'knocking-down' situations	To move from a non-resilient response to a resilient one, do this
Negative appraisal of the situation	'Even-thought edness' realistic optimism	Become familiar with your most common unhelpful thinking styles Master the thought record and use it to: Cultivate attitudes of acceptance for the things that cannot be changed Learn to positively frame difficult life events, i.e., learn to see the glass as half full for the things that can be changed Use the worry tree to manage worry and to push it away Use behavioural experiments to challenge some of your resistant unhelpful cognitions
Avoidance	Sitting still (Mindfulness)	De-link thoughts from reality, i.e., see thoughts as just thoughts Develop a mindfulness meditation practice Learn to lean into your most feared and painful situation including a fear of death Reintroduce avoided activities

Safety behaviours	Bouncing back (Resilience)	Drop your safety behaviours Develop choicefulness in your behaviours Develop your own set of resilience principles and apply them, remembering that the goal is not a positive outcome but to stay strong whatever the outcome
Increasing restrictions and inactivity due to avoidance and safety behaviours	Springing forward (Flourishing)	PERMA : Make sure you experience lots of positive emotion, engagement, good-quality relationships, meaning, and accomplishment Discover and develop your character strengths Work on your values to determine your valued directions and travel towards these despite your limitations Learn the art of letting go Integrate the reality of death into your life

Key Points from this Chapter

— When we think we have no control over the things that happen in our lives, we become depressed. This is what is known as learned helplessness

— We can train ourselves to be optimistic, to see the glass as half full rather than half empty. We do this by using the CBT techniques we learnt in Chapter 3

— Discovering and developing our character strengths causes us to have the foundations of flourishing

- According to Seligman, flourishing consists of having:

P – Positive emotion
E – Engagement in life
R – Relationships
M – Meaning and purpose
A – Accomplishment

- It is possible to flourish even in old age when physical faculties are on the decline
- Developing forgiveness towards ourselves and those who have harmed us is important for our own well-being and the well-being of the community
- Learning to be stoical about the things in our lives that cannot be changed is key to resilience and flourishing
- Integrating the reality of death enables us to lose our fear of life
- Developing the ability to sit still and be mindful on a regular basis enables PEACE
- Being able to bounce back quickly after being knocked down is the key to resilience
- Springing forward to embrace life in all its fullness while integrating or accepting the reality of death, is the essence of flourishing

REFERENCES

1. G.W. Allport, *Person in Psychology*, Boston: Beacon Press, 1968.
2. R. Biswas-Diener, *Practicing Positive Psychology Coaching: Assessment, Activities and Strategies for Success*, New Jersey: John Wiley and Sons, Inc., 2010.
3. N.J. Brown, A.D. Sokal, and H.L. Friedman, 'The Complex Dynamics of Wishful Thinking: The Critical Positivity Ratio', *American Psychologist*, 68(9):801–813, 2013.

4. K.T. Buehlman, J.M. Gottman, and L.F. Katz, 'How a Couple Views Their Past Predicts Their Future: Predicting Divorce from an Oral History Interview', *Journal of Family Psychology,* 5(3 and 4):295–318, 1992.

5. J.T. Cacioppo, and W. Patrick, *Loneliness: Human Nature and the Need for Social Connection,* New York: W.W. Norton & Company, 2008.

6. M. Csikszentlmihalyi, *Flow: The Psychology of Optimal Experience,* New York: Cambridge University Press, 1991.

7. D.D. Danner, D.A. Snowdon, and W.V. Friesen, 'Positive Emotions in Early Life and Longevity: Findings from the Nun Study', *Journal of Personality and Social Psychology,* 80(5):804–813, 2001.

8. A.L. Duckworth, and J.J. Gross, 'Self-Control and Grit: Related but Separable Determinants of Success', *Current Directions in Psychological Science,* 23(5):319–325, 2014.

9. R.I.M. Dunbar, R. Baron, A. Frangou, E. Pearce, E.J.C. van Leeuwen, J. Stow, G. Partridge, I. MacDonald, V. Barra, and M. van Vugt, 'Social Laughter Is Correlated with an Elevated Pain Threshold', *Proceedings of the Royal Society of London B: Biological Sciences,* 279(1731):1161–1167, 2012.

10. E. Erikson, *The Life-Cycle Completed: Extended Version with New Chapters on the Ninth Stage by Joan M. Erikson,* New York: W.W. Norton & Company, 1998.

11. B.L. Fredrickson, 'Updated Thinking on Positivity Ratios', *American Psychologist,* 68(9):814–822, 2013.

12. B.L. Fredrickson, and M.F. Losada, 'Positive Affect and the Complex Dynamics of Human Flourishing', *American Psychologist,* 60(7):678–686, 2005.

13. T.N. Hanh, 'The Pocket Thich Nhat Hanh', 9, (edited by) M. McLeod, Boston: Shambala, 2012.

14. N. Hutnik, P. Smith and T. Koch ' Using a Cognitive Behavioural Lens to Look at Resilience in the Stories of Centenarians in the UK'. *Nursing Open,* doi: 10.1002/nop2.44.

15. O. James, *Contented Dementia,* London: Vermillion, 2009.

16. C. Johnstone, *Find Your Power – A Toolkit for Resilience and Positive Change,* London: Permanent Publications, 2010.

17. C. Johnstone, and M. Akhtar, *The Happiness Training Plan,* London: Permanent Publications, 2008 Audio CD.

18. S. Kakar, *The Inner World,* New Delhi: Oxford University Press, 1978.

19. T.B. Kashdan, T. Julian, K. Merritt, and G. Uswatte, 'Social Anxiety and Post-traumatic Stress in Combat Veterans: Relations to Well-Being and Character Strengths', *Behaviour Research and Therapy*, 44:561–583, 2006.

20. M. Kataria, Laughter Yoga, 1995, *http://www.laughteryoga.org/index. php?option=com_content&view=article&id=197:dr-madan-kataria-a-profile&ca*, last accessed on 9 September 2016.

21. M. Kataria, *Laugh for No reason*, 2nd ed., Mumbai: Madhuri International, 2002.

22. S. Mehrotra, and R. Tripathi, 'Positive Psychology Research in India: A Review and Critique', *Journal of the Indian Academy of Applied Psychology*, 37(1):9–26, 2011.

23. C. Peterson, N. Park, and M. Seligman, *Journal of Positive Psychology*, 1(1):17–26, 2006.

24. D. Robertson, *Build Your Resilience: How to Survive and Thrive in Any Situation*, London: Hodder Education, 2012.

25. R. Rohr, *Falling Upward: A Spirituality for the Two Halves of Life*, London: SPCK, 2012.

26. M. Seligman, *Flourish: A New Understanding of Happiness and Well-Being – and How to Achieve Them*, London: Nicholas Brealey Publishing, 2011.

27. M. Seligman, T. Rashid, and A.C. Parks, 'Positive Psychotherapy', *American Psychologist*, 61(8):774–788, 2006.

28. M. Seligman, T. Steen, N. Park, and C. Peterson, 'Positive Psychology Progress: Empirical Validation of Interventions', *American Psychologist*, 60(5):410–421, 2005.

29. A. Srivastava, 'What Makes School Students Happy? An Exploratory Analysis', *Psychological Studies*, 53:164–169, 2008.

30. R.B. Stuart, *Helping Couples Change: A Social Learning Approach to Marital Therapy*, Paperback ed., London: Guildford Press, 2004.

31. E. Tolle, *Through the Open Door to the Vastness of Your True Being*, Colorado: Sounds True, 2006.

32. G.E. Vaillant, *Triumphs of Experience: The Men in the Harvard Grant Study*, Belknap Press, 2012.

33. I. Yalom, *Staring at the Sun: Overcoming the Terror of Death*, Chichester: John Wiley and Sons Ltd, 2010.

10

Pathways to Parivarthan: Pulling the Threads Together

My aim in this book was to facilitate you to become resilient, to move from fragility to flourishing using a CBT approach to thereby help you climb onto pathways of transformation. *Parivarthan* is the Sanskrit word for transformation and I think it encapsulates the idea of well.

Let us go over some of the ground we have covered together.

We looked together at the nature of depression and anxiety. You have filled in some questionnaires which will enable you to tell whether you are anxious or depressed. We then studied some fundamental concepts underlying CBT. We discovered how central and powerful thoughts are producing our emotions, behaviours and physical sensations. We looked at unhelpful thinking styles and began to teach ourselves how to transform our thinking into helpful thinking. Using the thought record, we learnt to identify the 'hot thought', which was the thought with the most emotional charge, the one that occurred just before we began to feel the emotion. We learnt to challenge this hot thought with facts, looking for the evidence for and against the hot thought. We then learnt to act as a judge in the courtroom of our minds, to create an alternative or balanced thought. 'Even-thoughtedness' is of great value in CBT. Taking this 'even' thought into the situation that triggered our emotions in the first place, we discover that if we think this thought rather than the hot thought, our distress usually, though not always, goes down. The thought record therefore is a powerful tool, enabling us to manage our moods.

Another very powerful tool for depression in particular, is behavioural activation. When we are depressed we tend to withdraw from social situations, we tend to ruminate, and our lives become dysfunctional. We thereby remove ourselves from opportunities for positive reward. In behavioural activation, we learnt to reintroduce into our activities of the week, those that will bring us pleasure. To counter our depressive passivity, we used the five-minute rule: do it for five minutes and consider the homework done. After five minutes, if we still want to continue in the activity then we should. Thus, we discovered the link between activity and mood. It is a strong one.

When we are depressed, we tend to fall into a malicious cycle of depressive rumination. We can break into the cycle by a) considering the costs and the benefits to us of this rumination activity and by b) mindfulness and acceptance. Thus, we turn our unfriendly Third Eye into a transcendent, helpful, friendly one.

The face diagram helps us access this transcendent, observing self. Stepping aside from our own lives and looking in, we are able to develop a much greater perspective on our situations, our thoughts, our bodies and the moods that we experience.

The antidote to anxiety is exposure. When we are anxious, we tend to avoid the situations that cause us anxiety. We also tend to develop a gamut of safety behaviours. This avoidance and indulgence in safety behaviours is counter-productive in the long run, though it brings us immediate relief in the short run. And thus, the process of working with anxiety is to drop our avoidances and our safety behaviours. This is frightening and unpleasant at first. However, research has shown that if we stay with our anxiety long enough, it dissipates within our bodies over time. We learnt therefore, to approach instead of avoid the very situations that cause us stress, with the faith that practice and repeated exposure will bring our anxiety levels down.

In addition, we realized that it is our overestimation of danger and underestimation of our ability to cope and of the resources that we have at hand to cope with things that cause us anxiety. The process of dealing with anxiety is to learn to become realistic about the level of danger we are facing and recognize the coping skills that we have already developed to deal with this danger. Thus, we made significant inroads into managing and getting rid of OCD, phobias, panic disorder, social anxiety, illness anxiety and generalized anxiety disorder. Even some forms of PTSD are amenable to change via self-help.

Learning to bring our bodies and minds together into the present moment is the essence of mindfulness. When we are mindful, we are at peace. There is joy and happiness in the moment. Or if our minds and emotions are turbulent, we usually discover that we have the skills to cope with whatever is been demanded of us now. Spiritual traditions have known this for many centuries. Psychology is only just opening its doors to this truth.

The essence of mindfulness is to disempower the potency of our thoughts by seeing our thoughts as just thoughts. Thus, instead of battling with our thoughts, restructuring them, challenging them and trying to get them in order so that they do not have this devastating effect on our emotions. Instead we let them be. We float them on a leaf down the river, so to speak.

Some psychologists see mindfulness as antithetical to the tools and techniques of classic CBT. I see them as complementary, each useful in different situations and with different people. Our thoughts do carry meaning and are powerful in producing our behaviour and emotions. Classic CBT has shown us that we have control over them, that we can change them and this will change the quality of our lives. Because we can control them, we can also let them go. The thought that 'thoughts are just thoughts' carries meaning. This meaning produces the 'letting go'.

ACT is a further development of mindfulness CBT. It builds on mindfulness concepts such as being present in the moment. However, it encourages us to explore our values and life directions and to take committed action towards travelling in those directions, despite the many difficulties and obstacles we face and the burdens we carry with us. We live lives of great integrity if we can do this.

By developing an awareness of our hidden strengths in everyday situations and transferring these strengths into the situations we find difficult, we find our resilience. We do this by opening our eyes to the fact that we are already resilient in certain situations. We can learn to abstract our principle of resilience from these situations and use them to face the larger life situations that threaten to knock us down thus practicing and strengthening resilience within us.

In addition to finding and using our hidden strengths in order to be resilient, we can teach ourselves to positively reframe difficult situations: we can learn optimism. Teaching ourselves to be optimistic, to see the glass as half full rather than half empty, is not to say that we force ourselves to be positive about the situations we find ourselves in. We are aiming for realistic optimism rather than positive thinking.

Having now learnt how to bounce back to position of greater robustness from having been knocked down, we are ready to enter the pathways of *parivarthan*. We are poised for transformation and flourishing. We put ourselves in the pathway of positive emotion, upping the level of joy, happiness and love in our lives. We put ourselves in the pathway of engagement, finding activities that will bring us regularly into the state of flow. We transform our relationships into positive ones by taking the necessary action to care for our loved ones and to respond actively and constructively to our loved ones' achievements. We search for and find meaning in our lives; be it in spirituality, politics, art or umpteen other sources. We undertake activity just for the sake of it because this feeds our need for accomplishment and achievement, be it in the short term or long term. As we enter the second phase of life, pathways of parivarthan take on different forms. We learn the art of letting go. We learn to accept the reality of death as we lose the people we love and those who have been important to us. We learn to adapt to the loss of the role and status as we let go of the very identities that made us in the first stage of life. In the second stage of life, we learn to mindfully accept increasing disability and decline. We learn to trust the fall upward. And thus we flourish. And are transformed. Parivarthan.

Index

Questionnaires

Important Blank Forms

List of Figures

Fig. 2.1: The Fight or Flight Response: Bodily Symptoms of Anxiety

Fig. 2.2: The CBT Model of Anxiety

Fig. 3.1: The Relationship Between Thoughts and Feelings

Fig. 3.2: The Hot Cross Bun

Fig 3.3: The Face

Fig. 4.1: The Vicious Flower

Fig. 4.2: Combined Model of Depression as Applied to Sunita

Fig. 4.3: Maintenance Cycle of Depression

Fig. 5.1: Exposure and Avoidance

Fig. 5.2: A Maintenance Cycle for Panic Disorder

Fig. 5.3: A Maintenance Cycle for Obsessive Compulsive Disorder

Fig. 5.4: A Maintenance Cycle for Illness Anxiety

Fig. 5.5: A Maintenance Cycle for Generalized Anxiety Disorder

Fig 5.6: The Worry Tree

Fig. 5.7: A Maintenance Cycle for Phobias

Fig. 5.8: A Maintenance Cycle for Social Anxiety

Fig. 5.9: A Maintenance Cycle for Post-Traumatic Stress Disorder